Social Work

Assessment

Intervention

BY

Steven Walker

and Chris Beckett

Russell House Publishing

First published in 2003 by:
Russell House Publishing Ltd.
4 St. George's House
Uplyme Road
Lyme Regis
Dorset DT7 3LS

Tel: 01297 443948
Fax: 01297 442722
e-mail: help@russellhouse.co.uk
www.russellhouse.co.uk

Reprinted 2004

British Library Cataloguing-in-publication Data:
A catalogue record for this book is available from the British Library.

ISBN: 1-903855–34–9

Typeset by Saxon Graphics Ltd, Derby
Printed by Cromwell Press, Trowbridge

About Russell House Publishing

RHP is a group of social work, probation, education and youth and community work practitioners and academics working in collaboration with a professional publishing team.

Our aim is to work closely with the field to produce innovative and valuable materials to help managers, trainers, practitioners and students.

We are keen to receive feedback on publications and new ideas for future projects.

For details of our other publications please visit our website or ask us for a catalogue. Contact details are on this page.

Contents

Introduction

The key purpose of social work has been defined as:

A profession which promotes social change, problem solving in human relationships and the empowerment and liberation of people to enhance well being. Utilising theories of human behaviour and social systems, social work intervenes at the points where people interact with their environments. Principles of human rights and social justice are fundamental to social work.

International Association of Schools of Social Work and the International Federation of Social Workers, 2001, in: BASW, 2002.

This powerful statement from a representative body of social workers from around the globe states quite clearly the twin elements that enshrine modern social work practice – the relationship between the external social world and the inner psychological experience of the individual that cause some citizens pain and suffering. In order to better understand how to help in these situations social workers need to develop the capacity to undertake assessments and interventions in a wide variety of settings with individuals, families, and groups. Such activity needs to be understood in the context of statutory duties, agency requirements, the needs and wishes of service users, and firmly underpinned by anti-racist and anti-discriminatory practice. Modern social work also needs to position itself within an increasingly globalised world where supra-national agencies and insti-tutions are impacting on previously unilateral policies and practices. The borders between countries are being eroded as a result of regional economic and geo-political pressures, migration for economic reasons, or to escape from war and ethnic conflict is on the increase. Cultural competence in social work is therefore a necessity and now an expectation of all public services that must reflect the increasingly rich, multi-cultural, religious and ethnically diverse society, country or region we inhabit.

Social work assessment and intervention are core skills for qualified social workers and fundamental learning requirements for trainee/ student social workers. These skills have relevance to the Human Rights Act and featured in recent guidance on practice competencies and the latest occupational standards guidance for the Training Organisation for Personal Social Services. This book combines the two practice elements of Assessment and Intervention in an integrated way that is consistent with contemporary practice and the foundational values and skills of classic psycho-social practice. It will be an invaluable guide to practitioners seeking to address the new occupational standards guidance and respond to the new regulatory and graduate training environment in modern social work. Assessment is usually separated from intervention in the literature and practice guidance. This book aims to provide social workers with the combined intellectual and practical resources to help improve practice in these crucial areas.

Practitioners know that the two processes cannot be separated from each other. Government guidance and the professional literature have begun to accept that assessment and intervention should be seamless parts of a continuous process. It also expects there to be a therapeutic dimension to this area of social work practice:

> *The provision of appropriate services should not await the end of the assessment but be offered when they are required by the child and family. The process of engaging in an assessment should be therapeutic and perceived of as part of the range of services offered.*
>
> DoH, 2000.

However, employers tend to emphasise assessment skills to the detriment of good, integrated, holistic practice. The trend towards retrenchment in social services and reduction of social work to bureaucratic care management is not meeting the needs of vulnerable service users who want more than administrative processing. Social workers who cherish their core helping skills will find this book supports and extends their practice. This book challenges the orthodoxy for compartmentalising practice processes that lead to narrow, resource-driven assessment procedures and eligibility criteria in statutory social services contexts. It also reminds staff that difficult decisions regarding rationing of human and physical resources are part and parcel of contemporary practice. We aim to offer social workers in a variety of qualified and unqualified roles and agencies a rich source of up to the minute resources to draw upon and enhance a psycho-social perspective to deliver empowering, ethical, service user-focused practice.

Recent SSI inspections have illustrated the need for social workers to rediscover their core skills of assessment and intervention, so that decision-making and care planning are based on sound analysis and understanding of the client's unique personality, history and circumstances. Social workers' own skills need to be seen as a resource to be used and offered in the subsequent intervention which should be based on client need rather than agency resource limita-

tions and where services should fit around the service user rather than the reverse (DOH/SSI, 2000). This book provides social work staff with an accessible, practice-oriented guide to their work in the developing modernising context of multi-disciplinary team working, joint budget arrangements, inter-agency collaboration and care management. The new graduate training environment, occupational standards, General Social Care Council, SCIE, TOPSS, and post-qualifying training requirements, all demand improvements in practice standards. This book responds to that demand and the needs of social workers to deliver high quality services in the contemporary context of practice.

National occupational standards

Six key roles for social work practitioners have been identified in the latest occupational standards guidance that together with the units and elements of practice provide detailed requirements expected of qualified professionals:

- **Key role 1.** Prepare for and work with individuals, families, carers, groups and communities to assess their needs and circumstances.
- **Key role 2.** Plan, carry out, review and evaluate social work practice, with individuals, families, carers, groups, communities and other professionals.
- **Key role 3.** Support individuals to represent their needs, views and circumstances.
- **Key role 4.** Manage risk to individuals, families, carers, groups, communities, self and colleagues.
- **Key role 5.** Manage and be accountable, with supervision and support, for your own social work practice within your organisation.
- **Key role 6.** Demonstrate professional competence in social work practice.

Evaluation, delivery and dilemmas

Within this broad occupational guidance framework some of the important tasks include the practical activities we aim to cover in this book. At the very beginning of the engagement process in social work you will be expected to review case notes and other relevant literature and liaise with others to access additional information that can inform initial contact and involvement. Evaluating all the necessary information in order to identify the best form of initial involvement is crucial. The advantage being that it can quickly bring you up to date on what might be happening in the life of a service user. The disadvantage is that the case file may be inaccurate, or other workers' perceptions are based on prejudice or misinformation.

It is important for you to be aware of your own prejudices and values when engaging with clients and to guard against making decisions based on preconceived assumptions about individuals and groups. Trying to evaluate what may be contradictory information or falsehood as a basis for deciding your next steps following a referral may not be as simple as it first appears. You are expected to inform clients about your own and your organisation's duties and responsibilities. Identifying, gathering, analysing and understanding information is a key skill. In addition you are expected to enable service users to analyse, identify, clarify and express their strengths, expectations and limitations. And you should be working with clients to assess and make informed decisions about their needs, circumstances, risks, preferred options and resources.

This all sounds straightforward enough until you start to consider the complexities presented by social work clients and the multitude of personal, environmental, and relationship problems they bring to your notice. You might also wonder whether you have the time and other resources to work in the way prescribed above. Social workers always have to defend their organisation's lack of ability to provide what service users define as their needs. It is not uncommon to then face the fury of people who have gone through with what feels like an inquisitorial assessment process to end up with very little in return for themselves. The likelihood of these tensions arising was acknowledged over 20 years ago in the first major inquiry into the role and tasks of social workers (NISW, 1982). The report described social work as comprising two strands of activity – counselling and social care planning.

The latter related to solving or ameliorating an existing social problem which an individual, family, or group experienced. All the subsequent evidence demonstrates service users' value the key counselling/therapeutic skills employed in assessment and intervention activity. Social care planning relates to preventive informal or formal work to develop and strengthen communities. The problem is that social care planning can be undertaken both by practitioners and managers, resulting in tension between staff trying to juggle finite resources. The dilemmas this situation produces are considered in this book in the context of rationing and eligibility restraints that operate more strictly in statutory agencies. We examine contemporary evidence for the delivery of competent assessment, intervention and risk assessment practice. The various elements that comprise a comprehensive model of assessment and intervention practice are drawn together to articulate a synthesis of practice based on empowerment and socially inclusive practice, integrated working, and evaluating effectiveness to contribute to the building of a coherent evidence base in social work.

The occupational standards suggest that you assess and review the preferred options of service users and assess their needs, risks and options taking into account legal and other requirements. Then you are expected to assess and recommend an appropriate course of action for your clients. The first part of this hints at the potential for disagreement between you and the service user. They may have a preferred option that conflicts with your legal duties to remove their child or to detain them against their will in a psychiatric unit. Your recommendation may not feel right for them, either because it is too much or too little of what they anticipated being offered. You will often be in a position of enforcing a course of action rather than recommending that it takes place. Assessment has been defined as:

an ongoing process, in which the client participates, the purpose of which is to understand people in relation to their environment. It is the basis for planning what needs to be done to maintain, improve or bring about change in the client, the environment or both. (Coulshed and Orme, 1998)

It therefore cannot be separated from inter-vention because of the reflexive interactive nature of the client/worker encounter.

Looking through these prescribed occupa-tional standards is an enlightening experience in as much as they tell you very little of *how* to achieve them. What you are expected to achieve is deceptively simple. There are different ways in which these aims can be achieved each of which is as valid as the next. The problem you face is that there is no way of confidently predicting which way is the best, easiest, or most cost-effective. And that is because every service user is a unique individual. You are expected in other occupational standards to tailor your practice to the needs of that individual thereby avoiding stereotyped, institutionalised practice.

You will also bring your own individual unique self to the task of social work practice – perhaps a history of personal problems that give you some degree of insight into particular difficulties faced by some clients. Or your motivation may spring from deeply held reli-gious or political imperatives that impel you to devote yourself to helping other citizens in trouble. Whatever the motivating factor, your interpretation of these occupational standards and the practice guidance that follows may be different to other social workers in small, subtle or large ways. You will also find differences in service standards between organisations. Each local authority, health trust, or voluntary agency has discretion and flexibility in terms of how it prioritises its responsibilities under various legislative and statutory duties. All of what follows therefore needs to be placed in the context of your own local professional environment.

This is linked to central government decisions about how to apportion the local government and health budget and the variety of formulae used to rationalise political decisions. Therefore, it is very difficult in practice to undertake the task of assessment and intervention without encoun-tering a degree of confusion, uncertainty and some dilemmas. Our aim is to bring clarity where we can, to explain where some confusion can be enlightening, but more than anything we hope this book will be a genuine resource for you to use in the complex, challenging and ultimately rewarding world of social work.

Assessment is now recognised as more than an administrative task, or as a form of gate keeping for resources, or even as a means of determining risk. It is an intervention and thereby like many of the orthodox methods and models of intervention can be applied in a variety of ways. The distinction between assessment and intervention is unhelpful and has always restricted the vision and creativity of social work staff. We combine both aspects of social work practice in this volume in order to permit an integrated, holistic, modern psycho-social practice rooted in the principles of social justice and informed by the highest level of ethical and evidence-based knowledge.

PART 1

Principles of Assessment and Intervention

CHAPTER 1

Contemporary Assessment Practice

Introduction

Social work assessment is often taken for granted, sometimes the subject of unwarranted attention, but always a potentially liberating and empowering experience for you and the service user. It is important that you understand how effective assessment takes into account people's needs, rights, strengths, responsibilities and resources. You need to reflect on how your individual practice enables you to identify clients' strengths rather than weaknesses, and work with their existing networks and communities. Organisational restrictions and resource constraints will militate against creative service user focused practice, but you need to overcome these. Understanding how oppression and discrimination influences contemporary assessment practice and service users' ability to function is an important task for your practice development. The following descriptions and analyses of the policy guidance on work with clients in the context of Mental Health, Community Care, and Children and Families work are designed to illuminate areas of creative potential. The legislative context and policy guidance derived from that will be considered in terms of the changes in emphasis expected from current social work practice. In order to negotiate this difficult terrain to your own personal satisfaction and ethical standards it may be helpful to think about the following as you are embarking on your assessment practice:

Good supervision: this is the foundation of professional social work practice although practitioners often feel they receive too little. On the other hand you might feel that the kind of supervision being offered is really a management/administrative supervision that is experienced as oppressive. Good supervision attends to the issues related to management of your caseload but equally attends to the emotional and relationship issues that invariably affect your practice. It goes without saying that a profession based on the primary helping relationship requires a model of supervision attuned to the discrete psychological processes at work within you as you experience stressful and distressing assessment situations.

Reflective practice: at its most basic is about learning from our mistakes. But it can be more useful to extend this concept and use it more actively during the process of your assessment work with service users. In other words reflecting about what you are doing as you are doing it. It also involves reflecting back on a piece of work ideally with a colleague or supervisor and evaluating what happened and what you might have done differently. We shall return to this subject throughout this book.

Whose responsibility?: at the start of a social work assessment or even before, it is worth spending a few minutes thinking about whether this referral is appropriate for you or your team or your agency. The work may have passed through the variety of eligibility criteria and initial screening measures that are typical of some organisations, yet still on closer examination seem to be inappropriate. The problem is that by the time you realise this you may have already encountered the client and begun to build the helping relationship. It will help if you ask questions of the referrer about their expectations and assumptions about what you can and cannot do. This can save time and trouble and avoid you taking on other agency's responsibilities.

Stress management: contemporary social work practice is typified by staff working with high levels of stress on a regular basis. Sometimes this is mitigated by supportive colleagues and a thoughtful supervisor; however it is worth considering adopting some self-preservation strategies as you begin to experience the demands and pressures of the job. An important factor is stress management. There are whole texts on this subject but for now it is important to recognise this need particularly in the context of your assessment work because so much else hinges on the quality of this work and the consequences that flow from it. There is considerable pressure to get it right, yet we can acknowledge how this is almost an impossible aim. Managing your stress will be as individual as what stresses you, but learning to say no; taking time out; time management; planning your work; seeking supportive supervision; personal insight and relaxation techniques can all help.

Understanding assessment

Assessment has been defined as:

> a tool to aid in the planning of future work, the beginning of helping another person to identify areas for growth and change. Its purpose is the identification of needs – it is never an end in itself. (Taylor and Devine, 1993)

Assessment is the foundation of the social work process with service users. It can set the tone for further contact, it is your first opportunity to engage with new or existing clients, and it can be perceived by people as a judgement on their character or behaviour.

A good experience of assessment can make service users feel positive about receiving help

and their attitude to you and your agency. A bad experience of assessment can make matters worse, offend, and make problems harder to resolve in the long term. You can regard it as little more than a paper chasing exercise, involving form filling and restricting peoples' aspirations. Or you can see it as an opportunity to engage with service users in a problem-solving partnership where both of you can learn more about yourselves. A good way of measuring your progress during assessment practice is to use the concept of systematic practice (Thompson and Thompson, 2002). This requires that you ask three questions:

- **What are you trying to achieve?** It involves considering what needs remain unmet, and acts as a focus for the assessment, helping avoid the pitfall of simply gathering a lot of information, with no clarity about what needs to be done.
- **How are you going to achieve it?** This relates to the need to develop a strategy for achieving the identified objectives – how do you intend to get to where you want to be.
- **How will you know when you have achieved it?** This helps to bring clarity to what can invariably be vagueness in the work process. It enables you to envisage the outcome of work and to recognise when this has been achieved – or not.

There are three types of assessment that most of you will encounter in some form or other in whatever agency you practice. They are designed to indicate the level of perceived need and seriousness and complexity of the service user's situation. These examples relate to child care practice but they are transferable to other contexts:

- **Initial assessment**: this provides a good basis for short term panning and can be used as part of eligibility criteria to determine the level of need and priority. In child care situations it is used to effect immediate child protection with a general requirement of a two week time limit.

■ **Comprehensive assessment**: this takes over from where an initial assessment finishes and where more complex needs have been identified. Or it has been initiated following changes in a service user's situation where basic, but limited information already exists.

■ **Core assessment**: this is used in child care cases and is a specific requirement under Children Act 1989 guidance for a time-limited assessment in order to help inform the decision-making process in legal proceedings. The key aim is to enable all stakeholders to contribute as much information consistent with effective outcomes.

Knowing the level or depth required from the assessment is a starting point. But you need to proceed with a framework or guide to the different elements making up the assessment. If you move beyond some of your agency constraints and believe in service user focused assessment as an interactive process rather than an administrative convenience, then Milner and O'Byrne (1998) describe a helpful framework as a base for effective assessment in a variety of practice contexts:

■ **Preparation**: deciding who to see, what data will be relevant, what the purpose is and what the limits of the task are.

■ **Data collection**: people are met and engaged with, difference gaps are addressed, and empowerment and choice are safeguarded as we come to the task with respectful uncertainty and a research mentality.

■ **Weighing up the data**: current social and psychological theory and research findings that are part of every social worker's learning are drawn on to answer the question: Is there a problem and is it serious?

■ **Analysing the data**: the data is interpreted to seek and gain an understanding of the service user in order to develop ideas for intervention.

■ **Utilising the data**: this stage is used to finalise judgements.

Practice guidance

The following sample of Acts of Parliament and associated practice guidance illustrate the wealth of material that provides the framework within which your assessment practice takes place. These are the rules of engagement that permit you to take some of the most important decisions that will affect the lives of many people possibly for years and generations to follow. Some of this is prescriptive and written in administrative language that probably feels alien to your caring compassionate instincts. You may also feel comfortable with the power and authority offered within the law and guidance. Or you may feel distinctly uncomfortable in the constraints imposed on your practice and better judgement. This is however the framework in which your practice takes place and what legitimates your social work role. Your task in managing this material is not helped by the artificial distinctions and divisions of your agency that compartmentalise families and communities into specialist areas of practice, when they are linked in all sorts of ways.

Legislation

■ National Assistance Act 1948 (section 21, 47)
■ Chronically Sick and Disabled Persons Act 1970 (section 2)
■ Adoption Act 1976 (section 1, 2)
■ Mental Health Act 1983 (section 2, 3, 4)
■ Disabled Persons Act 1986 (section 4)
■ Children Act 1989 (section 17, 37, 43, 44, 47)
■ NHS and Community Care Act 1990 (section 47)
■ Criminal Justice Act 1991 (section 3)
■ Disability Discrimination Act 1995 (section 1, 19)
■ Carers (Recognition and Services) Act 1995 (section 1)
■ Community Care (Direct Payments) Act 1996 (section 1)
■ The Family Law Act 1996 (section 1)
■ Youth Justice and Criminal Evidence Act 1999 (section 28)
■ Carers and Disabled Children Act 2000 (section 1)
■ Special Educational Needs and Disability Act 2001 (section 1)

Practice guidance

- 1988. *A Guide for Social Workers Undertaking a Comprehensive Assessment*. HMSO.
- 1989. *Caring for People: Community Care in the Next Decade and Beyond*. HMSO.
- 1989. *Working with Lesbians and Gay Men: Good Practice Guidelines*. NAPO.
- 1990. *The Kaleidoscope of Care: A Review of Welfare Provision for Elderly People*. HMSO.
- 1991. *Case Management and Assessment: Practitioners Guide*. HMSO.
- 1991. *Case Management and Assessment: Managers Guide*. HMSO.
- 1992. *Assessment Systems and Community Care*. DoH/HMSO.
- 1992. *Committed to Quality: Quality Assurance in Social Services*. SSI/DoH.
- 1992. *Caring for Quality in Day Care Services*. HMSO.
- 1993. *Community Care: Findings from DoH Sponsored Research 1988–1992*. HMSO.
- 1993. *Empowerment, Assessment, Care Management and the Skilled Worker*. HMSO.
- 1994. *The Children Act 1989: Planning Long Term Placements Study*. DoH/HMSO.
- 1995. *Multi-Disciplinary Teamwork: Models of Good Practice*. CCETSW
- 1995. *The Challenge of Partnership in Child Protection: Practice Guide*. DoH/HMSO.
- 1995. *Building Partnership for Success: Community Care Development Programmes*. DoH.
- 2000. *Framework for the Assessment of Children in Need and their Families*. DoH.
- 2003. *Every Child Matters*. DFES.

The national priorities guidance is another central government prompt to steer local authorities and other providers towards services and service user groups that it deems should receive particular attention – usually with financial incentives or penalties. So we can see already there are a number of layers of pressure that go towards affecting your assessment practice:

- Prescriptions for what you are meant to achieve in assessment practice occupational standards.

- Legislative injunctions setting out the legal powers and responsibilities defining your practice.
- Practice guidance documents based on research studies to offer some evidence of effectiveness and good practice examples.
- Central government budget allocations for local government that determine the scope of what your agency can provide.

We have selected the work contexts of mental health, community care and children and families to illustrate the issues, dilemmas and opportunities for your practice development in social work assessment. The government has set a variety of targets and service specifications for people with mental health problems, older people and children and families. These three broad areas cover the majority of practice situations but they are not a definitive list. Much of what follows will however, raise issues that are common to other service user groups and are therefore transferable to other areas of social work practice.

ACTIVITY 1.1

Review the above material and make a list of the legislative and practice guidance that is relevant to your work context. Now look for evidence of how these are translated into your particular agency eligibility criteria and service specification.

Mental health assessment

The 1983 Mental Health Act allows for someone with a serious mental illness (or suspected of having such a condition) to be compulsorily admitted to hospital for assessment, or treatment, or for both. These assessments are set up by approved social workers (ASWs) who have completed post-qualifying training. There are three grounds for such an admission:

- It is in the interests of the patient's health.
- It is in the interests of the patient's safety.
- It is for the protection of other people.

If one of these grounds is satisfied and the sufferer needs to be in hospital for assessment or treatment, then they can be admitted under the Act. However before this stage, any social worker may find themselves working in situations where they are concerned about the mental health of their client and making an assessment of the depth and severity of the client's human distress and what model of practice intervention is appropriate to their needs. For example, this might apply in the circumstances of an adult recently discharged from hospital following a compulsory admission, a teenager who had a history of self-harming or suicide attempts, or a single young mother with severe depression.

The Care Programme Approach is the current policy context which defines the way care is delivered to people with mental health difficulties and influences social work practice particularly in relation to duties under section 117 of the Mental Health Act 1983. The care programme approach was introduced in 1991 and its principle aim was to improve the co-ordination of care to people with severe mental health needs. Prior to this some people were not properly assessed, whether in the community or prior to discharge from hospital.

The care programme approach was designed to complement the principles underlying care management in the NHS and Community Care Act 1990. This means people should have an individual care plan based on a thorough needs led assessment which is designed taking account of the views and aspirations of the service user and carer. This plan should be implemented within multi-agency provision and co-ordinated by one professional who should be responsible for monitoring and reviewing the plan. A care plan is a written statement specifying the objectives for the future agreed between practitioners and users and their carers or family, and outlining the means by which those objectives are to be met.

Research shows that only minimum involvement of users and carers takes place under the care programme approach (Carpenter and Sbaraini, 1997). In order to more fully involve users and carers and to develop an inte-grated care programme approach the following elements of good practice have been identified:

- Ensuring that planning meetings involve carers, users, advocates, and professionals.
- Recording users and carers' views on services in the community or in hospital.
- Identifying and recording separately everyone's views on problems, needs, and aims, and noting disagreements.
- Formulating action plans to meet needs rather than accept existing services and agreeing a contract clarifying monitoring and review arrangements.
- Providing specific information about rights and services, including medication and complaints procedures.
- Making sure an explicit agreement is obtained by signature of everyone involved.

ACTIVITY 1.2

Make a list of the factors you think make it difficult to ensure the care programme approach is effectively implemented in this area of social work practice.

Commentary

Your list should address the evolving nature of the relationship between users and carers which may not remain static but will not be noted unless regular and sensitive review takes place. The process can be very time consuming and highlights lack of appropriate provision in the community. GPs are generally ill informed about the care programme approach and few are involved in developing or reviewing it. The approach may not of itself benefit multi-disciplinary team working.

The National Service Framework for Mental Health introduced in 1999 focuses on the mental health needs of working-age adults up to 65 and is based on the premise that one adult in six suffers from a mental health problem at any one time. The guidance included in the framework covers mental health promotion, assessment and diagnosis, treatment, rehabilitation and care, and encompasses primary and specialist care and the role of partner agencies. Working in partnership is a key strand-partnership between those who use services and those who provide services, between different practitioners and professional groups, between the NHS and local government; and with the community, voluntary organisations, and independent sectors. The guidance approaches mental health service delivery from a corporate or holistic perspective which looks at the spectrum of care and need, and attempts to meet that need across a range of sectors. However, forthcoming changes to the Mental Health Act are likely to involve a reversal of this philosophy with new guidance aimed at more compulsory treatment with less social work involvement.

ACTIVITY 1.3

Make a list of the advantages and disadvantages of working in partnership with professionals from other agencies.

Commentary

Your list will highlight the challenges in working jointly across professional boundaries, often using identical theoretical resources, but trying to maintain your professional distinctiveness. Many agencies work with mentally ill people but what is your role with this client group? Shared responsibility can relieve the burden of stress but can also involve negotiating disagreement. The different power and status of some professionals becomes apparent in partnership practice.

The CPA assessment is a core activity for all workers in mental health services. Its purposes are to:

- Evaluate the individual's strengths.
- Identify areas of need.
- Assess the level of risk.
- Identify the need for specialist assessment.
- Determine whether intervention from mental health service is appropriate.
- Identify the person's level of need.
- Establish an information base.

Working effectively with black and ethnic minority communities is highlighted throughout the framework. Standard one notes that some black and minority ethnic communities have higher diagnosed rates of mental health problems than the general population and calls for specific programmes of service development for these communities. Standards two to six discuss the need for performance assessment to include the experience of service users and carers, including those from black and ethnic minority communities.

ACTIVITY 1.4

What do you think are the factors influencing the higher rate of compulsory admission to psychiatric hospital for black and ethnic minority people?

Commentary

Here you will be able to review the social context of mental health, cultural variations in emotional expression, and the wider effects of racism in producing higher levels of stress and disadvantage among black and ethnic minority people. This is then compounded by practice in psychiatric services that are perceived to be institutionally racist and insensitive to individual needs. The development of psychiatry and theories of human growth and development constructed in the 18th and 19th centuries were based on white ethnocentric beliefs and assumptions about normality. The Western model of illness regards the mind as distinct from the body and defines mental illness or mental health according to negative, deficit characteristics. In non-western cultures such as Chinese, Indian and African, mental health is often perceived as a harmonious balance between a person's internal and external influences. Thus a person is intrinsically linked to their environment and vice versa.

The Western model of mental illness tends to ignore the religious or spiritual aspects of the culture in which it is based. However, Eastern, African and Native American cultures tend to integrate them (Fernando, 2002). Spirituality and religion as topics in general do not feature often in the social work literature, yet they can be critical components of a person's wellbeing offering a source of strength, and hope in trying circumstances. Clients for whom family and faith backgrounds are inseparable may need encouragement to feel comfortable in multi-faith settings. Social workers need to address this dimension as part of the constellation of factors affecting black people, bearing in mind the positive and sometimes negative impact spiritual or religious beliefs might have on their mental health.

Caring for carers

There are estimated to be one and a quarter million people caring for someone with a mental illness, but fewer than one in five knows that they have a legal right to an assessment of their own needs. New rights have been introduced that are aimed at ensuring that carers receive services to match those needs. The Carers (Recognition and Services) Act, 1995 gave carers the right to an assessment of their ability to provide and to continue to provide care. To be eligible a carer has to provide a substantial amount of care on a regular basis. But the carer has to request an assessment, and it is frustrating for a carer to be assessed and have needs identified if nothing is then provided to meet those needs.

The National Service Framework for Mental Health introduced in 1999 has the potential to influence practice so that carers receive an assessment at least annually and have a written care plan which is implemented in discussion with them. A care co-ordinator must closely monitor the care plan, take responsibility for co-ordinating care, and ensure that the plan is delivered and reviewed. A healthy and well supported carer can have a positive effect on the life of the person with mental illness. However, a stressed and poorly supported carer can become physically and mentally unwell and likely to eventually become a client themselves.

A high quality carer's assessment starts from the principle that long-term carers are expert in mental illness. Many simply need to know how to gain access to services, particularly out of normal office hours. Others need a regular break, by arranging respite care to the person being cared for. Some will require financial advice and support to ensure they have full welfare or social security entitlements. Others will want to be put in touch with fellow carers so that they can gain mutual support from people in a similar position. A good carer's assessment looks at the risk of disruption or breakdown in home support. A regular quality assessment can help to maintain family support and family care – the preferred option for many people with mental illness.

ACTIVITY 1.5

List the dilemmas you might face in trying to balance the needs of a mentally ill client and their carer.

Commentary

It is possible to see the inter-relationship between the client and carer that might have evolved over a long time so that mutual dependency makes it hard to disentangle their separate needs. The impact of any intervention planned to offer respite could have the opposite effect and prompt deterioration in the situation. Where children are involved the dilemmas are more complex because of your separate responsibilities and the need to liaise with other professionals. The challenges for you in implementing the policy direction consistent with your social work values are:

■ The need to understand the different needs of users and carers and to enable effective input from each.
■ Ensuring that the views of users and carers are actively sought and they are supported to participate equally.
■ How to achieve a common purpose between different professional groups in relation to the care programme approach and care management.
■ The need to ensure that expectations for staff competency are backed up by training which is relevant to diversity and need.

Community care assessment

The NHS and Community Care Act 1990 together with subsequent practitioners' guidance, forms the basis for assessment and intervention practice with elderly or disabled clients. In 1989 the government white paper *Caring for People* emphasised the role of care management as the means by which a person's needs were regularly reviewed, resources managed effectively, and they had a single point of contact in situations where their needs were numerous or involved significant expense. Research demonstrated that many elderly people were being placed inappropriately in residential care, and that agencies were often duplicating work or delivering home support in a haphazard way. A key part of community care strategy is for different contributions from health, social service, or voluntary providers to be co-ordinated through care management.

The Department of Health has produced detailed advice on care management (DoH, 1991; 1991) which is described as the process of tailoring services to individual needs. Seven core tasks are involved in arranging care for someone in need:

- **The publication of information**: making public the needs for which assistance is offered and the arrangements and resources for meeting those needs. Prospective users and carers receive information about the need for which care agencies accept responsibility to offer assistance, and the range of services currently available.
- **Determining the level of assessment**: making an initial identification of need and matching the appropriate level of assessment to that need. If an enquirer requests more than information or advice, basic information is taken about the need in question, sufficient to determine the type of assessment required.
- **Assessing need**: understanding individual needs, relating them to agency policies and priorities, and agreeing the objectives for any intervention. A practitioner is allocated to assess the needs of the individual and of any

carers, in a way that also recognises their strengths and aspirations. In order to take account of all relevant needs, assessment may bring together contributions from a number of other specialists or agencies. The purpose of the assessment is to define the individual's needs in the context of local policies and priorities and agree on the desired outcome of any involvement.

- **Care planning**: negotiating the most appropriate ways of achieving the objectives identified by the assessment of need and incorporating them into an individual care plan. The role of the practitioner is to consider the resources available from statutory, voluntary, private or community sources that best meet the individual's requirements. The aim is to assist the user in making choices from these resources, and to put together an individual care plan.
- **Implementing the care plan**: securing the necessary resources or services. The implementation of that plan means securing the necessary finance or other identified resources. It may involve negotiation with a variety of service providers, specifying the type and quality of service required, and ensuring that services are co-ordinated with one another. The responsibility of practitioners at this stage will vary according to the level of their delegated budgetary authority.
- **Monitoring**: supporting and controlling the delivery of the care plan on a continuing basis. Because circumstances change, the implementation of the care plan has to be continuously monitored, making adjustments, as necessary, to the services provided and supporting users, carers and service providers in achieving the desired outcomes.
- **Reviewing**: reassessing needs and the service outcomes with a view to revising the care plan at specified intervals. The progress of the care plan has to be formally reviewed with the service user, carers, and service providers, firstly to ensure that services remain relevant to need, and secondly, to evaluate services as part of the continuing quest for improvement.

The Single Assessment Process is being intro- duced as a response to criticisms of the way care management and the aim of multi disciplinary working has evolved. The NHS Plan (DoH, 2000) and the National Service Framework for Older People specifies ways in which assessment of elderly people should be standardised for use by professionals in joint health and social care teams. Agencies are expected to reach agreement on several contentious issues including:

■ Agree terminology and reach a common assessment language
■ Agree on shared values
■ Agree the link between medical diagnosis and assessment
■ Agree common assessment approaches

The SAP has not been rigorously evaluated but early indications suggest that in its desire to achieve effective practice and avoid dupli- cation, the government is making a crude attempt to construct an assessment tool that will not appeal to nurses or social workers. A recent Royal College of Nursing report found widespread dissatisfaction with the single assessment process among nurses who felt they were being used as social care staff inappro- priate to their training. Social workers equally fear that the SAP will be medically oriented and eventually marginalise the social aspects of an elderly persons experience.

ACTIVITY 1.6

What are the benefits of care management and the barriers to good practice?

Commentary

The benefits of care management are that it supports a needs-led approach to assessment and the use of resources, tailoring services to indi- vidual requirements. It involves a clear commitment to individual care planning, speci- fying desired outcomes. Care management requires a clear division of responsibility between assessment/care management and

service provision, separating the interests of service users and providers. It should result in more responsive services as a result of linking assessment and purchasing or commissioning.

Care management is designed to result in a wider choice of services across the statutory and independent sectors. It should enable part- nership practice in which users/carers play a more active part alongside practitioners in determining the services they receive. This could improve opportunities for represen- tation and advocacy and be a way of meeting the needs of disadvantaged individuals more effectively. Greater continuity of care and greater accountability to users and carers should result from these changes. Finally, better integration of services within and between agencies is envisaged as part of government aspirations for closer working between providers.

Policy guidance offers little in the way of addressing the dilemma of meeting potentially infinite demand within finite resources. This is especially so in the context of the increasing age profile of the UK population and individual expectations of service delivery. The implicit principle within the guidance is that users and carers will be empowered. Yet while practi- tioners are expected to seek the views of both carers and users, most weight is expected to be given to users' needs, and ultimately the assessing practitioner is responsible for defining the users' needs. The definition of need therefore remains a professional hegemony.

Guidance suggests that assessment should be simple, speedy and based on the principle of what is the least that it is necessary to know. This may not necessarily be the basis for good assessment practice. How is it possible to establish a relationship of trust on what appears to be superficial and brief contact? The policy guidance recommends establishing a balance between the needs of user and carer. It recog- nises that disentangling these needs would be a difficult task. Yet there is little in the way of concrete suggestions as to how this balance should be achieved especially as the users' views are still expected to carry most weight. The tendency to view carers as resources leads to the

...nption that the sole purpose of ...ntain carers in their role.

...ued that terms such as 'need' ...es people in a dependent position, ... rcing the perception that they are problematic. This leads to the tendency to focus on a person's deficits and difficulties rather than building upon their strengths and coping strategies. This is especially the case when practitioners are expected to use eligibility criteria – rarely made explicit to the user, to determine the level of need and priority. Integrated and co-ordinated working between agencies and professions is a fundamental aim of community care policy. Yet there are difficulties in putting this aim into practice due to lack of a common culture, values and agendas between agencies. Practitioners tend to rely on their implicit knowledge based on professional training, values and agency culture that differ.

The use of forms and assessment tools involving rather mechanical approaches to assessment can be criticised for simply justifying decisions already made. Consequently assessment tends to focus on physical functioning but the reason for such data collection is not apparent and does not appear to be interpreted or analysed in any meaningful way.

One of the major barriers to achieving good assessment practice concerns the resources available to develop innovative service options. Social workers often feel like rationers of care and services thus inhibiting them from probing too deeply into an individual's circumstances or spending time to develop a deeper professional, helping relationship. Identifying needs that cannot be subsequently met results in feelings of guilt, disillusionment and low morale.

Children and families assessment

The Children Act 1989 provides the legislative foundation on which subsequent policy guidance has been built to inform social work practice in assessment with children and families. *A Framework for Assessing Children in Need* (DoH, 2000) is the latest and most comprehensive guidance to emerge following implementation of the Children Act 1989.

Since 2001 all referrals to social service departments concerning children in need have been assessed under these guidelines in two ways. An initial assessment where the needs are considered to be relatively straightforward, such as a request for family support, and a core assessment where the needs are perceived to be more complex involving a number of concerns about emotional development or child abuse.

The guidance is a key element of the Department of Health's work to support local authorities in implementing Quality Protects – the government's programme for transforming the management and delivery of children's social services. This guidance has been incorporated into other government guidance on protecting children from harm – *Working Together to Safeguard Children* (1999). Research into the working of the Children Act 1989 showed that social workers were conducting child protection investigations but neglecting to assess fully the family's needs for ongoing support (DoH, 1995). Guidance has been driven as much by evidence from research as high profile child abuse cases under the full glare of the media spotlight where complexities are reduced to simplicities.

A recent research project found evidence that social workers find the framework cumbersome, over-reliant on prescribed formats, and expected to be undertaken in unrealistic timescales (Corby, Millar and Pope, 2002). The researchers found evidence that parents involved in these assessments felt their views were not being taken sufficiently into account. Key to parental satisfaction with the process was:

- Feeling that their perceptions about their children were taken into account.
- Reaching agreement about the nature of the problem.
- Maintaining optimism and a degree of sensitivity.
- Using the framework flexibly and creatively to maximise parental empowerment.

The principle underlying the assessment framework is that social workers need a framework for understanding and helping children and families which takes into account the inner world of the self and the outer world of the environment, both in terms of relationships and in terms of practicalities such as housing. This can be called an ecological, holistic, or psycho-social approach. The framework uses a triangular model to distinguish the elements of the assessment framework: the child's developmental needs, parenting capacity, and family and environmental factors. Within each of these elements social workers are expected to gather the following specific information for analysis:

Child's developmental needs

- health
- education
- emotional and behavioural development
- identity
- family and social relationships
- social presentation
- self-care skills

Parenting capacity

- basic care
- ensuring safety
- emotional warmth
- stimulation
- guidance and boundaries
- stability

Family and environmental factors

- family history and functioning
- wider family
- housing
- employment
- income
- family's social integration
- community resources

Successful implementation of the framework requires you to have a good grasp of the principles underpinning the framework and an ability to translate these principles into practice (Horwath, 2002):

- Assessments should be child-centred and rooted in child development.
- Professionals should recognise and work with diversity.

- Assessment practice means working whenever possible, with children and families and building on the family strengths as well as identifying difficulties.
- The quality of the human environment is linked to the development of the child.
- A range of professionals are the assessors and providers of services to children in need, therefore assessments should be multi-disciplinary.
- Assessment is a continuing process. Interventions and services should be provided alongside the assessment.
- Effective assessment practice is dependent on the combination of evidence-based practice grounded in knowledge with finely balanced professional judgement.

You will need to integrate multi-faceted knowledge of child development into your assessments from learning acquired from studies in human growth and development to be able to confidently use this framework (Beckett, 2002). Psychodynamic theory and learning theory are especially important tools to employ in this context. Also, two key concepts critical to the interrelationship between the inner and outer worlds are attachment and self-esteem. Children who are securely attached to significant adults in early childhood have been shown to develop good peer relationships and cope well with problems. Social work practice concerned with helping children who have lost attachment figures places great emphasis on providing these children with continuity of good alternative parenting experiences.

It is important to avoid being deterministic about some of these theoretical resources or to assume that adverse childhood experiences can cascade automatically through subsequent generations. Modern research has demonstrated the complexity and diversity of different children's responses to similar experiences. It is important to understand what may act as protective factors in children's lives which can mitigate the effects of negative experiences and promote resilience. And there are children who with ample social and family support have little capacity to cope with small amounts of stress.

Children vary in their vulnerability to psycho-social stress and adversity as a result of both genetic and environmental influences. Family-wide experiences tend to impinge on individual children in quite different ways. The reduction of negative and increase of positive chain reactions influences the extent to which the effects of adversity persist over time. New experiences that open up opportunities can provide beneficial turning-point effects. Although positive experiences in themselves do not exert much of a protective effect, they can be helpful if they serve to neutralise some risk factors; and that the cognitive and affective processing of experiences is likely to influence whether or not resilience develops (Rutter, 1999).

Evidence-based practice requires the gathering, testing, recording, and weighing of evidence on which to base decisions and the careful use of knowledge gained during work with a child and family. This helps the task of determining what is most relevant in a family's situation, what is most significant for the child, the impact intervention is having, and the judgement about when more or less action is required in the child's best interests. It is important to pay equal attention to all three domains in the framework and not be deflected by a child's behavioural symptoms to the extent that parental capacity and environmental factors are neglected.

Recent research demonstrates that assessments can become dominated by the agenda of social services departments thereby undermining the concept of inter-agency co-operation (Howarth, 2002). Also in the drive to complete recording forms within specified timescales anti-oppressive practice is given a lack of attention, while the pace of the assessment is inconsistent with the capacity of the family to cope. In the case of fostering and adoption work, research has highlighted practice based on diagnostic assessment of foster carers using psychodynamic theories, contrasted with practice based on task centred, functional analysis which applicants found more useful (Berridge, 1997). The important point is that you can locate and justify your chosen practice orientation and demonstrate how it fulfils the task requirement.

ACTIVITY 1.7

Write down the ways in which you think the guidance will help in your assessment of a child and family you might be working with, and the ways in which this guidance will hinder the assessment.

Commentary

Such a comprehensive guidance framework can seem daunting to social workers working under pressure on their available resources. Time is crucial in many situations and it is often difficult to obtain full information in risky circumstances. Interventions undertaken in one set of circumstances can impact on the quality of subsequent assessment – and vice versa. It is important to consider the purpose of assessment and the relationship between assessment and intervention, which can make it hard to separate their functions. The danger is that social workers will feel impelled to conduct lengthy detailed assessments following the framework rigidly rather than using it as a framework to guide practice across a multitude of different circumstances. The skill will be in focusing on the most important aspects of the framework relevant to particular situations.

Assessment as process

Organisational arrangements within social care agencies are driving the way assessment is conceptualised by social workers as we have already noted. It is therefore important that you adopt a wide definition of assessment if your practice is to be empowering and anti-oppressive. It is important to think of assessment as a process rather than a one-off event. There should be a seamless transition from assessment to intervention in a circular process that includes the crucial elements of planning and reviewing. Once completed, the circle begins again at the assessment stage of the process and so on. Think of it as a continuous, perpetual movement, punctuated by a range of activities involving major or minor interventions in the life of service users. Rather than adopting a one-dimensional view of assessment you could also perceive it as an intervention in itself – the very act of conducting an information-gathering interview could have a significant positive impact on a person's well-being. The simple idea that someone cares and is prepared to listen to their story could be enormously comforting to someone lonely, isolated and with low self-esteem.

No discussion of assessment can be complete without addressing the concept of need, as it is a word that frequently appears in much legislation, practice guidance and service providers' documentation. There are universal needs expressed in global documents like the UN declaration on the rights of children, there are special needs which although clearly discriminatory appear to be accepted as a useful signifier for certain groups in society. What this does is to permit rationing to occur under the guise of benign motives. If you consider the idea that every person has special needs, in the sense of their individual uniqueness, and replace this with the notion of rights then the concept of special needs becomes redundant. In our context of social work the concept of need has a powerful impact on assessment practice. It has been categorised in the following way to help us distinguish the subtleties in meaning and the way need can be defined (Bradshaw, 1972):

■ **Normative need**: decided by professionals or administrators on behalf of the community. Standards are set to minimum levels of service with stigma attached.
■ **Felt need**: limited by the individuals' expression of wants based on their perceptions, knowledge and experience.
■ **Expressed need**: these are felt needs translated into service demand but restricted by what the client feels is likely to be offered.
■ **Comparative need**: a comparison of need between two areas, or service user groups in order to reach standardised provision. Results in levelling down rather than up.

It is useful to bear these definitions in mind during the process of your assessment practice. They can help guide you and enable you to position yourself as you move from the role of client advocate articulating their needs through to the agency representative who is expected to

place a boundary or limit on resources. Social workers employed as care managers are to some extent insulated from these twin pressures by being separated from assessment but they too know what is required by clients in particular circumstances, understand the inadequacies of minimum provision and appreciate the negative consequences for service users. One of the aims of an empowering social work practice in keeping with the aspirations of disabled people for example, is to move to a system of client self-assessment. However, the continued emphasis on budget constraints limits the extent to which local authorities are prepared to relinquish their control in the determination of individual need, and self-assessment requires a partnership between social workers and disabled people which threatens that control (Oliver and Sapey, 1999).

Three models of assessment

It is sometimes suggested that social workers can either play a crucial role in understanding the problems of their client, or work alongside the person who has been identified as the client and other significant people in the situation. The task is to arrive at a mutual understanding of the problem and negotiate who might do what to help (Smale et al., 1993). A further distinction is to portray these two approaches as reflecting the questioning model or the exchange model of assessment. A third approach, perceived as a variation of the questioning model, is the procedural model whereby information is gathered to see whether the client meets certain eligibility criteria for services. The questioning model assumes the worker:

■ Is expert in people, their problems and needs.
■ Exercises knowledge and skill to form their assessment and identify people's needs.
■ Identifies resources required.
■ Takes responsibility for making an accurate assessment of need and taking appropriate action.

Whereas the exchange model assumes that the worker:

■ Has expertise in the process of problem-solving with others.

■ Understands and shares perceptions of problems and their management.

■ Gets agreement about who will do what to support whom.

■ Takes responsibility for arriving at the optimum resolution of problems within the constraints of available resources and the willingness of participants to contribute.

The difference between the questioning and exchange model of assessment is in how power is used and its impact on the service user. The latter appears to offer a more empowering experience enabling the person to be fully involved as an equal partner in a process of negotiating the nature of their problem and its possible solutions. In the questioning model it is assumed that questions can be answered in a straightforward manner and that the worker is able to accurately interpret what the client really wants. The danger is that the complexities of the communication process across bound-aries of race, gender, age, disability etc, can be underestimated or even ignored.

In the exchange model the worker concen-trates on an exchange of information between themselves and the service user and others involved. A definition of the problem and its resolution or management is arrived at by mutual understanding and sharing of percep-tions. The worker tracks or follows what others communicate and is careful not to be influenced by preconceived assumptions. Listening and communication skills are at their optimum effectiveness in this model of practice. The danger is that workers can be misled about the extent of a person's strengths or needs and be drawn towards over-optimistic or over-pessimistic judgements.

The procedural model is characterised by questions sometimes framed by pre-printed forms that define the eligibility criteria for services and enable judgements to be made about that should get access to resources. The questions are determined by those setting the criteria for resource allocation – not service users. This process attempts to:

■ Identify a particular level of dependency and categorise the client.

■ Define the nature of the client's needs in the terms that services are offered.

■ The client's definitions of their problems, or that of others, may or may not be included.

■ The process is invariably service-driven rather than needs-driven.

■ The agency remains central to the definition of problems and the range of available solutions.

■ Neither the worker, the service user or other involved persons are empowered by the process.

The procedural model is simple and quick to use. It can be controlled easily by managers and eligibility criteria altered to be responsive to changes in policy about resource allocation. Such procedures usually strive towards equitable allocation of scarce resources between competing demands by specifying detailed priorities. Workers often feel they are carrying out policy over which they have little influence. This can be frustrating, but equally they do not always want the burden of responsibility in deciding who gets a service and who does not. There can be a sense of safety in working to a strict set of procedures and guidelines where there is less room for interpretation and indi-vidual judgement. The danger is that workers can emphasise the negative aspects of a person's situation and underplay their strengths in order to ensure they fulfil the eligibility criteria for services. This distorts the overall level of demand and results in a deficit model of practice.

ACTIVITY 1.8

List the key features of the three models of assessment discussed above and describe their advantages and disadvantages.

Case illustration

Recent research into the experiences of disabled people has highlighted the difficulties in implementing policy designed to ensure that the right to an assessment actually delivers more appropriate social work intervention. This research discovered that the type of team with which disabled people made contact, was crucial to their experience of getting a proper assessment (Davis et al., 1997).

Standardised approaches to assessment based on a procedural model were set out in practice guidelines and decisions about access to assessment were influenced by risk-based service criteria linked to budget limits. However, social workers in specialist teams were more likely to open up access to assessment in collaborative ways and shift away from service-led agendas to identify and use community-based networks and resources.

Disabled people find social services contact confusing, fragmented, and often irrelevant to their concerns. Access to assessment produces feelings of uncertainty, marginalisation, and exclusion. Disabled people are fully aware of resource constraints but want creativity and flexibility from social workers to think of alternatives and priorities.

What disabled people want

- Partnership practice is highly rated and face to face contact preferred.
- Advice and information to enable options to be considered.
- Equal participation in the planning of services.
- Assessment should be informed by equal opportunities policies.
- Service charges to be explicit to enable informed choices to be made.
- Assessment practice should build on the strategies already used by disabled people and their carers to manage their lives.

Consumer studies and outcome research into helping relationships in social work, and other professional supportive relationships support the principles underlying the exchange model of assessment. The questioning and procedural models are based on management imperatives about service allocation from finite resources. They all raise questions about the notion of expertise and the use of power – especially in

risky situations where a measure of short-term control may result in longer-term empowerment or vice versa. All these models need to be applied in real circumstances in order to allow workers to evaluate their effectiveness and form conclusions about their usefulness. It may be that in practice you find there are elements of each appearing during different stages of a piece of work, or at different times with several contacts with a client. Another important factor is the particular practice context of your work. Each of these models may lend itself to a particular professional function with different service user groups. There are social work teams working in the short or long term across the spectrum of assessment and intervention roles. As always, it is important to be able to reflect on where you and your client are in that process.

Creative assessment practice

Accepting that assessment is an imperfect science is a good starting point for creative practice. Also understanding that it is a dynamic process requiring high quality communication skills is very important. Dynamic in the sense that it is not static – information can become out of date, a family's functioning can deteriorate quickly, while the very act of assessment can affect that which you are assessing. Assessment is therefore a purposeful activity. It is the art of managing competing demands and negotiating the best possible outcome. It means steering between the pressures of organisational demands, legislative injunction, limited resources and personal agendas. It includes having the personal integrity to hold to your core values and ethical base while being buffeted by strong feelings.

An assessment should be part of a perceptual/analytic process that involves selecting, categorising, organising and synthesising data. If it is conducted as an exploratory study avoiding labels it can result in a careful deliberation of a service users' needs and not just fit them into whatever provision exists. Remember that all assessments contain the potential for error or bias. These can be partly counteracted by following these guidelines (Coulshed, 1991):

■ Improving self-awareness so as to monitor when you are trying to normalise, be over-optimistic or rationalise data.

■ Getting supervision which helps to release blocked feelings or confront denial of facts or coping with the occasional situation where you have been manipulated.

■ Being aware of standing in awe of those who hold higher status or power and challenging their views when necessary.

■ Treating all assessments as working hypotheses which ought to be substantiated with emerging knowledge – remember that they are inherently speculations derived from material and subjective sources.

With government policy and organisational changes moving in the direction of more multi-disciplinary team working it is imperative that social work assessment skills in the context of practice with other professionals is both authoritative and creative. The values and knowledge base of different staff from other agencies will be reflected in the way they think about and undertake assessment. Your social work contribution is crucial and depends on having the capacity to work with other colleagues in partnership. Negotiation skills are paramount in order to enable you to challenge and confront when and where necessary to defend clients. Networking is considered a valuable social work attribute and you should be developing expertise in liaison, linking, communicating, and convening meetings.

Multi-disciplinary teams can become stressful places to work, particularly when the service is under pressure and energies are drained by resource shortages combined with high demand. It is easier to keep a low profile and grit your teeth in these circumstances rather than open up a painful or uncomfortable issue for discussion. However you will gain respect by voicing concerns about the service or the clients and showing a willingness to tackle difficult issues. Being open, client-centred and demonstrating sensitivity to the team dynamics will be helpful to others who probably feel the same. Your broader understanding of service users in their socio-economic context together with

your specific knowledge of child care, mental health or community care legislation will help clarify your distinctive and valued contribution.

Assessment is about making sense of the situation as a whole, and working out the best way to achieve change (Middleton, 1997). Creative assessment ensures that clients are included in the process and feel active in its determination rather than feeling that it is a series of coercive hoops to jump through before receiving a reward. It should be part and parcel of socially inclusive practice that enshrines the policy objective of social justice. These activities demonstrate that assessment can be, and is, inextricably linked to intervention and can be a therapeutic process in itself. Your practice will be more creative if you find yourself doing the following:

■ Spending time talking with the client.

■ Spending time with the client in their usual environment.

■ Spending time with the client doing things that they enjoy regularly.

■ Spending time with the client doing some of their regular activities.

■ Spending time with the client doing something they would not normally do and in an environment they are unfamiliar with.

■ Spending time with the client around other people both familiar and unfamiliar.

■ Spending time talking with other people involved in their life.

Chapter summary

We discussed the way organisational arrangements within social care agencies are driving the way assessment is conceptualised by social workers. It is therefore important that you adopt a wide definition of assessment if your practice is to be empowering and anti-oppressive. A useful starting point is to think of assessment as a process rather than a one-off event. There should be a seamless transition from assessment to intervention in a circular process that includes the crucial elements of planning and reviewing.

It should be apparent that the depth and complexity of the work involved in using official guidance places competing demands on practitioners who face numerous dilemmas such as: balancing the needs of clients and carers and individual liberty versus public safety. Time and resource constraints militate against the need for depth and analysis, while assessed needs can be hindered by service provision limits.

We noted how translating guidance into practical, visible and measurable practice is challenging and it is important not to become overwhelmed or deny the possibility of implementing change and rely on cynicism or complacency to excuse inaction. Guidance evolves as a result of research and evaluation of existing practice set against economic and social policy imperatives. Actively contributing to that process is part of ethical social work practice.

The care programme approach is the current policy context which defines the way care is delivered to people with mental health difficulties and influences social work practice particularly in relation to duties under section 117 of the Mental Health Act 1983. The care programme approach was introduced in 1991 and its principle aim was to improve the co-ordination of care to people with severe mental health needs. Prior to this some people were not properly assessed, whether in the community or prior to discharge from hospital.

We discussed how the benefits of care management are that it supports a needs-led approach to assessment and the use of resources, tailoring services to individual requirements. It involves a clear commitment to individual care planning, specifying desired outcomes. Care management requires a clear division of responsibility between assessment/care management and service provision, separating the interests of service users and providers. It should result in more responsive services as a result of linking assessment and purchasing/commissioning.

The use of forms and assessment tools involving rather mechanical approaches to assessment can be criticised for simply justifying decisions already made. Consequently assessment tends to focus on physical functioning but the reason for such data collection is not apparent and does not appear to be interpreted or analysed in any meaningful way.

One of the major barriers to achieving good assessment practice concerns the resources available to develop innovative service options. Social workers often feel like rationers of care and services thus inhibiting them from probing too deeply into an individual's circumstances or spending time to develop a deeper professional, helping relationship. Identifying needs that cannot be subsequently met results in feelings of guilt, disillusionment and low morale.

We suggested that the principle underlying the *Framework for the Assessment of Children in Need* is that social workers need a framework for understanding and helping children and families which takes into account the inner world of the self and the outer world of the environment. This includes relationships and practicalities such as housing. This can be called an ecological, holistic, or psycho-social approach. The framework uses a triangular model to distinguish the elements of the assessment framework: the child's developmental needs, parenting capacity, and family and environmental factors.

Assessment is a purposeful activity. It is the art of managing competing demands and negotiating the best possible outcome. It means steering between the pressures of organisational demands, legislative injunction, limited resources and personal agendas. It includes having the personal integrity to hold to your core values and ethical base while being buffeted by strong feelings. An assessment should be part of a perceptual/analytic process that involves selecting, categorising, organising and synthesising data. If it is conducted as an exploratory study avoiding labels it can result in a careful deliberation of a service user's needs and not just fit them into whatever provision exists.

CHAPTER 2

Contemporary Models of Intervention

Introduction

What do we mean by intervention? The orthodox literature tends to emphasise the separateness of assessment and intervention in social work practice, while practice guidance from central government unwittingly reinforces the impression. We think this is not helpful because in practice social workers understand that the two are in effect inseparable. Even before you make client contact, as a social worker picking up a new referral or taking over an existing case you will begin to form impressions and assumptions from the available information (however limited and inaccurate). This is inevitable but care needs to be taken not to let these ideas drive the process of your work. Rather they should inform it to the extent where they fail to fit with other information sources and your own impressions. In other words treat such evidence with caution and regard it as provisional until enough supporting material confirms the initial information.

Furthermore it is important to acknowledge that as soon as you interplay with the situation, you have already begun to intervene even before contact with a service user. An initial telephone call to another agency colleague might seem routine but the way you communicate and your selection of topics for discussion are already shaping the tone, style and content of your intervention. Your intervention is also not one-way it is already beginning to change you, as well as the situation. The responses you elicit from other people will be partly shaped by

your questions but also by what they want to tell you and what they feel you should be told.

Before long – and before client contact – you have started a process of intervention in which your perceptions and planning are being influenced directly and in subtle ways. A reciprocal relationship has begun between you and those connected to the person requiring help (Laing, 1976). A dictionary definition of intervention suggests it means to come between so as to prevent or modify the result or course of events. This definition does not imply success or a positive outcome – merely that the course of events is changed. It is important to bear in mind that for any social work intervention there is a potential spectrum of effects for people for whom the intervention:

- Has only benefits.
- Produces benefits which outweigh the disadvantages.
- Has very little or no effect at all.
- Produces disadvantages which outweigh the advantages.
- Has only disadvantages.

In other words bear in mind that your social work intervention begins before client contact and whatever the aim of intervention it may lead to different and quite unexpected consequences. How many times have you experienced directly or heard from colleague's reports of what appeared at first sight to be a straightforward piece of work that turned into a complex and challenging case? It is worth remembering to consider whether the referral is appropriate at all, even if eligibility criteria have been met, or whether you, or your agency are at this point in time the appropriate resource. You may feel under pressure to respond knowing there is nothing else available even though your role and task are unclear. Equally a case might not fit strict eligibility criteria but you are able to make an argument that some preventive work will stop a situation deteriorating and eventually require more expensive resources. Chapter 9 examines some of the evidence for evaluating social work assessment and intervention to provide you with some means for selecting what is likely to help, but there is as yet no definitive easy way of telling what intervention can, with certainty, produce a given outcome. Bear in mind that whatever your intentions the potential for making matters worse exists as much as the potential for making a positive difference or no difference whatsoever in the short, medium or long term.

The problem with theory

One of the contemporary issues in modern social work intervention is achieving the translation from theory to practice that has echoed throughout the development of social work as a profession. This is regarded as one of the hallmarks of any professional practice and can guide your practice towards the achievement of desired goals and outcomes. Several authors have drawn attention to the debate about terminology and sources of knowledge considered relevant to inform good practice standards. Social work is and should be promiscuous with regard to theory and knowledge from every relevant source whether philosophy, law, sociology or psychology. We should not constrain ourselves to what might be useful in making a difference to the lives of service users. Unfortunately accepting a wide theoretical panorama from which to choose means making the task of selection harder. It also can cause confusion about what to call the possible interventions that spring from the use of particular theories.

The concept of how to describe the particular piece of work you are engaged in probably occupies a disproportionate amount of non-practitioners' time compared to the time spent by practising social workers doing it. The terms method, model, orientation, approach, or perspective are all used interchangeably when social work students come to discuss and write about their practice placements. It is said that qualified practitioners rarely consider the particular theoretical base informing their practice, saying they are too busy to think. But when pressed they might confess to an eclectic approach, or list concepts such as empowering, anti-oppressive, feminist or partnership as indicative of the way they work.

Method is a term that can be used to identify four general forms of practice (Haynes and Holmes, 1994):

- work with individuals
- group work
- family work
- community work

Method is also defined in different ways altogether. It can be related to practice orientation to describe the four general types of practice above. And it can be used to describe practice methods or practice interventions that form part of a particular practice approach (Trevithick, 2000). The word model also suffers from multiple meanings and inconsistent usage in social work literature. Some authors distinguish between a social work model and a theory, identifying a model as a description rather than an explanation. Models therefore are used to define and describe phenomena; they can act as bricks in building theory (Howe, 1987). Others use the word model as a theory such as the medical model or social model of disability, and mix it up when discussing task-centred or client-centred work for example. However it is also used to describe specific types of intervention such as:

- task-centred
- crisis intervention
- behavioural

Trevithick (2000) offers a useful guide to locating your practice within what can easily begin to feel like a theoretical minefield that is as much a distraction to practice as it is a guide. She uses the term practice approach to describe practice that draws on a distinct body of theory that results in specific practice interventions such as:

- client-centred
- cognitive-behavioural
- task-centred
- crisis intervention
- psychodynamic or psychosocial
- systemic family therapies

Similarly she describes how the word perspective is loosely used in the literature and suggests that it is distinct from practice approach. Her contention is that a perspective is not linked to a particular theory and practice method. Therefore the main practice perspectives are:

- anti-discriminatory
- anti-oppressive
- anti-racist
- feminist
- users or survivors
- radical

Given the different meanings attached to the terms methods, models etc. it would not be surprising if this left the reader in a state of confusion when seeking to research the knowledge and theory base to inform practice interventions. We do not seek to add to the confusion but merely point out that there are differences and distinctions in the field of social work theory. The pragmatist will seek knowledge sources that fit with their internal concept of what social work should be about. If you believe that the problems of clients are caused by an unjust economic system that distributes wealth unfairly then a radical perspective combined with a client-centred approach might appeal to you. On the other hand if you feel that a client's problems stem from an emotionally deprived and neglected childhood you may be drawn to

offering an individual psychodynamic intervention. With experience you will begin to see the limited value of these dichotomies and understand that the complexities of people's lives cannot simply be ascribed to a particular experience. More likely they are a combination of socio-economic factors, intra-familial experiences, and a unique individual predisposition to dealing with stress. The important point is that you understand that you are more or less acting consciously within an intellectual framework that you can justify to defend your activity.

ACTIVITY 2.1

Having read the above material considers a recent piece of work you were recently involved in and try to identify the underlying theory influencing your practice.

Commentary

Whether you view service users' problems as the results of an unjust economic system or as the result of childhood abuse, any selected intervention requires the active consent of the client. You could also argue that both explanations are equally valid and are not necessarily mutually exclusive. The important point is that you do not get bogged down in theoretical wrestling, mystify your practice and alienate yourself from service users. The aim of using theory and basing practice interventions on the best available evidence of what is effective is to offer you resources to guide your practice and provide the justification for choosing certain courses of action.

The wider the gap between theory and practice the greater the distance you have to travel in your thinking. In some cases this might be a good experience but in many others it could feel like a hindrance. At its best theory can provide an anchor of stability in situations where stress and anxiety levels are high and confusion reigns. It can offer a light in dark circumstances when you feel that events are driving your practice rather than your planning determining the process of your work. The following interventions are described in order to provide you with some knowledge and understanding of the potential contemporary resources available to help inform your practice (Payne, 1997; Stepney and Ford, 2000; Milner and O'Byrne, 1998; Trevithick, 2000):

Crisis intervention

Work with any client group in a variety of agency contexts will sooner or later expose you to a crisis of some form or another. Crisis intervention has become a practice with a theoretical base and can be identified by certain characteristics. Drawing on psychodynamic principles it is aimed at strengthening the client's internal psychological resources through a personal relationship within which you can positively connote their coping strategies. Crisis theory is described as a time when a person finds themselves much more dependent on external sources of support than at other times in their life. It has been described as having three distinct phases (Caplan, 1964):

- **Impact**: recognising a threat.
- **Recoil**: attempting to restore equilibrium but failing leaving the person feeling stressed and defeated.
- **Adjustment/adaptation or breakdown**: when the person begins to move to a different level of functioning.

It is usually interrelated factors and triggers that produce a state of crisis, some of which can be anticipated while others cannot. Another concept to help understand what crisis means is that it is a stage of disequilibrium when tension and anxiety have risen to a peak and the individual's built in devices no longer operates. Rather than see crises as failures of individuals or systems it is useful to think of them as opportunities for significant interventions at times when stakeholders are more likely to engage with your strategy.

Characteristics of crisis intervention:

- Employs ideas from psychodynamic theory in understanding the way each person can be helped to gain insight into their functioning and discover ways of coping better.

- Is used in conjunction with risk assessment and risk management techniques.
- Is short term in nature?
- Relates a client's internal crises to external changes.
- Can help in cases of bereavement, loss, reactive depression, and trauma.
- Is based on the notion that people can return to previous level of functioning depending on the nature of the problem, and the quality of help provided.

Systems intervention

If you are employing a systems theory in social work practice this will be characterised by the key notion that individual clients have a social context which will be influencing to a greater or lesser extent, their behaviour and their perception of their problem. An important social context is that of the family and this has led to the practice of family therapy as a method of social work practice that springs from the systems theory. Different models of family therapy have evolved over time as the discipline itself develops and draws upon influences from behavioural or psychodynamic theories. It offers a broad framework for assessment enabling you to map all of the important elements affecting your client as well as a method of working with those elements to effect beneficial change. The theory is derived from general systems theory which assumes everything in society is linked and interacting, often at hidden and discrete levels.

Characteristics of systems intervention:

- Convening family meetings such as family group conferences to give voice to everyone connected to an individual's problem.
- Harnessing the strengths of families to support individuals in trouble.
- Using a problem–oriented style to energise the family to find their own solutions.
- Development of insight into patterns of behaviour and communication within the family system.
- Employing a circular rather than linear model of causality in order to avoid blame and scapegoating.

Pincus and Minahan (1973) suggest you assess a client's situation according to a classification of four systems: change agent, client, target, or action system. Clients turn to their resource systems to find help when encountering problems such as:

- **Informal or natural systems**: these include family, friends, neighbours who provide emotional support, advice, information and practical help.
- **Formal membership systems**: include trades unions, clubs, support groups, co-operative associations, or tenants associations providing more specialised help.
- **Public or societal systems:** include housing associations, hospitals, health centres, courts, social services offices, and schools, places of work and welfare agencies.

This can help identify in a structured way the complete picture of a service user's context and the resources within it. Classifying those resources as described enables you to mobilise those elements that can be most useful to help with the problem. We can use this as an overarching framework to help guide our social work practice. It is particularly useful to clarify situations where there is multi-agency and multi-professional involvement in client's lives. It can help the drawing of boundaries and sort out who does what in often complex, fast-moving, and confusing situations. This approach fits any area of practice equally well and aids assessment in that it locates and helps to formulate an action plan, linking all of the activities in a client's welfare system. Reviewing the systems provides a useful checklist for evaluation and prevents you from concentrating on only one part of the situation. Reassessment is therefore encouraged and the action plan maintained. It also helps you avoid the assumption that the client is necessarily the main target for intervention. On its own a systems model can help orientate you in a particular direction and together with good information-gathering skills, form a solid platform on which to build your assessment and intervention skills.

The main disadvantage of this model is it is too general and cannot achieve depth of understanding. Systems theory is used by family therapists and others working with families and other systems such as organisations and may therefore be too broad for some specific practice situations. It is a way of viewing the position, role and behaviour of various individuals within the context of the whole system but can feel rather mechanistic and reliant on prescriptive strategies. The concept that all individuals are influencing and being influenced by the wider system continually in a circular pattern negates individual power and responsibility especially in child abuse cases.

Psychodynamic intervention

The theories underlying this practice can enable you to enhance your assessment and intervention skills especially in complex situations which do not lend themselves to short term task-focused approaches. They offer a concept of the mind, its mechanisms, and a method of understanding why some service users behave in seemingly repetitive, destructive ways. It provides a framework to address profound disturbances and inner conflicts within people around issues of loss, attachment, anxiety, and personal development.

Characteristics of psychodynamic intervention

Key ideas such as defence mechanisms, and transference in the relationship between worker and client, can be extremely helpful in reviewing the work being undertaken, and in the process of supervision with your line manager. These can help you recognise and evaluate the strong feelings aroused in particular work situations, where for example a client transfers feelings and attitudes onto you that derive from an earlier significant relationship. Counter-transference occurs when you try to live up to that expectation, perhaps behaving as if you were their parent.

Psychodynamic thinking remains a useful way of attempting to understand seemingly irrational behaviour where it appears client's difficulties reside inside themselves rather than at the interface of them and structural inequalities in their environment. For example the notion of defence mechanisms is a helpful way of assessing men who have difficulty expressing their emotions. It also acknowledges the influence of past events and can create a healthy suspicion about surface behaviour. The development of insight can be a particularly empowering experience to enable people to understand themselves and take more control over their own lives. It is essentially neutral in its stance towards people's feelings and actions and is therefore useful in developing non-judgemental skills.

The theory has influenced a listening, accepting approach in social work that avoids over-directiveness. It can be used to assess which developmental stage is reflected in the person's behaviour, if there is anxiety and how severe it is. It can also enable you to assess how dependent or independent is the person, what ambivalences may be present. And it can help you note whether there are any repetitive themes in your client's life or whether the person has a strong attachment figure. The concept of resistance helps explain when service users are unable to express themselves freely, or do so in stilted ways because of fears about what might emerge and your reaction to it.

The conventional criticisms of this model are its genesis in a medical model of human behaviour that relies on expert opinion without too much account of the person in their socio-economic context. In its original form it pathologises homosexuality and negates gender power relationships. It is not considered an appropriate way of working with some ethnic minority groups and on its own cannot adequately explain the effects of racism. Like many theoretical models a little knowledge can be dangerous. This is so in cases of child abuse where explanations deriving from psychodynamic theory can appear to blame the victim. These can be wrongly attributed to inner or unconscious motives rather than locating motivation and responsibility within the perpetrator.

Cognitive-behavioural intervention

Social work practice with this theory is based on the key concept that all behaviour is learned

and therefore available to be unlearned or changed. It offers a framework for assessing the pattern of behaviour in service users and a method for altering their thinking, feeling, and behaviour. It aims to help people become aware of themselves, link thoughts and emotions, and enable them to acquire new life skills. Using this theory you might decide on the goals to be achieved with the client, those that are clear but also capable of measurement. For example where, when and how often is the new behaviour required? How would the client measure success? How will this differ from what is happening now? Why change now?

Characteristics of cognitive-behavioural intervention

The four major behavioural techniques include: desensitization, aversion therapy, operant conditioning and modelling. Working to this theory would be characterised by a formal structured programme of activity beginning with a baseline set for the current behaviours (wanted or unwanted). Details of how often they occur can then be used to decide whether the problem is one of unwanted behaviour or the lack of wanted behaviour. Certain questions can help the process of clarification:

- What behaviours need to be increased or decreased?
- How is unwanted behaviour being maintained or reinforced?
- Can these reinforcers be removed?
- What are the antecedents, or if the behaviour is acquired through modelling, can contact with the model be discontinued?

If wanted behaviour needs to be developed the behavioural model can help ascertain what new behaviour would be desirable, what antecedents are missing, what does the client consider rewarding, and what reinforcers are available or could be gained. Research into the outcomes of behavioural social work suggests that a combination of behavioural and cognitive approaches produce better results. The cognitive dimension considers how behaviour is guided by the perceptions and analysis of what we see, and how irrational thoughts or disturbances in perception lead us to process our view of the world incorrectly. The cognitive dimension therefore in attempting to explain irrational behaviour takes the notion of what psychodynamic theory would call defence mechanisms and applies a behavioural analysis. For example a person whose personality is characterised by withdrawn behaviour is perceived not necessarily as fixated at one stage of development. Instead the behavioural approach would see them as the result of frequent failure to attain desired goals.

Behavioural work has appeal for enabling you to undertake assessment because it offers a systematic, scientific approach from which to structure further work. The approach goes some way towards encouraging participatory practice, discouraging labelling, and maintains the client's story as central. The attention to detail helps expand the information data collected and helps expose all the variables in complex situations. The idea of learned helplessness has the potential to bridge the gap between psychological and sociological explanations of behaviour, maintaining the focus on both social and individual factors.

The disadvantages of this way of working is that usually it is only the immediate environment of the client that is examined. It is not as value-free as it claims. The instruments for measuring behaviour are basically masculine – a study into the assault on women of men charged with domestic violence, for example, found individuals' responses to questions about lack of control, were based on quite irrational beliefs. The scientific nature of behavioural assessment rests on modernist assumptions about certainty. There is often in practice a tendency to rush a solution after a limited assessment where the theory is bent so that the individual client changes to accommodate their circumstances rather than the other way round. The potential to use the theory to employ anti-oppressive practice is limited because much of the theory is based on white, male, western norms of behaviour. It is quite directive and to be successful requires a high level of service user commitment.

Task-centred intervention

Task-centred social work is often cited as the most popular base for contemporary assessment and intervention practice, but it may be that it is known as a set of activities rather than as a theoretically-based approach from which a set of activities flows. It can be adapted for use in a wide range of situations. The key elements are that it is based on client agreement or service user acceptance of a legal justification for action. It aims to move from problem to goal, from what is wrong to what is needed. It is based around tasks which are central to the process of change and which aim to build on service user strengths as far as possible. Task-centred work is focused on problem-solving and is short-term and time-limited, preserving client self-esteem and independence as far as possible.

Characteristics of task-centred intervention

Task-centred practice is open to other approaches and can be combined via tasks. It develops and changes by continuing evaluation. If there is one key activity to this approach then it is negotiation – where a client is able to participate in the process and be clear about the mandate for work undertaken. This offers the opportunity for effective intervention. It offers a highly structured model of practice using a building block approach so that each task can be agreed and success or not measured by moving from problem to goal. The approach prefers to assess while intervening, rather than before, therefore time must be spent carrying out an appropriate assessment. It involves a lot of attention being paid to partnership principles in respecting the service user's point of view with effort put into good communication. You may find yourself helping a client perform a task by simulation and guided practice.

This practice is suitable for any specific, acknowledged psycho-social problem that is capable, with some help, of resolution by the service user's own action. It can serve as a basic approach for the majority of clients. In this approach the problem is always the problem as defined by the client. It therefore respects their values, beliefs and perceptions. This approach encourages service users to select the problem they want to work on and engages them in task selection and review. It lends itself to a collaborative and empowering approach by enabling social workers to carry out their share of tasks and review them alongside the clients'. It offers a unique problem classification and problem clarification process. Time limits and task reviews aid motivation and promote optimism.

Although this approach has the capacity for empowerment, it can sometimes prohibit active measures by social workers to ensure it does. Although you may believe this approach to be value-free and intrinsically non-oppressive you should continually reflect on your practice to make this explicit. The coaching role of the social worker could be open to abuse, or permit you to become overly directive. The emphasis on simple, measurable tasks may focus attention on concrete solutions that obscure the advocacy role of social work practice. The approach requires a degree of ability and motivation in the client that in some cases will be lacking.

Community work intervention

This intervention might seem at first glance to relate to the place of the actual work you do – it is outside an institution where practice takes place with clients who are not living in their own homes. In the context of government and practitioner preference and research evidence it is accepted that helping people in their own familiar surroundings is better. However there is evidence that for some people institutional care better meets their needs, while care in the community can be inadequate. But community work also describes a form of social work practice that is rooted in social justice and concerned with mobilising the collective strengths of people. The theoretical base is unashamedly political and can be traced to socialist, non-conformist ideologies embracing feminist and anti-capitalist thinking. In its narrowest definition it might exclude statutory social work and identify it with voluntary activity, pressure group action, or work carried out by community outreach staff. A broader

definition would include it in mainstream social work practice because it epitomises the philosophy and practice of psycho-social social work.

Characteristics of community work intervention

Non-directiveness is a hallmark of community work practice. It has been described as comprising these elements (Henderson and Thomas, 1987):

- galvanising
- focusing
- clarifying
- summarising
- gate keeping
- mediating
- informing

In order to practice community work, social work practice should be located in areas of need. It is a practice that is able to respond to short-term problems as well as building resources to help in the long term. Social workers using this intervention will take a broad and holistic view of the neighbourhood or community in which problems occur. A needs analysis using data from local councils or central government census can be used to identify the specific characteristics of the community. Levels of unemployment, rented accommodation, and single parent households together with other social indicators are useful in measuring need and the likely demand for services. Partnership, anti-discriminatory, empowering practice are the keystones to community practice, with good evidence of effectiveness in reducing social exclusion and fostering self-help (Holman, 1983). The aim is to network by bringing people together to construct a shared agenda for improving their environment. Community social work is par excellence the socially inclusive model of practice. It is a pro-active and preventive intervention intended to intervene before a situation deteriorates, and before a service is demanded.

The disadvantage in this work is that often clients who are homeless or in crisis are not linked directly to their neighbourhoods or kinship networks of support, therefore it is difficult to galvanise help for them or enable them to accept any help offered. The concept of community is full of ambiguities and debates about its precise meaning. Attempts to unite a community or neighbourhood neglect to address the deep divisions along racial, class, economic, and religious lines that are resistant to outside interference. It is argued that modern communities are alienating, hostile, and oppressive and essentially beyond intervention other than reactive, authoritarian measures of social control. The definition, design and delivery of contemporary social work services militate against community practice. Service managers and elected local politicians have budget limits within which to make decisions that tend to avoid investment in preventive services thereby reinforcing a low level of expectation from service users and staff.

ACTIVITY 2.2

Select a piece of work you undertook recently and review it so that the theory underpinning the intervention you used is highlighted and made more explicit. You could do this with a supervisor or other colleague to explore some of the clarities, confusions or contradictions you encountered during the process of the work. Then reflect on whether in hindsight you would do the same again or something different and the reasons why.

Post-modernism and social work

Post-modern ideas have been influencing social work in recent years as practitioners seek ways of resolving the dilemmas inherent in modern practice that is constrained by managerialist values while demand for services increases. Post-modernism seeks to challenge received wisdom about what social work interventions are valid, based on apparent empirical certainty. Post-modern theorists have articulated a theory that requires us to continually question the prevailing orthodoxy and to deconstruct

theories and practices based on old certainties. Replacing these notions with a more flexible, less constrained perspective enables practice to embrace a plurality of intellectual resources from which to guide your work. The growth of the voluntary sector, devolved budgets and decision-making, horizontal management structures and retraction of local authority social services departments, are all stimulating the expansion of post-modernist thinking as creative and innovative ways of delivering social work interventions are being engendered (Walker, 2001).

Post-modern theorists are also highlighting the significance of power relationships within social work practice and arguing for an analysis of how this impacts on intervention practice through the prism of a commitment to social justice and human rights (Leonard, 1997). By attending more closely to the barriers constructed between yourself and service users you can begin to appreciate how professional language is a way of preventing understanding rather than enabling useful communication.

Narrative as a root metaphor can replace old modernist certainties derived from the classic theoretical paradigms derived from medical models informing assessment and intervention practice. A more refined social work practice can become a dialogic-reflexive interaction between client and worker using language and the social construction of meaning to define the parameters of the helping process.

If you are interested in a social work practice that seeks to challenge social inequalities and embrace radical ideas based on, for example, feminist or green politics then you can begin with a structural analysis of power in society that produces exploitation of marginalised citizens. The post-modern paradigm advocates the importance of diversity, devolution, decentralization, and interdependence. An example is offered by Ahmad (1990) who invites social workers to take risks with their own personal world view by revising their perceptions of colleagues, friends, or other professionals and then learn something new about them. An integrated model of social work drawing upon these notions searches for an understanding of the experience of the service user. Explanation or interpretation is still important but in the context of social understanding that is pluralistic where a range of explanations can co-exist and be part of a larger chain of enquiry that challenges discrimination in all its manifestations (McLennan, 1996).

Social work practices have become burdened by the demands for efficiency, calculability, predictability and control. The relentless obsession with cost effectiveness implies that only things that can be counted are important, and that the standardisation controlled by technology ensures predictability. The ensuing conformity and globalisation of practice has been highlighted by Dominelli (1996) resulting in privatization of welfare services, new organisational structures in social work agencies, and a redefinition of the social work task leading to a deterioration in the relationship between social worker and client. This conflict between the bureaucratic context of your practice and the values that attracted you into social work lie at the heart of contemporary intervention practice. Post-modernist thinking offers a liberating perspective to help you locate your practice in the wider social context and within your personal value system.

ACTIVITY 2.3

Consider the following case scenario. Decide which intervention you might use and describe the process of your intervention.

Paul, a five year old has been accommodated for two months at his mother's request following bruising to his right leg and right upper arm. She lost her temper after Paul had a tantrum. Paul's father is unknown. Kayleigh is two and a half years old and lives with her mother. Previously perceived as a happy child developing normally, her behaviour now seems to be regressing. Their mother, Lucy, is 25 years old, single and expecting her third child in five months. She finds it hard to cope and is asking for help. She has poor health and a past history of physical and sexual abuse. Lucy was in care herself from five to eight years of age and is isolated from family and friends. A review meeting has recommended a comprehensive assessment.

Commentary

The primary aim of this assessment is to assist the decision-making process about Paul's future by assessing Lucy's parenting. This should be made explicit with Lucy. The needs of all family members should be addressed and the elements of the assessment clarified so that Lucy knows what is going to happen, when, where and how. However, you are also intervening at the same time so your choice of working practice needs to be informed by theory that can at least partly, explain the situation. In doing so they can also guide the way forward.

The legal context needs to be explained and the possibility of Paul returning home or care proceedings being commenced. The assessment could be used in evidence but you should avoid any hint of threat or coercion. An empowering approach would explain the rights of Lucy to decline to participate in the assessment, even though this might precipitate care proceedings. The areas for assessment need to be discussed and negotiated so that Lucy's concerns can be acknowledged and valued and what you are expecting her to achieve is made explicit.

Your assessment should include what impact the child protection system has had on the family and acknowledge that their functioning will be affected in that context. A wider focus will include the current role of the grandparents and father of Kayleigh, and what support they might be prepared to offer in future. The details of the plan for assessment and intervention can be incorporated into a written agreement. Lucy should be encouraged to obtain legal or other expert advice throughout the process to ensure she is fully aware of her rights and responsibilities. She should be able to contribute formally to the final report and express any disagreements or alternative interpretations.

A combination of various models for different aspects of the assessment process might be appropriate, as would using other professionals in contact with the family, to contribute their perspective. For example, a psychodynamic model could help you explore with Lucy the effects of past experiences on her current parenting capacity. A task-centred model could assist in mapping out the steps necessary for Paul's return, while a systems model could enable all the important aspects of the family's context to be included. Your model of assessment and intervention will be influenced by your own evolving social work identity and the functional role within the work context. An empowering approach will facilitate the appropriate environment in which to assess Lucy's parenting and ensure practical arrangements such as transport are in place.

Anti-discriminatory and anti-oppressive practice

Having reviewed some specific practice interventions, reflected on their advantages and disadvantages and considered their applicability, it is important to locate your use of these theoretical resources in anti-discriminatory and anti-oppressive practice. It has been argued historically in social work that theoretical models have rarely sat easily with the concepts of empowerment and anti-oppressive practice – because they essentially reflect the existing power relationships dominated by white, middle class, heterosexual, male, healthy, employed, Westerners. It is argued that there is a fundamental problem for social workers attempting to practice in anti-oppressive ways because they are part of the superstructure of social control and state sanctioned oppression. Equally it is argued that while government policies emasculate citizens and the economic system is inherently contradictory, there are many opportunities to satisfy your aim of practising in more empowering ways. Some of the features of anti-discriminatory or anti-oppressive practice are:

- Work collaboratively.
- View users as competent.
- Help users to see their strengths.
- Develop their confidence by affirming their experiences.
- Help them seek diverse solutions.
- Help users build and use informal networks to increase access to resources.

The use and abuse of power is at the centre of anti-oppressive practice. It is a significant element in every relationship but is not necessarily negative. Rather than becoming monitors of sexism, racism, disablism, or homophobia, you might find it more useful to think in terms of ensuring you and your clients have access to equal opportunities in your environment and in the assessment and intervention plan you formulate. Effective anti-oppressive practice requires a clear theoretical perspective to inform the value base that permits anti-oppressive work (Payne, 1997). To practice in an anti-oppressive way means seeking to bridge the gap between you and the service user in order to facilitate a negotiation of perceptions.

Always be aware that gender is central to power issues and as workers or clients men need to be made aware in every situation of their potential to oppress (how maleness affects their perception of problems), and to be oppressed because of assumptions about masculinity. Feminist social work practice engages both the personal and the social by focusing on the whole person and examining the interconnectedness between people and the structures they live within. It provides a powerful explanatory tool to use in assessing situations involving child abuse and domestic violence, for example, where social workers inadvertently end up blaming mothers for failing to protect children, instead of understanding the dilemmas and impossible predicament faced by women.

Gender permeates aspects of social, political, and economic life and the organisations that maintain society. Anti-oppressive practice requires the active challenging of dominant masculine discriminatory attitudes, beliefs and practices. In practice this means raising issues about which team member is the most appropriate to work with certain service users. It also means resisting the simple notion that a female worker should necessarily work with a female client. The important point is that the issue is acknowledged and discussed instead of being avoided. A wider theoretical perspective suggests that your practice should be informed by ideas about how people behave in relation to, and therefore influence, others and the effects of social factors such as stigma, stereotyping and ideology on behaviour in groups (Hogg and Abrams, 1988). In this context empowering practice is both a goal and a process for overcoming oppression.

Similarly anti-racist practice requires an acknowledgement of the combination of institutional and personal racism that privileges white western culture and norms of behaviour whilst denigrating and obscuring black culture. The effects of racism have been measured and quantified as recently as the Macpherson inquiry into the murder of the black teenager Stephen Lawrence, and over the years revealing systematic discrimination against black people in terms of housing, employment, and educational opportunities. In the youth justice system and the psychiatric system young black males are over represented compared to other groups in society, while in the care system black children are likely to face multiple disadvantages. It is important to keep the issue constantly in mind so that in every proposed intervention you are actively considering how your practice can resist and challenge overt and covert racist assumptions and beliefs.

ACTIVITY 2.4

Divide an A4 sheet into two columns. In the first column write down five issues and concerns that are important to you when considering anti-discriminatory practice. In the second column, list the abilities and skills you currently have or need to be developed, to deal with the issues and concerns you have identified.

Commentary

If one of your concerns was about the use of professional power, you may have been able to recall skills which allow you to use your power productively on service user's behalf – for instance where you have done your best to listen and encourage dialogue. If you were concerned about the use of interpreters, you may have thought about the transferable skills you use when translating professional jargon

into everyday speech. Or you may have considered the implications of communicating clearly and simply within one language or across two or more languages.

Perhaps you have wondered about your ability to manage difficulties that occur within the service user's cultural context, and your ability to interpret accurately feelings expressed in ways unfamiliar to your culture. You will probably have reflected on your own racial and cultural prejudices, and the way they influence your attitudes and behaviour. This would enable you to anticipate work with your client's own cultural prejudices and fears so that you can establish an open working relationship.

ACTIVITY 2.5

Read the following case study then list the risks involved in attempting to assess the possibility of maintaining the client in the community and weigh these against the rights of the client to self-determination:

Susan is a 44 year old woman who has been diagnosed as having a persistent delusional disorder. She has been admitted more than once to psychiatric provision, but currently lives on her own in the community with little or no contact with family members. She feels persecuted by various authority figures and has previously threatened police, housing officials and her doctor. Susan refuses to co-operate with the psychiatric consultant, take medication, or participate in the care planning process. She has previously lived in poor accommodation where she was neglecting herself. As her allocated social worker your task is to monitor her mental health; improve her self-care; reduce the intensity of her threatening behaviour; and try to find ways of reducing her emotional distress. Slowly, over time your persistence has enabled Susan to accept an offer of council accommodation, a laundry service, and regular meetings.

Commentary

Susan is still isolated and her refusal to comply with medication constitutes a significant risk. Her link with support services is fragile and she could slip further into self-neglect.

There has been no significant reduction in the role played by her delusional thoughts. There is a risk she may carry out planned threats or continue abusive behaviour. Susan has gradually come to accept regular social work intervention. There is now a monitoring system in place co-ordinated by the social worker. So far, she has not carried out any threats to harm others. Susan has accepted permanent accommodation and this might reduce her feelings of isolation and paranoia.

Intervention skills

Some of the key skills identified in good social work intervention practice are (Coulshed and Orme, 1998):

■ **Partnership**: the ability to engage with colleagues, allocate tasks and give feedback.
■ **Negotiation**: making clear what outcomes for self and others are desired; compromise and confrontation.
■ **Networking**: gathering and disseminating information, linking people and establishing mutual support groups.
■ **Communicating**: writing effective reports, speaking and writing in non-jargonised ways.
■ **Reframing**: offering different perspectives by placing the problem in a wider frame of reference and discussing alternative ways of seeing the problem.
■ **Confronting**: assertively challenging a dominant view.
■ **Flexibility**: learning from the skills of others.
■ **Monitoring and evaluation**: measuring outcomes and modifying methods or goals accordingly.

Fundamental to using these skills is the ability to engage with clients. This is harder than it seems if we consider some of the potential barriers to engagement identified by Compton and Galaway (1999):

■ **Anticipating the other**: this is connected to pre-judging the situation and happens when we fail to listen carefully if we believe

we know beforehand what the other person is going to say. The message and subsequent communication is anticipated and you drift into automatic language rather than reading between the lines of what the other person is saying.
■ **Failure to make the purpose explicit**: if we fail to make the purpose of contact explicit, then you and the client may have different, even contradictory ideas of what the purpose is and will interpret each other's communication in the light of different ideas. As the subtle distortions continue, the two will be heading in entirely different directions.
■ **Premature change activities**: efforts to produce change will fail without clearly understanding what the service user wants and whether that change is feasible. To urge change prematurely may create a barrier to communication and can lead to directive approaches that are often ineffective in the absence of trust.
■ **Inattentiveness**: if your mind wanders during the contact, then the communication process is compromised. This happens when you are tired; thinking about the last or next visit, bored or even frightened and upset. The situation you are confronted with might remind you about your own family or a deeply personal experience that has suddenly come into your mind and is distressing or distracting.
■ **Client resistance**: the barriers that some clients create can be seen as forms of resistance against entering into a problem-solving process. They can stem from discomfort and anxiety involved in dealing with a strange person and a new situation; or from cultural or sub-cultural norms regarding involvement with service agencies and asking for help; and some clients may be securing a degree of satisfaction from their problems.

In order to overcome these barriers to engagement you need to prepare fully and follow some relatively simple guidelines during the initial contact. These first steps to effective intervention can lay the future direction and pattern for the service users' contact with your agency and other helping relationships. Do not underestimate the importance of this. First you need to examine your own inner prejudices and assumptions about the client's situation and try to suspend these to prevent them compromising good practice. Encountering early hostility, silence or non-compliance should be expected from involuntary clients and not seen as reflecting your social work skills.

Previous negative experiences or the dynamics of the practice situation may not permit the service user to perceive you as an individual person but rather as a representative of a potentially disempowering agency service. Remember client behaviour in the early stages of an encounter is unlikely to have much to do with your specific actions. The best strategy is to be clear, honest and direct but in a non-defensive way – clarifying your role and the agency mandate and working hard to project a calm, patient, uncritical image will help in the long run. Avoid contradicting the service user even on matters of fact, it is much better to listen respectfully and acknowledge their right to express different values and preferences.

Designing a care plan or participating in a planning process with others can be informed by asking two fundamental questions derived from the person-centred planning approach (Sanderson 1997):

1) Who are you and who are we in your life?
2) What can we do together to achieve a better life for you now and in the future?

The characteristics reliably identified that are better at producing effective intervention outcomes are when social workers are (Smale et al., 2000):

■ **Empathic**: more than placing yourself in another person's shoes and convincing yourself that you understand the service user's predicament. Empathy in social work is about experiencing another person to the extent that they feel you understand the core issues of relevance to them. It is more than

sympathising with their situation as well, it means having the capacity and courage to challenge a person's assumptions and perceptions.

■ **Respectful**: more than token acknowledgement of difference or superficial knowledge of ethnic or cultural customs and practices. Respect is a fundamental social work value that comes through your humanitarian principles of concern for other human beings and egalitarianism.

■ **Warm and friendly**: clients know when you are pretending to like them and they can spot false warmth a mile off. You need to harness your inner feelings of compassion combined with a desire to improve matters to enable the warmth and friendliness of a genuine equality of brotherhood or sisterhood to touch every gesture and tone of voice in your communication.

■ **Authentic**: behaving consistently as a rounded human being rather than adopting a stilted professional role or hiding behind an obscure therapeutic strategy. Demonstrating proper professional standards based on reliability, clarity, and limitations need not be done in a cold matter of fact way. Bringing something of your own unique personality into the work reveals your humanity and can help a service user to re-examine their own assumptions about what to expect.

■ **Rewarding and encouraging**: do not be afraid to praise success where it occurs or even effort if a task is not achieved. People thrive on encouragement so make much of small successes and suggest more is possible.

■ **Confident**: be sure of your ground and always strive to convey a sense of authority. You can be authoritative about not knowing something provided you admit to this and can assure the service user of your capacity to obtain accurate information. Knowing your own professional and legal boundaries will help establish the limits to your remit and enable you to be confident in what you are doing.

■ **Interested**: try to find something special or unique about the person you are trying to help and show interest in this. Focusing away from the problem for a while might relieve a stressful situation and introduce information which helps the person see themselves or the situation differently. You can concentrate on the problem of course but if this is done in a routine or even indifferent way you may be creating unhelpful barriers to the process of change.

■ **Challenge in a non-confrontational way**: easier said than done especially in heated situations where the potential for harm or abuse exists. Keeping a calm tone, maintaining appropriate eye contact and remembering to use positive language, will help service users hear your perceptions of the situation. It is important to keep the flow of conversation going and providing every available opportunity for the client to express themselves.

Chapter summary

In this chapter we have considered the advantages and disadvantages of six examples of contemporary intervention practice. In exploring them in this way we have illuminated difficulties and dilemmas which can be presented when evaluating their effectiveness in taking proper account of service users' needs, rights, strengths, responsibilities and resources. Case studies have been employed to develop further understanding of these issues particularly to highlight the potential for oppressive and discriminatory practice.

We considered how social work intervention begins before client contact and whatever the aim of intervention it may lead to different and quite unexpected consequences. Accepting a wide theoretical panorama from which to choose means you are making every effort to find the right approach for the particular service user you are helping, but it makes the task of selection harder. It also can cause confusion about what to call the possible interventions

that spring from the use of particular theories. The pragmatist will seek knowledge sources that fit with their internal concept of what social work should be about.

If you believe that the problems of clients are caused by an unjust economic system that distributes wealth unfairly then a radical perspective combined with a client-centred approach might appeal to you. On the other hand if you feel that a client's problems stem from an emotionally deprived and neglected childhood you may be drawn to offering an individual psychodynamic intervention. With experience you will begin to see the limited value of these dichotomies and understand the complexities of people's lives.

We reviewed the contribution post-modernism has made to contemporary intervention practice as it seeks to challenge received wisdom about what social work interventions are valid, based on apparent empirical certainty. Post-modern theorists have articulated a theory that requires us to continually question the prevailing orthodoxy and to deconstruct theories and practices based on old certainties. Replacing these notions with concepts of ambivalence uncertainty and a critical stance is harder than succumbing to the quickest and least demanding solution.

Finally we discussed the skills and qualities required for effective relationship-building but warned of the use and abuse of power that is at the centre of anti-oppressive practice. It is a significant element in every relationship but is not necessarily negative. Rather than becoming monitors of sexism, racism, disablism, or homophobia, we argued that you might find it more useful to think in terms of ensuring you and your clients have access to equal opportunities in your environment and in the assessment and intervention plan you formulate. Effective anti-oppressive practice should not diminish anyone involved in the helping process.

CHAPTER 3

Risk Assessment and Risk Management

Introduction

Assessment of risk and its management has become a dominant theme in social work in the past decade. As with other aspects of the profession – such as the move to competence-based training and the increased emphasis on evidence-based practice – the concern with risk assessment has been a reaction to a wider demand for greater public accountability of professionals in all spheres. In social work several highly publicised failures to protect our clients and the public from dangerous people have ensured that the spotlight of concern has been kept on practice standards. Despite the fact that the highly publicised failures – mainly in child care and mental health work, represent a minority of social work cases, their impact on practice has been considerable. This has led to policy and practice in relation to risk and its management, becoming focused on dangerousness, particularly so in work with offenders and mental health and significant harm in relation to children and elders. This puts undue pressure on work that is already highly sensitive in many cases and paradoxically may provoke the very behaviour that it seeks to prevent.

The social construction of risk

Definitions of concepts such as risk, dangerous and significant harm are ambiguous and widely agreed to be determined by social, cultural and historical factors. There is no absolute definition of dangerousness that is independent of any social and cultural context. For example verbal abuse may be considered by some to be aggressive behaviour, a possible precursor to physical violence. Others may consider verbal abuse to be a 'safety valve', which if handled appropriately can actually reduce the risk of physical violence. Cultural factors, based on class, gender and ethnic differences for example, are important in an individual's definition of what constitutes verbal aggression.

What a social worker from a white, middle class, professional background considers verbal abuse, a black teenager immersed in rap culture may think of as no more than 'telling it like it is'. The well documented disproportionate rates of compulsory admissions to psychiatric hospitals of black males suffering from schizophrenia has been accounted for in terms of cultural differences in modes of verbal and physical behaviour. Similarly, the definition of significant harm is relative. The legal debates about the acceptability of physical chastisement (smacking) of children, is an example of this. In some European states this is illegal; it is currently not in England and Wales although there is an ongoing debate about whether it should be so. Many consider such parental behaviour to be physical abuse with the potential for significant harm to the developing child; others believe that sparing the rod spoils the child. This lack of absolutes and the ambiguity it brings has profound implications for social work practice in relation to risk. This is epitomised in the tension between care and control.

ACTIVITY 3.1

Think about a recent piece of work in which you were considering the risks in the situation. On reflection, do you now feel you underestimated or overestimated the risks, or got them about right? What do you now think were the factors leading you to that perception?

Care, control and partnership

This tension between care and control and the ambiguity from which it arises is apparent in the guidance enshrined in occupational standards in that whereas partnership practice figures prominently elsewhere, it is not mentioned in the elements on risk with their greater emphasis on protection and control. This points to the apparent conflict between an emphasis on working in partnership with service users – which is fundamental to modern social work practice – and the statutory requirement to protect vulnerable adults and children from themselves and others (Jack and Walker, 2000).

Whilst the values underpinning partnership practice and the evidence of its efficacy are fairly unequivocal, this is not the case with the requirement to protect and control where there is much greater ambiguity about both the values on which it is based and the practice methods which it involves. We have discussed the problem of the social and cultural relativism of concepts of dangerousness and significant harm that create uncertainty for practitioners. Similar problems exist in relation to the values underpinning practice in relation to control and protection.

The contention over the Mental Health Act (1983) and its requirements in relation to compulsory admission, where a client is expressing suicidal ideas, exemplify this values dilemma. Should social workers be involved in removing an individual's right to end their own life? Self-determination is a long cherished value underpinning social work practice – removing an individual's autonomy and self-determination is thought by many not to be in keeping with the duties social workers have

under this Act. It is argued that assessors of risk should be working towards a model in which self-management of risk by the service user is paramount (Strachan and Tallant, 1997).

In relation to the efficacy of practice which seeks to control behaviour, there is widespread concern over, for example, behavioural techniques employed to this end in children's homes. The behavioural regime employed in some children's homes in the 1980s which involved enforced isolation and deprivation of privileges in an attempt to control behaviour deemed unacceptable, is an extreme example of the uncertain nature of practice in this context. The questionable benefits of incarcerating teenagers in young offenders prisons – with the high rates of suicide and self-harm which these institutions have – is another example.

Thus both the underpinning values and methods associated with practice in relation to control and protection are fraught with uncertainty and seem far removed from the aspirations of partnership. As we progress we will repeatedly encounter these tensions and recognise that a defining characteristic of assessment practice is the need to balance the competing demands within different forms of practice. These try to maintain our commitment to the value base of the profession whilst fulfilling our duty to both care and control.

Partnership practice

Partnership practice whilst apparently being at odds with some of the requirements of social work is in fact one of the methods through which this balance can be sought – if not always attained. The next activity is intended to clarify this.

ACTIVITY 3.2

Write a paragraph describing how you think working in partnership with service users can help to integrate the requirements of both care and control. In doing this you might find it helpful to briefly re-read the section above on the social construction of risk.

Commentary

In the section on social construction we discussed the social and cultural factors involved in the definition and perception of dangerousness. Working in partnership involves a genuine commitment to the attempt to understand the world from the client's perspective and communicating this effectively without necessarily condoning any particular behavioural expression of their perception of the world. Partnership however also involves mutuality – there is an expectation that the client will be willing to make a similar attempt to understand the perceptions and behaviours of others. Obviously the worker has the professional responsibility to enable clients to work on problems in this way when initially the nature of their problems may inhibit the flexibility which this entails. This will involve entering the social and cultural context of the client – rather than attempting to promote change by imposing an alien cultural context.

For example, in the case of verbal behaviour which is causing problems for the 'rap' fan due to the perception of it as abusive, the worker may begin by encouraging the teenager to share their tastes in music. Whilst not directly confronting the issue, this approach may eventually enable the teenager to understand the origins of the problem and work on it in ways which are rooted in their social and cultural context – rather than demanding they conform immediately to cultural standards which are alien to them.

In such ways partnership practice can work with the social and cultural relativity which, as we have seen, is a characteristic of assessment practice. What may be seen as the problem of ambiguity and uncertainty which in some circumstances leads to draconian attempts to control, can in this way be turned into a positive strength in the attempt to care and enable. The above example demonstrates the integration of knowledge, skills and values which we discuss further in Chapter 8. In this case, knowledge of cultural diversity, the skills of interpretation and negotiation in building partnership, and the values of individualisation and respect for uniqueness and diversity are the foundation of such partnership practice. It is important to acknowledge that the commitment to partnership should not be misinterpreted as an invitation to relinquish boundaries in professional relationships. Loss of boundaries can place social workers at risk.

Risk to social workers

An interesting aspect of the moral panic about risk and dangerousness is that the risk to social workers from dangerous people and the adverse attention of politicians and the media has not been of such concern. The risk of abuse and physical threat or attack for social workers is considerable. Social workers – particularly in residential settings – are among those who share the highest risk of assault at work. The recognition of this risk should be an important consideration for all social workers, their managers and the organisations within which they work.

As we shall see later, too narrow a focus on assessing risk to others can lead to a neglect of risk to self. Disregarding the wider context in which clients exist – psychologically and socially – can result not only in inadequate assessment of their needs but also of the dangers to workers which may be inherent in this context. Service users may experience the bureaucratic requirements that form part of assessment processes as a further burden or imposition from a system perceived as hostile and inaccessible. Already frustrated by the problems of their immediate context, the service user may find a ready scapegoat in the worker who can come to represent and embody the problem. Unacceptably, though unsurprisingly, this can result in misplaced aggression directed at the worker. Two factors that can contribute to this potential for misplaced aggression are:

Neglect of the client's context

In attempting to fulfil the requirement to protect allegedly vulnerable others, the worker may unwittingly reinforce the client's perception that they are being labelled remorselessly as the problem. Systems theory points to the way in which family and social systems manage problems by identifying them as caused by individuals which are in fact a result of dysfunctional systems – not any particular individual within them. In focusing too narrowly on assessment of the alleged problem person this theoretical insight and the practice which should lead from it are forgotten.

The result being that the scapegoating which may have contributed to the client being identified as the problem in the first place is reflected for the client in the assessment process. The client may then respond – as they perhaps have in their social context – with aggression. Thus, by neglecting the client's systemic context, the worker becomes part of the dysfunctional system and any therapeutic potential of the professional encounter is reduced dramatically – sometimes to the extent of verbal or physical violence occurring.

This is a further example of the necessity of integrating theoretical knowledge with the skills and values of social work if practice is to be effective. It is also a necessity if the well documented dangers which social workers encounter are to be minimised. We have given an example of how the skills and values of partnership practice can contribute to the effective assessment and management of risk. We have also suggested that the aspiration of partnership practice can lead, in unskilled hands, to the loss of professional boundaries which itself can put workers in danger.

Failure to maintain boundaries

Unfortunately partnership practice can easily be misinterpreted as 'standing in the client's shoes'. The attempt to empathise with the client is often described in these terms – but empathy, or understanding, is not standing in their shoes. In any case, this is impossible and can be misperceived by clients as the creation of a mutual acceptance of their position and their response to it. This can be a flawed position in the sense that inevitably such misperception – if shared by worker and client – will result in the worker eventually having to belatedly affirm the difference of their position. In turn, this can

lead to feelings of rejection and betrayal in the client and the resultant danger of aggressive reactions.

Because the professional role entails empathy and understanding of all the participants' positions in the dysfunctional system – the worker can not create alliance with any one participant. The acceptance and acknowledgement of this difference between worker and client is the skill of working in partnership – which involves, not only empathy with the client, but negotiation of the difference between them in terms of roles and relationships. Failure to establish this difference – and the boundaries between them – is a potential source of risk to workers.

Partnership practice is based on a negotiated – often written – contract to mutually explore the client's context. In this contract the worker's responsibility is to attempt to understand without prejudgement the client's experience – not to accept or condone its attitudinal or behavioural outcomes. The values of individualisation and recognition of diversity are fundamental to this. But so too is a considerable knowledge of the nature and role of modelling in the professional relationship. Failure to establish the boundaries' nature of this partnership not only deprives the client of the possibility of learning (through modelling) about negotiating such boundaries and their value in managing their own problems, but will inevitably lead to problems for workers. These may, at worst, include verbal or physical aggression from clients who will understandably experience disillusion and betrayal by their misperceived ally.

Well intentioned but ill informed attempts at partnership in risk assessment can therefore be dangerous for both client and worker. If serious aggression occurs, the client is left with yet another experience of failure, and the worker may not only have been ineffective but also physically harmed. The process of effective partnership practice involves risk – but should not invite danger. Tension and ambiguity is inherent in working with risk, but it is unambiguously unprofessional to court danger. This is further evidence that assessment can not be understood as separate from the wider process of social work intervention.

We will now move on to explore the difference between danger and risk and the importance of regaining an understanding of the social work process in assessment. As we shall discover, it is simply not possible to provide unambiguous check lists to identify dangerous people, or rules to reliably eliminate risk to self or others. What is possible to acquire is the knowledge, skills and values of the social work profession and integrate them in a social work process in order to minimise danger and manage risk as effectively as possible.

One of the consequences of pressures to reduce risk and eliminate danger from social work has been an obsession with the production of check lists such as eligibility criteria, assessment schedules and risk assessment scales. As recent DoH reports have acknowledged this has been at the expense of attention to the process aspects of social work intervention. The tendency has been for practice to become narrowly focused on aspects of the individual such as dependency or dangerousness, rather than on the whole person-in-context. This is counter to – and in extreme cases can threaten – the established values and effective practice of social work which emphasise individualisation, respect for the person and a holistic approach which takes full account of the social and cultural context.

There is some evidence that effectiveness in assessment and intervention can be enhanced by the use of well validated assessment scales. Additionally, in terms of accountability, social workers must be able to demonstrate that they are aware of and make appropriate use of all available aids to best practice. However, the consensus from research presently is that such tools are useful adjuncts to competent professional judgement – not substitutes for it. In relation to the assessment and management of risk there is a need therefore to resist the reductions tendency to focus exclusively on assessment of risk conceived as danger and intervention as risk control. Risk can be conceived also as opportunity and intervention as risk management – as opposed to elimination.

ACTIVITY 3.3

Make some brief notes describing several disadvantages of viewing risk solely as danger and intervention as about risk control.

Commentary

Ironically the danger of such practice is that in pursuing the ultimately unattainable goal of entirely risk free practice workers may:

Overlook the risks attached to intervention: Removing a child allegedly in danger from its family opens the child up to other dangers which can be equally damaging.

Neglect the rights of individuals in order to control the risks they pose to themselves or others: Removing an elderly person from their home under the National Assistance Act (1948) on the grounds that they are living in unsanitary conditions raises ethical issues about how far the state should dictate how individuals live.

Lose sight of the individual-in-context, their strengths and the creative potential for development and growth this brings: TOPSS Values Requirements include recognising the uniqueness, diversity and strengths of individuals. Focusing too narrowly on one aspect of the individual (e.g. dangerousness) may limit opportunities for interventions that can enable clients to build on their strengths to become less dangerous.

Overlook the risk to the social worker: Over-eagerness to control risks posed to others can expose workers to unacceptable levels of risk to themselves. This can result not only in serious harm to the worker, but add to the guilt and other problems experienced by the client involved in violence against the worker.

Defining risk

The TOPSS occupational standards guidance demonstrates the tension in risk work between care and control. Some of the requirements seem to be based on a perspective of risk as containing positive opportunities for personal development. Other requirements suggest that risk must be viewed as something entirely negative to be controlled and eliminated. In order to be able to achieve a balance in practice between these apparently conflicting requirements, it is helpful to consider these perspectives in more detail. You can do this by thinking about two approaches to risk in social work. As social work develops its understanding and practice in relation to risk, two contrasting approaches have emerged. The safety first approach which can be paraphrased as CYB – cover your back and the risk taking approach which subscribes to the view that risks are an inherent part of social life. If individuals are to be fully engaged in social life some risk is inevitable. Both terms are problematic:

■ Competent social work should not be entirely 'defensive' and preoccupied with covering your back.
■ Risk taking has connotations of an advocacy of taking risks which is counterintuitive to many and easily misconstrued as irresponsible in view of the vulnerability of many service users.

For these reasons risk control and risk management are used here and some of the implications identified.

Characteristics of the risk control perspective

Definition: risk is negative – danger, threat.
Priority principles: professional responsibility and accountability.
Practice priorities: identification (assessment scales) and elimination (procedural, legalistic).

Characteristics of the risk management perspective

Definition: positive – risk is part of life, balancing risks and benefits is part of individual's development, being self-determining and personally responsible.
Priority principles: self-determination, anti-oppression.

Practice priorities: solution-focused, partnership practice, empowerment.

The benefits of the risk management perspective are that they are in keeping with the values and practice of modern social work; emphasises process of maximising benefits as well as minimising risks, rather than procedure of identifying and eliminating risk; and builds on strengths. The drawbacks are that it relies heavily on highly developed professional competence and judgement and requires commitment of client to partnership. It also requires intellectual/cognitive competence of the client. This approach involves ambiguity and uncertainty, is poorly understood by the public, and requires supportive management practice and organisational policy. Risks to social workers are virtually ignored. As understanding and practice in relation to risk develops it becomes clear that there needs to be an integration of the best of both approaches. Eliminating or totally controlling risk in social work is impossible. It is undesirable to think of risk and the social work task in relation to it in this way because:

■ Evidence and intuition suggests it is impossible and thus resources are wasted.
■ Risk is part of social life.
■ Practice which is effective in terms of promoting individual responsibility and social competence can not be reductions – it must recognise the person-in-context and build on strengths.
■ Social work agencies have responsibilities in law in relation to certain client groups. Individual social workers must neither neglect these responsibilities nor accept unlimited liability – whether or not there are legal requirements.
■ The social and individual costs of control can outweigh the social and individual benefits.
■ Social work routinely brings its practitioners into contact with dangerous people and entails professional judgements which are potentially castigated by management, organisations and the media.

It is possible to minimise risk. For example by appropriately employing well validated risk assessment scales where they are available. Other ways of minimising risk would include being aware of the meaning of risk and its role in the personal development and social life of service users. Ensuring practice is evidence-based and in accordance with statute, government guidance and agency policy. Managing decision calls – don't be rushed, ensure immediate safety of all parties involved, be appropriately assertive, and be sure a decision has to be made and by whom. The capacity to share responsibility, involve where possible and support the subject of the decision, report back to referring agency, ensure continuity, and debrief as soon as possible with your manager/supervisor is important.

Clearly identifying specific risks and the contexts in which they might occur is a helpful skill to develop. Fully engaging clients and significant others in risk assessment, management and recording accurately is crucial. Multi-disciplinary sharing of risk management with other involved professionals while clearly recording risk assessment and management plans, relating them to specific legal requirements as appropriate is necessary. You should always ensure the availability of supervision and recording key decisions from it. Finally never forget that managing risk to self is a priority of professional practice.

ACTIVITY 3.4

Review the material above and list three priority factors you consider could improve your current risk assessment and risk management practice.

A generic framework for risk assessment practice which can take into account the two perspectives on risk and the tensions between the various practice requirements has been influential since first described by Brearley (1982). His framework is based on the clear definition of danger, risk, predisposing and situational hazards, and strengths as follows:

Dangers: undesirable outcomes.

Risk: the chance of loss or the occurrence of an undesirable outcome as a result of a decision or course of action. The chance of gain and a desirable outcome.

Social work, for reasons discussed above, can focus too narrowly on potential losses – thereby missing the potential for gain. Competent practice involves weighing up the pros and cons of both possibilities, which Brearley describes in terms of hazards and strengths. A hazard is an existing factor that introduces or increases the possibility of an undesirable outcome. He identifies two types of hazard:

Predisposing hazards: these are factors in the person's background – such as their experiences and personality – which make an undesirable outcome more likely.

Situational hazards: these are factors specific to the current situation which make an undesirable outcome more likely.

This distinction between the two types of hazard is useful because it helps you to focus on those aspects of the risk situation which may be more amenable to intervention and change.

Strengths: any factor which reduces the possibility of an undesirable outcome occurring. The dangers we have discussed of a too narrow focus on hazards are reduced by this requirement to identify strengths. This may seem an obvious requirement of holistic assessment which fully takes account of the person-in-context, but it is one which can be easily neglected in the pressured environment of risk work. We shall return to a consideration of this environment and how environments can be more or less supportive of effective risk work towards the end of the chapter.

Listing the hazards and strengths provides a way of quantifying the balance between them. You need to then identify what other information can be obtained to help analyse the whole situation, before reaching a conclusion and making a judgement about the decisions to be made.

Thus far we have discussed some generic aspects of risk assessment and management in terms of principles and practice. Now we will move on to describe aspects of risk assessment in relation to three of the most vulnerable and largest client groups – children and families, those with mental health difficulties and elderly people.

It is important to recognise at this point that this book is not a specialist text in child protection, working with mentally distressed or elderly people. What follows is intended to provide you with a discussion of some of the important issues in practice with these client groups. For more specific theoretical and practice guidance you will need to consult other sources. Throughout the text and in the bibliography you will find pointers to specialist texts.

Risk assessment in child care

Government policy

There is a very extensive body of government policy and practice guidance in relation to risk assessment in child care. These are a selection:

- 1988 Protecting Children: A Guide for Social Workers Undertaking a Comprehensive Assessment.
- 1989 Children Act.
- 1995 Child Protection: Messages from Research.
- 1996 The National Commission of Inquiry into the Prevention of Child Abuse.
- 1998 Responding to Families in Need.
- 2002 Quality Protects.
- 1995–1999 The Children Act Report.
- 2000 Framework for the Assessment of Children in Need and their Families.

Government guidance on assessing children to safeguard and promote their welfare is continually evolving in the light of research and the inspections carried out by the Social Services Inspectorate. In 1988 an influential guide was published by the DoH and formed the basis of local authority practice in this field (DoH, 1988). The DoH subsequently commissioned 20 research studies on child protection, the results of which were published in *Child Protection: Messages from Research* (DoH, 1995). In 1998 the government's eight objectives for children's social

services were set out in the Quality Protects initiative. Since when further publications have emerged including the draft consultative document *Framework for the Assessment of Children in Need and their Families* (1999) from the Department of Health. A comprehensive summary of these publications, recent research and policy development is to be found in *The Children Act Report* – 1995–1999 (DoH, 2000). This report can be found on the Web at www.doh.gov.uk/scg/chactrep.htm and is essential reading for those with a special interest in child care.

Several recent reports on assessment in child and family work affirm that many of the general issues about assessment which we have discussed already apply specifically to child care and child protection. Perhaps the most significant is the effects which have been found of the over-emphasis on risk control which followed the Children Act and various child protection failures. One report concluded that child protection appeared to have a de-skilling effect on social workers who were only expecting to respond to families in crisis, and where children were at risk of significant harm. Social workers therefore gained little experience beyond this in developing work with families (DOH/SSI, 1997b).

It described a very worrying picture, with departments continuing to respond to child protection and looked after children cases to the exclusion of support to other families of children in need. Therefore too narrow a focus on danger can lead to neglect of the wider picture whereas a strategy of risk management which takes the wider context into account is more likely to effectively meet need. This has been recognised in the most recent practice guidance *Framework for the Assessment of Children in Need and their Families* (2000) which requires that any assessment of a child and family will take account of three interacting domains:

- The child's developmental needs.
- The parenting capacity of the child's carers to respond to those needs.
- Relevant wider family and environmental factors.

This is part of a growing recognition that since the Children Act (1989) practice has focused too narrowly on assessment of risk rather than need (of which risk is only a part).

In 1996 a national commission of inquiry into the prevention of child abuse recognised the need for a more holistic approach. It included in its definition of child abuse not only direct and acute forms (such as violence) but also indirect forms such as poor housing, family health and poverty (DOH, 1996). Nonetheless the narrow view has persisted and has led frequently to a failure to provide supportive services to children and families in need such that:

- Over half the estimated 160,000 children subject to child protection enquiries each year receive no further services.
- Inter-agency work is often relatively good at the early stages of child protection enquiries; its effectiveness tends to decline once child protection plans have been made.
- Discussions at child protection conferences tend to focus too heavily on decisions about registration and removal rather than on focusing on plans to protect the child and support the family.

The first of these points reminds us of the issue discussed earlier about the tendency that has developed over the recent past to view social work assessment as separate from intervention.

Assessment: stage or process?

Whether assessment should be regarded as a stage or part of the ongoing process of intervention is clarified in a recent DoH publication on the working of the Children Act. It asserted that the provision of appropriate services should not await the end of the assessment but be offered when they are required by the child and family. The process of engaging in an assessment should be therapeutic and conceived of as part of the range of services offered (DoH, 2000). Other findings from SSI inspections on assessment and decision-making in child care which reflect the generic issues discussed before include:

- Social workers did a great deal of fact gathering but were less good at structuring it and drawing conclusions from it.
- It was difficult to discern how decisions were reached on the basis of the information recorded. Decision-making needed to be more explicit. Plans should flow logically from the assessment.
- In responding to referrals, social workers followed local custom and practice rather than agency procedures.
- The child protection register is not consulted for 60% of children for whom there is some child protection concern.
- Referrers were not notified of the outcome of their request for service.
- Decisions affecting families' welfare were not formally conveyed to them.
- Managers did not sign the case record to indicate their endorsement of the social worker's action.

ACTIVITY 3.5

What are the implications of these shortcomings for the effective management of risk in your agency context?

Commentary

Decision-making needs to be more explicit. Plans should flow logically from the assessment. There is a need for a guiding framework. If decisions are not clearly linked to the findings of assessment accountability for actions is difficult to support. In the event of unsuccessful outcomes there is no way of analysing which aspect of the situation could account for this and how future interventions could be amended in the light of it. Following local custom and practice rather than agency procedures leads to inconsistency in practice, is open to complaint from service users on the grounds of inequity of treatment, and is in any case insupportable in terms of professional accountability.

Assessment should take account of any relevant information about predisposing and situational factors – of which the child protection register is a readily accessible source. Neglect of this basic source would be subsequently indefensible in terms of professional accountability. Not notifying referrers of the outcome of their request for service can result in disillusion among colleagues from other agencies (and concerned members of the public) about the worth of such referral, leading to potentially hazardous situations for vulnerable people who should be referred. It is essential for continuing multi-disciplinary risk work and it is professionally impolite (Jack and Walker, 2000).

Failing to convey decisions affecting families' welfare undermines the potential for partnership practice currently or in the future. It also (as with the above) means that there is not a clear audit trail linking referral, assessment, intervention and outcome. Managers failing to indicate their endorsement of the social worker's action means there is no record of the agreed intervention which is mutually binding and which may lead to disagreement later about what was in fact agreed. This can be potentially hazardous to the social worker in situations where harm occurs to clients or others. Having explored this particular aspect of risk work we will conclude our discussion of risk work in relation to child care with a summary of some general implications for practice drawn from the discussion so far.

Competent practice in risk work should:

- Adopt a systemic, holistic perspective on need (as well as identifying risk).
- Appropriately employ well validated criteria of risk within a coherent framework of assessment and consequent, clearly related intervention.
- Explicitly involve parents and children, recording their perceptions and opinions.
- Avoid gender bias in assessment, recommendation and intervention (attention often focuses unreasonably on mothers in abusive situations).
- Utilise multi-disciplinary processes of assessment and decision-making.
- Be explicitly shared in supervision, recorded and endorsed at every stage by managers.

Risk assessment in mental health

Government policy

As with child care, partly as a result of highly publicised cases of murder and assault by psychiatric patients, there has been a considerable volume of government policy and practice guidance in mental health. Some of these reports are listed below:

- 1983 Mental Health Act.
- 1990 Code of Practice.
- 1995 Building Bridges.
- 1998 Modernising Mental Health Services.
- 1999 Still Building Bridges.

As in child care, risk and dangerousness have increasingly become the focus of policy and practice during the past decade; to some extent threatening the multi-agency, holistic approach to need which has also been a feature of government policy during this time.

The Code of Practice for the Mental Health Act 1983 (DoH and Welsh Office, 1990) asserts that a broad range of contextual factors – in addition to the health and safety of the patient – should be taken into account in any decision on compulsory admission. These include:

- The patient's wishes and view of their own needs.
- Their social and family circumstances and cultural background.
- The needs of the patient's family.
- The need for others to be protected from the patient.

The Code provides specific guidance on risk assessment related to the protection of others, it includes the need to take account of:

- Reliable evidence of risk to others.
- Relevant details of the patient's medical history and past behaviour.
- The degree of risk and its nature. Too high a risk of physical harm, or serious persistent psychological harm to others, are indicators of the need for compulsory admission.

■ The willingness and ability to cope with the risk, by those with whom the patient lives.

■ Consideration of any prognosis of future deterioration of mental health.

This apparently holistic approach continued in the DoH guidance on multi-agency collaboration in mental health care *Building Bridges* (DoH, 1995). This stressed that the Care Programme Approach had not been intended to be a bureaucratic system, but was intended to ensure that people in the community received the treatment, care, support and monitoring they needed to stay as well as they could, and to remain safe. However, at the same time doubts had arisen about the effectiveness of the CPA in this regard as a result of several highly publicised murders by psychiatric patients. Many see the Patients (in the Community) Act 1995 – which amends the Mental Health Act (1983), extending powers of authorities to cover people in the community, as the culmination of this.

The government strategy document *Modernising Mental Health Services* (DoH, 1998), was published partly in response to public concern about safety and risk in relation to people with mental health problems. It stressed the need for services to be safe, sound and supportive. This increasing concern about risk and dangerousness is despite research which has shown a 3% annual decline between 1957 and 1995 in homicides committed by people defined as mentally ill (Taylor and Gunn, 1999). In 1999 the SSI published the results of its inspection of 15 social services authorities reporting that it was very concerned about several aspects of risk assessment procedures. It found:

■ Only one authority had an agreed risk assessment procedure.

■ A complete lack of risk assessment in some authorities.

■ Different models of risk assessment being undertaken within the same agencies.

■ Lack of coherence between in-patient risk assessments and implications for discharge.

■ Lack of acceptance by different professionals that everyone has a contribution to make in undertaking risk assessments.
Still Building Bridges. DoH/SSI 1999: 6.

Risk and dangerousness in mental disorder

There is considerable research evidence from the UK and abroad – much of it from longitudinal studies with very large samples – which suggests that assessing risk in this field, is particularly difficult. Predictors of actual suicide (as opposed to self-harm) are highly unreliable – a recent study in the UK found that the majority of people who committed suicide were not seen as high risk. Also, predicting violence is very difficult – over-prediction of violence especially from men and ethnic minorities, is common and where accuracy is greater it is a result of anticipating who will not be violent. Violent women are under-predicted by professionals. There is also little research about the protective factors in individuals' lives that serve to reduce the risk to self and others. However there are a number of other findings that do provide useful guidance for assessors:

■ Whilst the link between mental disorder and violence is contested, where mental disorder occurs with substance or alcohol misuse violence is more likely, and in addition it is more likely where delusions are present, and where the diagnosis is anti-social personality disorder.

■ Aspects of social networks and social support have been shown to be associated with increased violence in people with a diagnosis of mental illness e.g. if they are financially dependent on others.

■ People with a mental disorder are far more likely to be a risk to themselves.

■ Risk of suicide among those with schizophrenia is 8.5 times that of the general population, opiate dependence increases the risk by between 14 and 20 times and a history of self-harm combined with drug abuse among women increases their risk by 87 times.

In summary this research evidence suggests that even individuals who fit into high risk categories, may actually pose no risk to others, and – as in risk assessment generally – it is important to have an holistic approach. In particular, it is inadequate to have a static conception of violence as a characteristic of an individual regardless of the changing factors of clinical process and social context (Parsloe, 1999).

Risk assessment with elderly people

Government policy

There is a relative dearth of government policy and practice guidance in relation to risk work with elderly people. Whilst the National Health Service and Community Care Act (1990) lays out policy and practice guidance in relation to adult service users generally who are mainly older people and people with mental disorder, it is does not deal specifically with risk assessment related to elders. As part of the reform of health services at that time GPs' contracts were changed to require that primary care groups offered annual assessment to all people over 75 in their area. These developments led to a growing body of mainly medical literature dealing with assessment, some concerned with issues of risk and assessment (Beales, Denham and Tulloch, 1998). As we shall see there was a Law Commission report on mental incapacity in relation to elders and a subsequent green paper (1997) which made no recommendation for substantive changes in the law despite intensive lobbying by pressure groups such as Age Concern.

There have been a series of reports from the Social Services Inspectorate into aspects of community care provision for elders (DoH/SSI, 1996; 1997a; 1997c) and most recently one dealing with community care for black and ethnic minority elders (1998). These reports provide valuable insights into progress and problems in implementing the NHS and CC Act in relation to elders.

The relative lack of statutory guidance is due in part to elderly people being to some extent covered in such guidance as is available in relation to vulnerable adults generally, for example, the Mental Health Act 1983. There is a well documented and enduring ageist tendency within social work and other professions which has historically relegated work with elders to the least prestigious realms of the profession where the least well qualified work in some of the least well resourced environments. This has led to the neglect until comparatively recently of the risks faced by elders, and the role of social work in protecting them. The statutory framework for protective work with elders specifically is minimal in comparison with the extensive legislation available to guide practice in child care and mental health.

Despite this there is an extensive body of academic literature and research on elder abuse – much of it American. However recent UK publications which provide valuable evidence-based practice guidance include Bennett and Kingston (1993), Pritchard (1995), Eastman (1994) and McReadie (1995). More recently Professor Olive Stevenson has drawn informative comparisons between child protection and elder care (Stevenson, 1996; 1999) and provides us with a concise overview of the issues in risk work with elders in Parsloe (1999).

Most risk assessments are done as part of a more general assessment of need. It seems very important that the interaction of need with risk be at the heart of the process. In this way, the implications of the assessment, including the elements of risk, will be considered creatively, with a search for imaginative solutions to the tensions between autonomy and protection. The principle of needs-led assessment has been distorted and impoverished by current resource constraints and the mental set of workers caught up in over bureaucratic systems (Stevenson, 1999). The fundamental tension, which we have noted in relation to risk work generally, between care and control in relation to older adults can be reconceptualised in terms of the balance between autonomy and protection.

Autonomy versus protection

It is accepted in our society that part of being adult is the right to autonomy. Within the bounds of law and the mores of social life,

autonomy is perceived as a definitive characteristic of adulthood in democracies. This is not so
in relation to children who are defined as ill-
equipped because of the incompletion of the
developmental process, to exercise autonomy
and bear the consequences and responsibilities
which this brings. Much of the risk work arising
with elders involves individuals who by dint of
dementia or other degenerative disease, are
incapable of fully exercising autonomy because
they are either insufficiently aware of the consequences of so doing or physically incapable of
coping with them.

Social workers and other professionals
therefore have to balance the ethical and
statutory requirements to protect vulnerable
adults whilst recognising their right to
autonomy. Unlike child care and mental health
there is very little in UK social policy and legal
statute to guide workers in managing this
dilemma. This lack of guidance was recognised
by the government in 1997, when it stated that
there was a clear need for reform of the law in
order to improve the decision-making process
for those who are unable to make decisions for
themselves or who cannot communicate their
decisions. Despite acknowledging that elderly
people were some of the most vulnerable
people in our society this did not lead to
reform. Thus you are left with the dilemma.
There is some limited guidance, however, from
the Law Commission's enquiry that led to the
green paper in which they proposed four principles for assessment in this situation in relation
to mental incapacity. These are that assessment
should take account of:

■ A person's ascertainable past and presents
  wishes and feelings.
■ The need to permit and encourage the
  person to participate.
■ The views of other people concerned with
  the person.
■ Whether the required action or decision can
  be achieved by less restrictive methods.

You will inevitably draw the conclusion that
this very limited official guidance points to the
value of the holistic social work assessment of
risk which we have described, and for which

social work, because of its integration of
knowledge, skills and values is particularly well
equipped. It seems very important that the
interaction of need with risk be at the heart of
the process. In the relative absence of specific
policy, practice and statutory guidance we will
now draw on what we have learned of the social
work process to identify some practice guidance
in relation to risk work with elders.

Implications for practice

The particular dilemmas of risk work with
elders centre around the tension between
autonomy and protection. As we suggested in
the introduction to this chapter, the social
construction of risk is an aspect of assessment
work that can not be ignored if assessment
practice is to be effective. Ageism in caring
organisations and the professions who work in
them reflect the socially constructed ageism of
wider society in terms of the procedures and
practices adopted. Awareness of this has a key
role to play in effective assessment of risk in
working with elders.

Ageism and assessment practice

Ageism as with any other prejudice involves the
ascription to individuals of the socially ascribed,
stereotypical characteristics of a group. In
relation to elders in western society this involves
attributing to individuals the largely pejorative
stereotypical attributes of inevitable decline,
incompetence and dependency. Ageism can
affect assessment both in terms of organisational
procedures and professional practice.

The referral may be allocated to an untrained
worker as is routine organisational policy with
older people – thereby denying the client
properly qualified assessment. The elderly
person may not wish to have been referred in
the first place and may not be been asked their
permission for a visit and or assessment –
thereby invading their privacy and denying
their autonomy. In view of the elderly person's
age and diagnosis of dementia, assessment may
focus on the aspects of their personality and
capability damaged by the dementia – not on
the whole person-in-context. Thereby failing to

take account of factors such as a supportive social network which if mobilised, could mitigate the currently limited effects of their condition.

Preoccupation with the symptoms of the elderly person's condition may lead to the neglect of their wider personality much of which might remain intact – leading not only to neglect of their strengths but to denial of their uniqueness and individuality. An assumption of inevitable decline and complete dependency based upon the stereotypical characteristics of advanced age and of dementia may lead to a neglect of the possibility of rehabilitation.

Focusing on the hazards of the current situation and an eagerness to eliminate, rather than manage risk can lead to neglect of the hazards of intervention – particularly in this case those involved in the removal to residential care including loss of independence and autonomy through admission to residential care. Awareness of the impact of ageism on assessment is therefore essential to effective practice, but what does research tell us about which elderly people may be most at risk of losing their autonomy and independence?

High risk factors in elderly people

A review of research evidence on risk factors that provides a practically useful summary and concise typology of risk shows that high risk factors include advanced age, recent hospital discharge and recent change of home. Medium risk factors include recent bereavement, living alone and social class v. Low risk include lack of social contact, childlessness, and never having been married. Beales and Tulloch (1998) in discussing this typology raise several caveats in relation to it, which mostly reflect the kind of limitations shared by all such risk assessment schedules we mentioned in relation to child care and mental health.

Whilst it is useful to be aware that most elders at high risk will be of advanced age, it is equally true to say that most people of advanced age are not. Age alone is therefore an unreliable indicator. Overly narrow focus on age and disability which such assessment schedules

frequently encourage leads to a preoccupation with hazards and a neglect of strengths in Brearley's terms. For example, living alone and never having married may well point to an independence of character that can in fact enable the individual to manage debility and its hazards better.

Recent bereavement whilst posing potential hazards, need to be seen in context. We know that most informal care of severely disabled elders is carried out by spouses who are themselves aged. Whilst bereavement will inevitably lead to a period of grief – it may also signal the end of a distressing and physically demanding responsibility and an opportunity for a renaissance of energy and social contact. Gender and ethnicity are often ignored in such schedules as in this one, despite the fact that these are influential factors in debility, disadvantage and the social context within which they occur. This brief discussion of risk assessment typologies once again reminds us of the limitations of procedural, check list approaches to assessment and the pressing need to resist the reductionism they can entail in favour of the process approach we have advocated throughout.

Elder abuse and assessment

As we pointed out at the beginning of this chapter on assessment with particular client groups, this book is not intended as a specialist text. We have referred to some of the most recent of these. The extent of elder abuse in the UK has been disclosed as much greater than previously believed and still remains, despite this, a low priority for social policy and legislative action. Both the belated recognition of its extent and the lack of government action are symptomatic of the endemic ageism of our society. Elder abuse is not only widespread both in residential and domestic settings, but is multi-faceted and often not recognised as such by its perpetrators – both organisational and individual. Abuse may be physical, verbal, emotional and financial and may take the form of neglect which may not be immediately dangerous but which can result in significant harm in the longer term.

Abusers frequently don't recognise what they are doing as abuse because they do not regard aged people as fully adult, rather perceiving them as dependants who require protection from themselves. Such ageist attitudes can result in relatively minor forms of abuse such as referring an elder to social services without their consent, and to major forms of brutality such as tying elderly people in chairs to prevent them moving around in under-staffed residential facilities. In one such case recently not only did the staff involved in perpetrating such brutal abuse in an NHS hospital claim it was acceptable practice, but senior managers seemed to assert that because it was common practice with elders it did not actually constitute abuse.

Thus, elder abuse is as much a social construct as any other aspect of risk work we have discussed. Ageism is so endemic that it prevents people from recognising the brutality they have inflicted on elders actually constitutes abuse. How much greater, therefore, is the danger posed to effective assessment by professionals who themselves are exposed to the pervasive ageism of our culture? As in risk work with any other group, attention to the person-in-context – not narrowly focusing on the attributes of the client which allegedly put them in danger, is the foundation of effective practice.

In the light of this it is clear that holistic assessment of the whole context of elders at risk is essential if it is to be effective, either in promoting their continued autonomy or protecting them from harm. Many of the issues raised in relation to elders at risk thus reflect our discussion of risk work in general, and in risk work specifically with children and people with mental distress. This affirms – perhaps justifies and legitimates – the point we consistently make in this book. That the social work process is a well tried and tested one, which has value and relevance beyond the politically driven moral panics which have shaped practice in relation to client groups with a higher political profile than elders. A moral panic the results of which – in terms of overly narrow definitions of risk and danger – have been detrimental to professional practice and those it serves.

Towards holistic risk assessment

ACTIVITY 3.6

Review this chapter and consider some of the fundamental principles we discussed. Now apply these to your practice environment and make notes of how you might integrate them in your work.

Commentary

It is suggested that social work has a distinctive contribution to make to risk work because it has a socially-informed, user centred perspective which can counterbalance diagnostic and behavioural approaches (Davis, 1996). These have become overly concerned with attempting to eliminate risk at the expense of other important aspects of assessment practice. According to Davis there are four essential components of risk work which stress the values underpinning practice which is person centred and empowering, whilst being aware of the need to protect. These are:

- practice principles
- interpersonal encounters
- practice locations
- organisational support

Many of the elements she points to in terms of practice principles and interpersonal encounters we have addressed earlier in this session and we will list them only briefly to remind you of the issues involved. Davis's points about the practice environment of risk work which can be more or less supportive of it are addressed in a little more detail as we have not specifically discussed this before.

Practice principles

- Empowerment of clients through choice and opportunity.
- Recognition of individuality, self-determination, personal responsibility, autonomy.
- Counterbalances loss of client autonomy in reactive over-protectiveness and control.

■ Attention to competence, its limits and creative ways of working with all levels of it.

■ Involvement of service users, practitioners and managers in reviewing principles.

Interpersonal encounters

■ Quality of assessment is linked directly to the establishment of relationship, trust, and empathy this takes time – there are no short cuts.

■ 'Risk consuming work' – getting to know individuals, building trust and confidence.

■ Allowing time for mistakes, failure and return to the task.

■ Listening closely to the person in distress – even if apparently irrational.

■ Enable expression of feelings whilst calmly pursuing purpose of minimising risk.

Practice locations

Aspects of practice environments which are supportive to competent assessment practice include minimising the negative risks of harm and harassment so that workers and service users both feel secure in working with risk, is very important. Physical safety must be ensured through adequate arrangements for protection and care should the need arise – including physical aspects of working environments and working practices. Maximise opportunities for positive risk taking for change and empowerment would include multi-disciplinary, co-working and partnership practice. Policy and practice which reflect agreed practice principles is crucial especially as SSI reports have disclosed that many authorities and organisations involved in risk have no policy and practice guidance specifically relating to and supporting it.

Provide support for clients in risk taking from other service users as well as staff so that support from existing informal as well as professional networks can be offered in supporting clients taking on the challenge of positive risk taking. Support for staff engaged in stressful work with competent and regular supervision and consultancy, co-working and forums for peer support, all contribute to developing a culture of positive and creative risk taking

which is not based on 'covering your back'. Forums to address separate and shared concerns of service users and staff are necessary. Whilst confidentiality is a major concern in building trust, the isolation for both professionals and service users which can characterise risk work can be reduced through group work. This can itself be a powerful method of building trust between agencies, workers and service users.

Organisational support

Workers who fear organisational blame become anxious and defensive encouraging entirely negative interpretations of risk, the pursuit of risk elimination and the growth of a 'cover your back' culture can contribute to professional isolation and a fear of encouraging positive risk taking for fear of failure. Supervision is essential to effective practice; it is a venue for self-reflections in terms of striving for the integration of knowledge, skills and values which we have stressed as being essential, for accountability and for confidence building. Managers should review assessment practice and support required with workers and clients, expanding the managerial role to include not only monitoring and ensuring accountability, but also the development of an appropriate organisational culture and commitment to its shared values and practices both among workers and clients.

Inter-agency policy and practice should support and promote social work assessment. It is not only a legal requirement in some cases, but is essential to effective practice. Differences of professional culture and organisational policy and practice can inhibit this and lead, again to defensive practice. There is a need to work with these differences, understand and manage them in the interests of effective assessment. This will involve working towards a shared value base, policy and practice in relation to creative – not defensive – assessment practice.

Chapter summary

The increasing focus on risk assessment in modern social work practice has led to policy and practice in relation to risk and its management becoming focused on dangerousness, particularly so in work with offenders and mental health and significant harm in relation to children and elders. We noted that this puts undue pressure on work that is already highly sensitive in many cases and paradoxically may provoke the very behaviour that it seeks to prevent. The risk of abuse and physical threat or attack for social workers is considerable and social workers – particularly in residential settings – are among those who share the highest risk of assault at work. We argued that the recognition of this risk should be an important consideration for all social workers, their managers and the organisations within which they work.

We then went on to discuss what is meant by the 'social construction of risk' and how this knowledge contributes to effective practice. Describing Brearley's framework for risk assessment enabled us to usefully differentiate between risk, hazard and danger. We explored tension and potential conflict between rights and risk, care and control and illustrated how effective practice achieves a balance between them. The benefits of the risk management perspective are that they are in keeping with the values and practice of modern social work;

emphasises process of maximising benefits as well as minimising risks, rather than procedure of identifying and eliminating risk; and builds on strengths.

We noted however that the drawbacks are that it relies heavily on highly developed professional competence and judgement and requires commitment of client to partnership. It also requires intellectual/cognitive competence of the client. It involves ambiguity and uncertainty, is poorly understood by the public, and requires supportive management practice and organisational policy. Throughout the chapter we have stressed the need to work in partnership with colleagues and service users to identify and analyse potential risk of harm, abuse, or failure to protect and explored how such general principles and practices underpin effective risk work with three particular client groups. Finally we discussed Davis's four components of effective risk work – practice principles, interpersonal encounters, practice locations and organisational support and, in particular, how practice environments can contribute to positive practice and the minimisation of risks not only to clients but to social workers.

PART 2

Dilemmas in Practice

CHAPTER 4

Role Conflicts in Assessment and Intervention

Introduction

This chapter begins a new part of the book in which we look at some of the difficulties and dilemmas that arise when we try and apply practice principles in the context of contemporary social work, particularly in statutory social services. Here we look at the diversity of roles that are played by social workers and the conflicts that can occur between these roles. Social workers play very different roles in various agency contexts and with different service user groups. For example a social worker employed by a small voluntary agency working with homeless adults will play a very different role from a social worker in a community mental health team, or a child protection social worker, or a social worker who manages a residential home for the elderly. But what we will look at in particular in this chapter is the diversity of roles that a social worker can play *within* a single context. These roles do not always sit very easily or comfortably together.

Diversity of roles

In their book *Constructive Social Work* Nigel Parton and Patrick O'Byrne (2000: 134) write:
It is perhaps 'assessment' more than any other aspect of the work, which distinguishes social work from counselling or therapy. Social workers perform a whole range of roles which differ fundamentally from those performed by counsellors or therapists even though some of the techniques and strategies used reflect the skills and applied

knowledge of counselling and therapy. Below are some of the main roles, grouped into broad categories. We have not included 'assessment' in this list because we feel that assessment is not a role in its own right but is more properly seen as a *task* which social workers need to carry out as part of their various different roles. Assessment may be carried out for rationing purposes, for example, or for care management purposes, or indeed as part of a piece of therapeutic work.

Care management: the setting up and co-ordinating of a variety of services provided by workers other than the social workers themselves.

Advocacy: speaking on behalf of a service user, or helping service users to speak for themselves.

Rationing: collecting information to be used for decisions about the allocation of resources or participating in the decision-making process itself. (We will return to social work's inevitable involvement in rationing – and consider the principles involved in the next chapter.)

Quasi-parental care: both residential and field social workers, and not exclusively in the child care field, are frequently involved in performing a variety of activities – from arranging doctor's appointments, to taking children from A to B, to providing a shoulder to cry on – which are analogous to those performed by parents for children. Such activities may be delegated to others – foster-parents or care assistants – leaving the social worker with a 'care management' role in relation to them. But it is frequently the case that social workers must perform these tasks by default and often the case that the social worker is the most appropriate person to perform them. For instance a residential social worker is clearly *in loco parentis* when a child is distressed or needs some attention that would in other circumstances be provided by a parent. A field social worker may also have to take this role in situations where there is no other quasi-parental figure, such as a foster-parent, available.

Exercising quasi-parental responsibility: another quasi-parental role that social workers play in respect of children in care, but also in respect of some adults whose own decision-making capacity is limited (such as old people with dementia, adults with severe learning difficulties) is making plans on their behalf. In the case of children subject to care orders, there is an explicit legal expectation that the local authority shall: '(a) have parental responsibility for the child; and (b) have the power to determine the extent to which a parent or guardian of the child may meet his parental responsibility for him.' (Children Act 1989, s33 (3)).

All these tasks are core social work roles. Many social workers spend much more of their time performing these roles than they do on anything that might be described as counselling or therapy. The challenge is in employing those skills and applied knowledge characteristic of counselling and therapy at an appropriate level consistent with the demands of the particular role. Social workers neither are nor usually employed as counsellors or therapists but no employer would expect them to conduct their work without recourse to those essential helping/communication skills which we might define as follows:

Counselling and therapy: professional use of self, through some form of structure conversation or interaction, as a catalyst for change.

Indeed, some social workers do no counselling or therapy at all. Social workers often complain that 'we only do care management now, we don't have any time to perform real social work' which is an indictment against the increasing retrenchment and re-definition of social work occurring in statutory services. Something like this was observed by Andrew

Pithouse (1998) in his study of the daily interactions in a social work office:

> *Among the child care workers there is an embracing perception that all administrative regulation detracts from the 'real' work of visiting consumers...In the area office, administrative work is perceived as an intrusion and higher management the culprits of this diversion from 'real' work.*
>
> Pithouse, 1998: 18.

Clearly people do not go into social work because they want to fill out forms or sit in front of a computer screen all day, but we should nevertheless be clear that social work has never just been about counselling or therapy. Care management has always been part of the role, even if not always under that name. So has advocacy, rationing (the old term for a hospital social worker, for instance, was 'almoner' which originally meant 'distributor of alms') as well as what we have called quasi-parental care and the exercise of quasi-parental responsibility. Not just the paperwork but too much of the direct contact that social workers have with service users is connected with roles such as these rather than with the counselling or therapy role.

But there is one more key social work role which we have not yet mentioned which is absolutely central to child care social work and mental health social work as they are practiced in the UK – and a significant feature of social work with the elderly, with drug users and many other groups. This role we will call 'policing'.

Policing

Policing is the regulation and enforcement of boundaries of socially acceptable behaviour, using statutory powers if necessary or otherwise using the implicit authority that comes from the possession of statutory powers.

ACTIVITY 4.1

Thinking about social work as you have practised it, or have seen it practised, which of the roles that we have listed above predominate? The roles are summarised below. What proportion of a social worker's time is typically spent on each of them? Bear in mind that many activities, such as recording or interviewing service users, or meetings with other agencies, may at times be linked with different roles. (If you are filling out an eligibility criterion form then that is to do with the rationing task. If you are making a note of some key points that emerged in a direct work session with a child, then that is to do with counselling or therapy, though both activities could be described as 'recording'.)

- care management
- advocacy
- rationing
- quasi-parental care
- exercising quasi-parental responsibility
- counselling or therapy
- policing

Commentary

You may find that it is sometimes difficult to tease out the separate roles, which are often closely interwoven. For example: if you spend 45 minutes with an elderly person completing an assessment of needs, you could say that the time you spent was primarily to do with care management and rationing, but depending on the circumstances, the interview may have had an important counselling component as well and may have raised issues for which advocacy might be appropriate.

Acknowledging that there are difficulties in dividing a social worker's activities neatly into our list of roles, we suggest nevertheless that it is unlikely that the amount of time spent on counselling or therapeutic tasks will amount to more than 50% and in some areas of social work the proportion may be much lower than that.

On the other hand – in child care social work – the policing function may well take up at least 50% of a social worker's time if you include court work, attendance at case conferences and core groups, child protection investigations and all the visits and administrative work that flow out of these jobs. A substantial proportion of the remainder of the time may be spent on care management (though it is not so commonly referred to by this name in the child care field.)

A social worker involved in administering the community care system, on the other hand, probably spends nearly all their time on care management and rationing tasks and only a relatively small proportion of their time either on policing or on counselling or therapy tasks.

Conflict of roles

The difficulty of playing so many different roles is that at times they can come into conflict with one another or become confused. The care managing and rationing roles, for instance, can be difficult to combine with the counselling or therapy role. Most therapists would agree that a therapeutic relationship works best when unencumbered by other things. If your therapist or counsellor is also your access point to a variety of services, or is in a position to provide you with financial assistance (as local authority social work agencies are empowered to do under Section 17 (6) of the 1989 Children Act) then this, in our experience, can create a number of difficulties:

- Are service users entering into a counselling or therapeutic relationship with the social worker because they actually want to, or are they doing so because they believe that this is the way to gain access to services or material assistance?
- If entering into a counselling or therapeutic relationship is required to gain access to other services is this ethical?
- If the counsellor or therapist are also the care manager, they will probably need to share information about the service user with others. Can they separate out the information that they have obtained in a 'counselling' role from that which they have obtained as a care manager? (In other words: is it possible to provide the level of confidentiality that counsellors and therapists can normally offer?)
- The social worker's judgement on whether services and material assistance are given or

withheld is likely to be influenced by their understanding as counsellor or therapist. This creates an additional layer of complexity to the power relationship between client and counsellor.

- If the social worker, in their care manager capacity, decides that it is not appropriate to accede to a request for a service or material assistance, this is likely to have a significant impact on their relationship with the service user as a counsellor or therapist.
- Conversely, fear of upsetting the counselling or therapeutic relationship, may make it difficult for the social worker to make fair and objective decisions about whether or not to provide material assistance or services that are asked for.

ACTIVITY 4.2

You are working with a service user who we will call Linda. You are doing some work with her on building self-esteem and helping her to cope more assertively with others. You have established a good working relationship with her and feel that you are making progress. She has told you that she trusts you and that she feels that you 'really listen to her'. During one session she tells you that she is aware that your agency is able to give financial help in some circumstances and she asks you for a cash grant.

You are aware that the funds available for this purpose are very limited and you are not sure that the purpose for which Linda is requesting the grant can really be regarded as very high priority. What sort of position would this put you in?

Commentary

Different people would deal with this in different ways. However, we would suggest that, for you to say no to the request might create some difficulties for your therapeutic work with Linda. Equally, if you said yes, simply in order to avoid creating these difficulties, this in itself has some implications. Are you going to have to say yes to every such request? Would this be fair to other service users? Is your counselling work

going to be the same once it has been established that, as well as offering the opportunity to talk and reflect, you are also a source of material help? A lot of social workers would sidestep these issues by passing the decision about the financial help to a manager (and in many agencies this sort of decision would have to be made by a manager – something we will come back to in the next chapter), but even so the problems do not entirely disappear.

Another conflict that can occur is between 'advocacy' and 'rationing' roles. At the time of the introduction of the 1990 NHS and Community Care Act, the current legal framework for adult social work, the tension between these two roles came to the fore because local authorities were required:

- To carry out 'needs led' assessments of adult service users. That is they were asked to make an assessment of what the client's needs were without pigeonholing people into the services that were actually available.
- To manage a substantial community care budget.

In pursuit of the former aim, government guidance and staff training programmes encouraged social workers to look holistically at service users, to consider all their needs and to find creative ways of meeting those needs. If, to give an illustration, an elderly man asked for a place at a day centre, then social workers were encouraged not just to consider him 'a day centre case', but:

- To explore what needs a day centre was supposed to meet. These might be the need for company or stimulation, perhaps, or the need for someone to keep an eye on him when his carer was not available, or the need for his carer to have a break.
- To consider whether there were other ways in which these needs might be better met.
- To consider whether he might have other needs which a day centre would not meet – and consider how these too might be met.

What was being suggested, then, was that social workers – or care co-ordinators – should not merely be officials arranging access to various services, but should act as a kind of advocate for the service user, getting a picture of their needs 'as the service user saw them' and then working on behalf of the service user to get those needs met.

At the outset, not surprisingly, many authorities went over budget and, as a result, complex new screening procedures involving eligibility criteria became part of the process, inevitably dampening down initial hopes of a more creative, user-led service. The question is, can social workers, or care co-ordinators, in this field, carry out genuine needs-led assessments and act as advocates for the service user in trying to get these needs met and yet *at the same time* take responsibility for rationing resources and therefore limiting access to services? Bateman (2000) suggests six ethical principles for advocacy of which the first two are: 'Always act in the client's best interests' and 'Always act in accordance with the client's wishes and instructions', but those involved in rationing resources cannot put the best interests of one client before everything else and are expected to set the interests of one client in the balance against the interests of others.

Some specialist advocacy services can concentrate entirely on advocacy but local authorities had no choice to reconcile these two roles as best they could, whatever the tension between them. But was it feasible for one person to carry out both roles at the same time? There are arguments both ways on this, and we will be exploring them further in the next chapter. For the moment we will just note that there are, at the least, tensions between acting as a whole hearted advocate for a service user within the system and, at the same time, acting on behalf of the system to protect it against being overwhelmed and to help it distribute its resources as fairly as possible. These tensions occur not just to social work under the NHS and Community Care Act, there are tensions too between the quasi-parental role and rationing. A social worker's capacity to provide quasi-parental care is clearly limited, not least by the fact that they may be assigned new cases. In the context of a resi-

dential home, pressure to free up residential beds may mean that the child is swiftly moved on.

But perhaps the most difficult of role conflicts relate to tensions between social work's 'policing' roles and its other roles, particularly the counselling or therapy role and the advocacy role. It is this policing role, and the way it impacts on these other roles, that we will explore for the rest of this chapter.

ACTIVITY 4.3

Before going any further you might like to take stock by considering your own experience of social work and asking yourself what are the most difficult role conflicts that you have encountered?

Policing, oppression and social control

The dichotomy between what we have called 'policing' and other aspects of social work is sometimes presented as *care* versus *control*. We will therefore begin by noting that this is something of a false dichotomy. In life, control can often be caring. A parent who made no attempt to control their toddler next to a busy road would not be very caring, to give an obvious example.

But the role that we have called 'policing' *is* of course part of the 'social control' aspect of social work, an aspect that many social workers are uncomfortable with, sitting uneasily as it does with the social work values of promoting empowerment and self-determination. The policing role often *feels* oppressive and this makes it seem difficult to reconcile with the idea of anti-oppressive practice. It is sometimes necessary to remind ourselves that, for example, to leave a small child in a situation where they are being used by adults for sex would be much *more* oppressive than to use statutory powers to intervene and prevent the abuse from happening.

Or in the case of a man who is having terrifying paranoid delusions as a result of an acute psychotic illness – and who has shut himself off from family and friends and all other sources of help as a result of those delusions – it might be much more oppressive to leave him to suffer than it would be to use the powers given by the Mental Health Act to take him to a hospital and get him treatment. The latter might involve asking the police to break down his door and remove him by force. This would therefore feel very oppressive and brutal, but it could be that when he was well again this service user would thank you for doing it nevertheless, or might at any rate have a much better quality of life.

We should bear in mind too that the policing function is not the only aspect of social work that is connected with social control. It is simply the most obvious one. In fact many would argue that the therapeutic role played by social workers, psychiatrists and others is *also* about social control. Critics of social work have pointed out how 'explanations in traditional social work reduce complex social problems to individual psychological ones' (Payne, 1997: 216, discussing McIntyre, 1982) as a result 'blaming the victim' and making the client responsible for problems which are really social and political in origin. Parton (1991) draws on the work of Foucault (1977) to discuss how this process of defining problems in terms of individual psychology has the effect of increasing the power of various professional groups to regulate the behaviour of others, legitimised by discourses drawn from 'human sciences' like medicine, psychology and psychiatry.

We will not go into this further here, however. Having noted the complexities of the relationship between what we have called 'policing' and social control, we will now look at the policing function of social work as it exists in the various different specialisms before moving on to look in more detail at the way the policing function can conflict with other roles.

The policing role in social work with older people

Section 47 of the National Assistance Act 1948 (as amended by the National Assistance Amendment Act 1951) allows local authority social services departments to apply to a magis-trates' court for an order authorising them to remove a person 'in need of care and attention' from their home and to take them to a hospital, residential home or some other 'suitable place' if:

- The person is 'suffering from grave chronic disease or being aged, infirm or physically incapacitated, is living in unsanitary conditions'
- 'Is unable to devote to themselves, and is not receiving from other persons, proper care and attention',
- The person's removal from home is necessary, 'either in their own interests or for preventing injury to the health of, or serious nuisance to, other persons'.
- The community physician has supplied evidence in writing to the local authority to this effect.

Seven days notice needs to be given to the person concerned or to someone who is 'in charge of' that person. If the court is satisfied by the evidence presented it can make an order lasting up to three months, under Section 47 (4), which can be further renewed by the court for a further three months. In an emergency an order can also be obtained from a single magis-trate without giving the person concerned any prior notice, if the community physician and another doctor state that it is 'in the interest of that person to remove him without delay', under Section 1(1) of the National Assistance (Amendment) Act 1951. An emergency order of this kind can last up to three weeks.

The use of the National Assistance Act in this way is not a common event in social work with the elderly, but it does occur. Social workers with the elderly may also adopt a policing role when there are allegations of elder abuse. Working with people who have Alzheimer's disease or other forms of dementia may also at times involve social workers making decisions to overrule service user's stated wishes in the interests of their own safety or wellbeing, though arguably this is an instance of operating in a quasi-parental role rather than a policing one (the two shade into each other.)

The policing role in mental health social work

The Mental Health Act 1983 places social workers in a unique position of authority which is not found in any other social work specialism. Social workers 'approved' under the Act are the professional group given the task of deciding whether people should be detained, and even given treatment, against their will. Section (2) of the Act makes provision for a 'patient' to be admitted and detained for assessment on the grounds that:

- He is suffering from mental disorder of a nature or degree which warrants the detention of the patient in a hospital for assessment (or for assessment followed by medical treatment) for at least a limited period: and
- He ought to be so detained in the interests of his own health and safety or with a view to the protection of other persons.

Application must be made by an approved social worker, on the recommendation of two medical practitioners. A person can be detained under this section for 28 days.

Likewise detention for treatment – permitting not only compulsory detention but compulsory treatment – under Section (3) of the Act is made by an approved social worker on the recommendation of two medical practitioners on the grounds that:

- The patient is suffering from mental illness, severe mental impairment, psychopathic disorder or mental impairment and his mental disorder is of a nature or degree which makes it appropriate for him to receive medical treatment in a hospital: and
- In the case of a psychopathic disorder or mental impairment, such treatment is likely to alleviate or prevent a deterioration of his condition: and
- It is necessary for the health or safety of the patient or for the protection of other persons that he should receive such treatment and it cannot be provided unless he is detained under this section.

There is also provision for a emergency application to be made under Section (4), on the recommendation of one medical practitioner under which a 'patient' can be detained for 72 hours.

The interesting thing to note here is that it is the social worker who actually decides whether to make the application. The medical profession, normally viewed as more powerful and prestigious, is placed in the position of simply making recommendations.

The mental health social worker's policing role does not end here, either, since they will also be involved in, for instance giving evidence to tribunals which review the status of patients detained under section and deal with appeals from patients. What is more, the existence of these powers inevitably casts a sort of shadow over other areas of the mental health social worker's activity. Service users will be aware that social workers have these powers. If the social worker attempts to offer counselling or therapy, the service user will be aware that information that they disclose might be used at a later date in a decision as to whether to apply for a section under the Mental Health Act.

The policing role in other areas of adult social work

Historically, the professionals involved in work with adults with learning disabilities were heavily involved in policing this group of service users in regard to all aspects of their lives, particularly in regard to sexual behaviour. Active steps were taken to prevent the possibility of adults with learning difficulties from having sexual relations.

With the advent of community care and a greater awareness of the rights of people with learning difficulties to be regarded as citizens like the rest of us, this attitude is somewhat in decline. However professionals working with this client group are still frequently involved in making judgements as to whether or not service users have the capacity to make decisions on their own behalf, or whether it is necessary for professionals and others to make decisions for them. Of course it is debatable whether paternalistic control of this kind comes under our category of 'policing' or under our category of 'exercising quasi-parental responsibility' – as noted earlier the two merge into one another.

Social workers in drug and alcohol services also work in an area where there is a policing element in the role, alongside care management, advocacy and counselling or therapeutic roles. Service users of such agencies may be required to submit to tests, including urine tests, in order to get a service (for example: in order to become eligible for referral to a treatment unit.)

The policing role in children and families work

The policing role in children and family social work is perhaps the form of social work 'policing' most widely known to the public at large and the one that rouses the strongest and most ambivalent passions. Social workers take children away from their families. Unlike mental health social workers they do not exercise this power on their own account, however, but make application to courts to make orders which will allow them to remove children from their parents or to obtain access to them.

Section (47) of the 1989 Children Act sets out a local authority's duties when it receives information about a child within its area who may be suffering, or likely to suffer, 'significant harm'

- It should make sufficient enquiries to allow it to determine what action needs to be taken to protect the child.
- It should arrange for the child to be seen, unless sufficient information can be obtained without doing so.
- If denied access to a child, or refused information about the child's whereabouts, it should apply for a court order. This might be an emergency protection order (Sections (44–46)) a child assessment order(Section (43)), a care order or a supervision order (Section (31)).
- More generally it should decide whether it is in the interests of the child whether to initiate court proceedings.

But even if the case is not taken to court, the multi-disciplinary arrangements under *Working Together* (Department of Health, 1999), create an environment – case conferences, core groups, strategy meetings – in which parental behaviour is placed under scrutiny and parents are expected to comply with the Child Protection Plans put in place by the multi-agency system. Such plans do not, in themselves, have statutory force but parents will be aware that failure to comply places them at risk of being taken to court in the ways described above. And we should note that, while this is a multi-agency system, only two agencies can take on the key worker role of co-ordinating the overall effort, convening core groups, preparing reports for case conferences and only these two agencies have the job of (if necessary) taking the case to court. Those agencies are local authority social service departments and the NSPCC – both social work agencies.

ACTIVITY 4.4

Looking at the area of social work with which you are most familiar, consider to what extent a policing role is part of the social work task. How do you think the existence of the policing role impacts on the relationship between social worker and service user?

Policing versus therapy

The 'policing' role undertaken by social workers is important. Some people cannot take full responsibility for managing their own lives, either because of their own capacity (people who cannot think clearly as a result of mental illness or dementia, people with profound learning difficulties) or because of their powerless position (children, frail elderly people who may be unable to stand up to abusive carers). It is appropriate that powers should exist to intervene in order to protect such people, or to act to prevent them from endangering others, in certain clearly defined circumstances. However, in all areas of social work, the existence of the policing role has the potential – as we put it earlier – to 'cast a shadow' over other roles. This is particularly the case in relation to the counselling or therapeutic role, since counselling and therapy are generally agreed to work best in an atmosphere of trust, confidentiality and what Carl Rogers called 'unconditional positive regard' (Rogers, 1967: 47).

Rogers suggested that it was important in a therapeutic relationship to convey 'a warm acceptance and prizing of the other person as a separate individual' (Rogers, 1967: 38). It is most important that social workers do attempt to give this message to service users in *any* context – social workers are certainly not there to pass judgement on anyone's value as a human being – but it is much harder to give this message convincingly when you are also (for example) involved in a court case where you are arguing that this person is not parenting their child adequately. In such a context it is, of course, also much harder to receive such a message.

We would suggest that in such a context, while it is possible for the social worker to convey to the service user that they are respected as a person, it is challenging for both service user and social worker to expect them to establish the kind of context that is necessary for counselling or therapeutic work. And if this is the case in respect of the extreme situation in which the social worker and service user are on different sides of a court case, then it may be the case too in somewhat less extreme situations:

- The social worker is key worker under child protection procedures and has recommended that a child's name be placed on the child protection register.
- The social worker has expressed some concerns about the service user's parenting. The social worker has not invoked child protection procedures or legal proceedings, but the service user is aware that these possibilities exist.
- The social worker has not expressed any concerns about the service user's parenting, but the service user is aware that the social worker is employed by a child protection agency.

These examples come from children and family work and we suggest that conflict of roles is particularly acute in this area, though not because the statutory powers of children and family social workers are necessarily more extensive than those of others. In fact a good case could be made that it is mental health social workers who have the most powers in that respect, since they are empowered on their own account to apply for compulsory detention. What does make the clash of roles especially pronounced in children and family social work is that, in this field, social work agencies are simultaneously placed in the position of being the agency on whom primary responsibility is laid for 'policing' families, *and* the agency primarily responsible for *bringing about change* in families. In the mental health field, social work is not the primary agency responsible for bringing about change: this is a collaborative task with health as the lead agency. Nevertheless the clash between policing and counselling or therapeutic roles is undoubtedly keenly felt in the mental health field too.

ACTIVITY 4.5

(a) Suppose that you are parent under a great deal of stress. You have on several occasions felt a murderous rage towards your children and you are genuinely frightened that you may hurt them. How willing would you be to disclose these fears to an independent counsellor? And how willing would you be to disclose them to a child protection social worker?

(b) Suppose that you have recurring mental health problems and have been detained in a mental hospital in the past. Suppose you become aware that certain frightening and delusional ideas are becoming more and more insistent in your mind. How willing would you be to disclose this to an independent counsellor? How willing would you be to disclose this to a social worker who had applied for you to be detained under section in the past?

Commentary

(a) People can and do disclose such feelings to social workers, but you will probably agree that many people would be more reluctant to talk to a social worker about such things than they would be to talk to an independent counsellor, because of a fear that the social worker would take away the children, or a fear that in some other way the social worker would take over.

(b) Clearly if detention under the Mental Health Act had not been a positive experience for you, you would be extremely wary what you told the social worker who had put you in that position.

Implications for assessment

Most of us are wary what we tell people who we perceive to have power over us and are reluctant to disclose private, personal information about ourselves unless we trust the person we are talking to and are confident that the information will go no further without our permission. Since part of the assessment process consists of information-gathering, assessment is unavoidably compromised when the person carrying it out is perceived to be in a position of power, or is perceived not to be able to keep the information to themselves. Both these circumstances apply when the social worker is acting in – or could move into – a policing role. (We should note in passing that these circumstances apply too if the worker is acting in a rationing role.) We cannot expect completely open communication under such conditions and we should be very careful not to leap into labelling service users as 'unco-operative', 'unwilling to engage', 'anti-authority' and so on, if they are cautious about, or resistant to, sharing information.

When working with a child protection social worker, a service user – parent or child – *should* of course be able to be confident that their social worker will not gossip about their case to friends or to other clients. But, that aside, they cannot be given any guarantee of confidentiality as this would normally be understood, for the worker can give no undertaking that they will not disclose information about the case to other people. On the contrary, they are obliged to record the substance of what a service user says to them in files to which others have access. They are obliged to discuss the content of their conversations with the service user with their supervisor (who in turn must pass on any concerns they may have to *their* own supervisor). In the event that the social worker is told things that raise child protection issues, then they will have to discuss these with professionals from other agencies. If the matter comes to a case conference or a court, the social worker is obliged to include any salient information from their files in their reports. So, for instance, if a parent tells the social worker that she sometimes feels like killing her child, she may later have to hear the social worker talk about this in front of a dozen professionals in a case conference, or read it in a statement prepared by the social worker for a court.

In an introductory handbook on counselling (Milne, 2002: 10) writes: 'Generally speaking, whatever theories the counsellor is familiar with the basic requisites are the same. These are that the counsellor provides an environment of privacy, safety and assured confidentiality, is non-defensive and shows respect for the client at all times.' This is clearly a difficult environment for a child protection social worker to create, at least in respect of privacy, safety and assured confidentiality.

Nor is loss of privacy by any means the only implication of disclosing a piece of information to a social worker. A teenager who is being sexually abused might wish to find a professional with whom they can discuss the situation and decide, within the safe confines of that professional relationship, what they ought to do next. However a social worker cannot offer that safe space (nor actually can any other professional involved in the child protection system). Having heard an allegation of sexual abuse they have no choice but to act on it. There are people to whom the social worker *must* talk, systems that *must* be set in motion. The teenager will find that, having spoken of their abuse to a social worker, the question of what to do next is largely taken out of their hands. It is a very far

cry from a controversial confidential counselling service such as is offered by the
Samaritans, who guarantee not to pass on
anything they are told, even the most serious
allegations and confessions.

The basic conditions for a counselling relationship quoted above from Milne (2002)
included *safety*. If you make a disclosure only to
find that you have started off an intrusive
process over which you have no control, this is
clearly not going to make you feel safe at all
even though the consequences may be
improved safety. Roland Summit (1983) went so
far as to describe a specific 'Child Sexual Abuse
Accommodation Syndrome' under which
children who have disclosed abuse experience
such a frightening loss of control as a result that
they then retract the allegation as a means of re-
establishing some control.

As Beckett (2003: 42) has suggested elsewhere, one could make out a hypothetical case
for requiring social workers to caution their
clients at the beginning of an assessment in the
manner of the police: 'You have the right to
remain silent, but anything you say will be taken
down and may be used in evidence.' Even
though a caution like this is not given in so
many words, it is important to be honest with
service users about the true position and
important to be aware that service users are
understandably cautious about what information they are prepared to share and what
information they will keep to themselves.

And the policing role does not impact only
on the *service user's* handling of the assessment
relationship. It also inevitably impacts on the
social worker. A child protection social worker
investigating alleged abuse clearly cannot necessarily go at the client's own pace. Inconsistencies
must be challenged, awkward questions asked. A
social worker investigating abuse cannot simply
be accepting of the service user's 'world and
himself as he sees them' (Rogers, 1967: 38) but
must be suspicious and even confrontational.
The same is true to varying degrees for social
workers operating in other areas; in drug and
alcohol services; in agencies that work with
adult offenders, or in aspects of mental health
work.

ACTIVITY 4.6

Before reading further you might like to pause
and consider your own experience of social
work. How is the assessment process affected, in
your experience, by the existence of social
work's 'policing' role? How do service users
respond to questioning by social workers?

Implications for intervention

The policing role casts a shadow over the
assessment process in social work, because it
creates an understandable reluctance on the part
of service users to engage in open communication. How does it impact on social work
intervention? In fact, since assessment and intervention overlap, we have already begun to look
at this. Open communication is not just
important for assessment purposes but for any
counselling or therapeutic intervention. We
have already discussed the ways in which,
because of their policing 'hat', the social worker
cannot easily adopt the conventional stance of
the counsellor or therapist, on going at the
client's own pace and respecting the client's own
choices, and offer privacy, confidentiality and
safety in the way that these are normally understood. A child who discloses abuse will find that
a process of intervention starts to unfold from
that point, whether or not they wanted it to do
so. In the mental health field a client who admits
to the recurrence of delusional ideas may
likewise find that processes are set in motion
over which they have no control.

Can a social worker in a policing role also
undertake counselling or therapeutic work?
Our suggestion would be that it is still possible
for a social worker in a policing role to
undertake useful direct work with a service
user, but that it is important to be clear that this
is very different to counselling or therapy as
these are generally understood. The temptation
for an inexperienced social worker can be to
minimise this difference and to draw a veil over
their policing role, in an effort to give a sense of
confidentiality and safety for the client *which is
in fact spurious*. This is a strategy which is likely to
backfire, since if the social worker has not been

honest from the outset about their dual – or multiple – roles, then the sense of betrayal will be all the greater on the part of the service user at a later date when the social worker has to suddenly switch from counselling to policing. In any case, it is unethical for a social worker to lie to service users, even if this is allegedly to spare the service user's feelings. It is commonly said that information is power. Misinformation, by the same token, is profoundly disempowering.

However by being very clear from the outset about the different roles and responsibilities, it is often possible for the social worker to establish a working relationship of trust and respect, albeit of a limited kind, and to be able to work with a service user on specific problems. Establishing clear ground rules, in other words, is key to working successfully in a context like child protection or mental health where the social worker may have no choice but to hold a policing role while at the same time trying to enable the service user to make changes in their life. These ground rules – and we suggest that it is helpful to put them in writing because people do not always retain everything they hear, especially when distressed – should include a statement about the limits to confidentiality and about the circumstances under which the social worker might intervene using statutory powers. A social worker in this context cannot offer unconditional confidentiality but can offer openness and honesty. These are qualities which, in our experience, are very much valued by service users. It can be reinforced by ensuring that the service user is kept up to date with what is going on, and by for instance, sharing case recording with the service user so that they can see for themselves what is going into the file.

Ethical considerations

If combining a policing role with elements of a counselling role is difficult for social workers, we should be careful not to forget that it may be much more difficult for the service user on the receiving end. We suggest that if counselling or therapeutic work is to be included in a child protection plan, or any other kind of care plan

with which a service user is required to comply, then service users should have some choice as to who they do that work with. If they feel uncomfortable about doing the work with the social worker who, as key worker, is also monitoring their performance, then this should be respected. Since the social worker cannot offer what is normally regarded as a conducive environment for counselling, the service user should not be labelled as unco-operative if they do indeed feel that what the social worker can offer is not for them.

One strategy to deal with dual roles is to split the task, with one social worker taking on most of the policing functions while another worker offers the counselling or therapeutic role. If both workers are from the same agency, however, it is unlikely that they will not talk to each other and co-ordinate their efforts and it remains important to be honest about this, otherwise the kind of 'spurious safety' and 'spurious confidentiality' that we mentioned earlier is simply being reproduced in another form. Even if the two are from different agencies the multi-agency system means that they are likely to be linked in the same information-sharing and decision-making network. If tasks are to be split, then the nature and limits of that split should be made clear and not used manipulatively and dishonestly in order to entrap or prejudice the powerless service user.

We will conclude by saying that counselling and therapy are a highly personal matter. What is helpful to one person is profoundly unhelpful – even damaging – to another. Few of us would be willing to enter into a counselling or therapy as a client (even in an entirely 'safe' and 'confidential' context) without being able to choose who we entered into it with. Equally, there are clients who may find the concept of therapy incomprehensible yet benefit enormously from the social work practice informed by the approach deriving from it. A social worker should never use their 'policing' powers to insist that a service user enter into a counselling or therapeutic relationship with themselves, or indeed with any other specified person. On the other hand social workers who attempt to practice without the advantages of a theoretical framework that can help guide their own emotions and those of the service user, is unnecessarily hampering their effectiveness and the capacity of the client to change.

Chapter summary

This chapter has looked at the difficult combination of roles that social workers typically have to play and considered the contradictions that exist between them. We suggested that the main roles could be categorised as:

- care management
- advocacy
- rationing
- quasi-parental care
- exercising quasi-parental responsibility
- counselling or therapy
- policing

We considered the conflicts that can arise between the counselling/therapy role and the care management and rationing roles, potentially resulting in one undermining the other. We also discussed the conflict between advocacy and rationing roles which creates tensions in the community care system and conflicts between quasi-parental roles and rationing. We then moved on to look at the policing role in particular, having identified major conflicts between the policing and counselling/therapy and advocacy roles. We looked at the relationship of policing to oppression and social control, cautioning against a simplistic assumption that the policing role is necessarily oppressive or that other roles necessarily are not.

Looking at the policing role in more detail we briefly considered what it involves in, firstly, social work with the elderly and secondly, mental health social work. We discussed the policing role in social work with other adult client groups and finally child and family social work (probably the area of social work where the statutory powers of social workers are most widely known.)

In considering the ways in which a policing role clashes with the counselling or therapy role we discussed the implications for assessment, pointing out that information-sharing is inevitably compromised by the existence of a social worker's statutory powers. The same is true in respect of social work intervention. A social worker with 'policing' responsibilities cannot offer the privacy, confidentiality and safety that are normally regarded as appropriate to a counselling or therapeutic relationship. We suggested that useful direct work *can* still take place in this context, but only if the ground rules are clearly spelled out.

We concluded by suggesting that therapy and counselling as such must be entered into voluntarily and that social workers should not use statutory powers as a means of coercing service users into therapy or counselling. Equally, social work practice that fails to draw on those foundational skills and communication techniques is impoverished.

CHAPTER 5

Working with Limited Resources

Introduction

The existing social work literature, both on assessment and on intervention, seems to place surprisingly little emphasis on the issues associated with managing within limited resources. And yet, one of the purposes of social work assessment is to determine a service user's eligibility for the allocation of specific resources and to determine the priority to be given to the service user's case vis-à-vis the cases of other service users.

When a social worker in a children and families team, for example undertakes an initial assessment or core assessment of need, they are not simply assembling a picture of a family's needs. The social worker is also determining whether those needs fall within the brief of their agency to meet, and, if so, how those needs should be measured against the competing claims of other service users for the limited time and resources of their agency. The same is true of an assessment carried out by a social worker in a team assessing the social care needs of elderly people. The social worker will be required to come to a view as to the service user's eligibility or otherwise to varying levels of service provision. Both of these examples relate to formal assessment processes, but even the most informal decision-making processes carried out by social workers require constant judgements to be made about resources. As we will discuss, even simply deciding how to allocate one's limited timed between different cases is, for instance, a resource allocation process that is no different in principle from deciding, say, how to allocate limited funds available for domiciliary care.

Nor are resource issues relevant only to our thinking about the assessment process. We would argue that responsible planning of interventions cannot take place in some theoretical vacuum, but must take into account the availability of resources. It is our proposal that clear thinking about resources should not be regarded as a necessary evil, or as a distraction from the real business of social work, but as an unavoidable core part of the job in all of the following ways:

- Decision-making about the allocation of resources is one of the main purposes of assessment in many circumstances.
- Negotiation over scarce resources where there are competing claims is a crucial social work role and an essential part of care planning.
- Making decisions about the best way of deploying resources are a key responsibility of any social work agency, statutory or voluntary.
- Any responsible intervention requires that adequate resources are properly secured in order to be able to carry the intervention through.

Even when they decide how to allocate their time between different cases on their caseload, or between different tasks, a social worker is involved in deciding between competing claims on resources.

Rationing in social services

> The language of government guidance requires us to target resources at those most in need...Targeting is rationing dressed up in more acceptable language.
>   Bamford, 1993: 35.

Social services – like other public services which are not directly funded by their own users – are rationed, though words like 'targeting', 'eligibility' and 'prioritisation' may be used. This is true both in the state sector and the voluntary sector because supply is limited by the resources available and cannot expand to meet demand unless additional resources are provided. If you were running a commercial organisation (let us say a biscuit factory) increased demand on your services would generate new income for you and – in due course – allow you to take on additional staff or manufacturing plant to meet the demand. But if you are part of a team of social workers delivering a children and families social work service to a given neighbourhood, then you will have to continue to manage all the referrals on children and families that come from that neighbourhood among yourselves even if demand increases. This kind of comparison is often used to justify resource constraints throughout the public sector but it is unreliable because consumer market economics are subjected to different fiscal dynamics than the broader and necessarily more complex dynamics of public welfare provision.

Increased demands on the services of your social work team will not generate new income and, unless you can persuade your employers to provide you with additional resources, you will still be expected to manage the new demand between you. Additional business is good news for a private company. For a public service, though, it may be an additional source of stress and create increasing difficulties in providing an adequate service. The high levels of long-term sickness and poor recruitment and retention statistics are testimony to the short-sighted

nature of management responses. Feelings of guilt are generated particularly by managers who are charged with the responsibility of maintaining budgets and responding to impossible demands. These feelings can translate into cold disengagement, or a brutalising style that engenders low morale and team disenchantment. 'There is one characteristic which makes the management of public services different in principle from managing private service:' as Flynn (1997: 11) writes, 'the fact that they are not actually sold to people at a price which yields a profit and are not withheld from people who cannot afford them.'

Over the past 25 years there has been a major change in the political context under which public services operate, not only in social work and social care, but across the board: in health, education, the police, housing and social security. Writers on social policy (see, for instance, Clarke et al., 2000) speak of 'new public management' or 'new managerialism' to describe the ethos under which managers of public services have been expected to make their agencies more 'businesslike' and more like commercial organisations. We have seen, for instance, the introduction of the purchaser-provider split in health and in social care and the introduction of performance tables for schools intended (in theory) to allow consumers to exercise informed choice.

We have seen the introduction of various performance measures to highlight strengths and weaknesses, in the way that the financial bottom line provides a measure for private business. There has been a concern to improve the economy, efficiency and effectiveness of public services at the expense of quality, user-driven, and socially inclusive practice. There is widespread opposition to these trends combined with a retreat into defensive practice and cynicism about what can be achieved. However the need to ration represents a fundamental point of difference between public services and private companies. Lord Laming (2003: 11), in his report on the Victoria Climbié tragedy, criticised social services departments for seeming to 'spend a lot of time and energy devising ways of limiting access to services, and adopting mechanisms to reduce service demand.' Given that their resources are finite, and their staff human, social services departments has no choice but to limit access to services – and can only hope to do so as fairly, as rationally and as humanely as possible. This goes directly against the aspirations and humanitarian principles that draw many to consider social work as a worthwhile occupation.

Rationing in voluntary organisations

Most of the discussion in this chapter will relate to statutory agencies and reflect a concept of social work practice that is undergoing some re-definition as the social policy imperative to increase the amount of voluntary and independent social care provision gathers apace. The new degree qualification and occupational standards are raising expectations of quality social work provision that to many seem at best unrealistic or at worst disingenuous. Certainly it is in the statutory services that we characteristically see elaborate bureaucratic filtering mechanisms intended to ration out resources on the basis of risk and need. These tend to be much less evident in social work agencies run by the voluntary sector, especially in the smaller local agencies. But rationing does occur in the voluntary sector too. The reason that rationing is less evident in the voluntary sector is that voluntary agencies are not required to provide a universal service and can therefore control their workload in other ways. For example:

■ By dealing only with a small and specific client group (for example: a mental health day centre that offers an open door service to people with mental health problems in a small market town). Because they do not have to make service users jump through elaborate hoops, in the form of assessments of need and eligibility, such services may feel much more user-friendly than many statutory services.
■ By taking on a fixed number of cases at any given time (for example: a family assessment unit that takes on X number of families for an agreed period of time), after which they

are simply 'full' and do not take on any new work until a vacancy arises. Because they can control the type and/or amount of work that they take on in ways like this, voluntary agencies may be able to do a much more thorough job than statutory agencies. And, unlike statutory agencies, voluntary agencies operating on this kind of basis can proceed with their work without there being a risk that at any moment an even higher priority piece of work will come along requiring them to drop what they are already doing.
■ By negotiating service level agreements under which voluntary agencies agree to take on tasks on behalf of statutory agencies that specify the type and volume of work to be taken on. For these kinds of reasons voluntary agencies may be able to offer better services in many respects than statutory ones. However it is important to bear in mind that it is the existence of the statutory services (as a safety net to pick up those cases which fall outside their brief) which make possible this distinctive role for voluntary agencies.

ACTIVITY 5.1

Before going any further you may like to consider your own experience of social work. In the contexts where you have seen social work practised:

■ What mechanisms existed to determine how resources should be allocated between different cases?
■ What proportion of social work time was taken up with servicing these mechanisms? For example by writing reports for and attending panels whose purpose was to determine how resources were allocated – or filling out forms intended to establish eligibility.

Needs versus resources

On the whole, books about social work practice tend not to discuss how to go about rationing.

This reflects the traditional division that occurs not only in social work agencies but in other public services in which resource decisions are made by managers while casework decisions, such as intervention strategies, are made by practitioners. Academic discussion of social work practice sometimes seems to reflect this split by offering an image of social work in which resources are not an issue – or at any rate are of little concern to the professional social worker. We would argue however that limited resources are integral to the nature of social work, as they are to any service which is not paid for by its users. Practice guidance which is directed at social work may simply not be applicable when it comes to modern social work in which resources are limited and decisions about resource allocation are central to the daily task.

Thus Bamford (1993: 38) argues that the ideal of user choice – is 'rarely more than rhetoric' when it comes to the provision of social care services for the elderly. 'Choice requires surplus capacity if it is to be real'. He goes on:

> *The real choices…are in practice whether or not to accept a service. The rhetoric of choice obscures the unacknowledged conflict between user choice and needs-led assessment.*
>
> Bamford, 1993: 38.

This point can be overstated as there are often important choices which service users can make even within the constraints imposed by resources. But the fact remains that the amount of choice that can be offered is limited – and this is a factor that has to be taken into account when establishing principles for contemporary practice.

The manager-practitioner split

The traditional division, in which managers deal with resources and practitioners deal with casework, has some advantages for those involved. It allows front-line practitioners to blame their managers for not making resources available to service user. And it allows managers to blame practitioners for pieces of casework that go wrong or to dissociate themselves from the day to day

contact with human distress. The Climbié Report, for instance, comments (in paragraph 1.26) on the ways in which senior managers attempted to distance themselves by saying, for instance, that their role was 'strategic' and that they were not responsible for the 'day-to-day realities' (Lord Laming, 2003: 5). In reality, though, resource decisions and casework decisions are closely interrelated: neither type of decision can really be made without reference to the other.

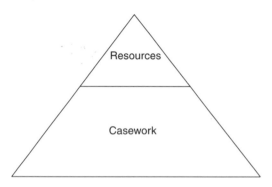

Figure 5.1   The traditional manager/practitioner division (Acknowledgements to Colin Green)

It is worth asking the question as to whether the traditional split of responsibilities between managers and practitioners, which could be represented by Figure 5.1, is necessarily the healthiest way of running a social work agency. As we've seen, It does have the benefit to both front-line staff and managers of reducing anxiety by allowing responsibility for some painful decisions to be pushed away onto others. McCaffrey (1998) relates this division to the psychological defence against anxiety known in Freudian and Kleinian psychology as 'splitting', and suggests that it is likely to be harmful because it allows front-line workers and managers respectively to project negative, uncomfortable aspects of their job onto one another. McCaffrey suggests that it would be better therefore to try as far as possible to 'heal the unconscious splits' which 'would mean that the rationing task and the clinical task must be held in mind at the same time.' (McCaffrey, 1998: 103). In short: responsibility for managing within resources and responsibility for case work decisions should be taken on board by the agency at every level, as represented by Figure 5.2.

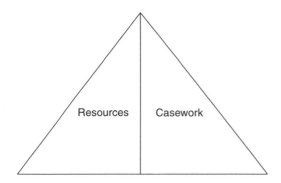

Figure 5.2 Joint manager/practitioner responsibility

There are various ways in which this could happen. During the early days of the NHS and Community Care Act it was suggested that care co-ordinators could be assigned a budget to use as they thought best (rather than drawing up a care plan for each case and then bidding for funds). Under this scheme the front-line practitioner would be responsible for keeping within their own budget, but they would have the freedom to spend it in whatever way seemed to work best for the service user. They could then be able to develop their own network of local resources to meet local needs.

This particular system has not in practice been widely adopted, perhaps partly because it presupposes that the social worker will have a wide range of purchasing options at their disposal, which is not necessarily the case in practice. However it is worth considering, in any given area of social work, whether devolution of budgetary responsibilities to front-line staff or service users, far from inhibiting creative casework, might actually promote it. For example, if you were a children and family social worker who had negotiated for an adolescent service user to be given a place at a residential assessment unit (which usually costs in excess of £1,000 per week), would it be helpful if you were told that, if you preferred, you could have the money that would have been spent on residential care to put together a package which would allow the young person to remain at home?

On the other hand you could argue that in many situations the split between resource and casework decision-making are a necessary division of labour which results in a useful creative tension. And it is possible to argue that a division of labour makes everyone's task more manageable. As McCaffrey (1998: 105) comments: 'Splits are to some extent inevitable and, up to a point, can be helpful in allowing different groups or disciplines to carry bearable amounts of anxiety.' 'Splitting' is a well-known psychological defence and these defences exist for a reason. Given that resources are limited and that time is in itself a resource, any system needs to be able to keep track of overall expenditure and not to be excessively time consuming.

ACTIVITY 5.2

Before continuing, you could try and list the advantages and disadvantages of splitting resource decisions from casework decisions. In your opinion, do the advantages outweigh the disadvantages or vice versa? Would your view vary depending on the type of context and the client group?

Direct payments

A more radical extension of the idea of devolving budgetary responsibility to front-line staff is the idea of devolving responsibility to service users. In Britain, under the 1996 Community Care (Direct Payments) Act, local authority social service departments are empowered – if this is wanted by the service user – to make cash payments to service users 'instead of arranging the services it has assessed the person as needing' (Department of Health, 1996: 4). 'Day-to-day control of the money and care package passes to the person who has the strongest incentive to ensure that it is spent properly on the necessary services and who is best placed to judge how to match available resources to needs' (Department of Health, 1996: 3).

Some service users welcome the freedom to put together their own package of care and the direct payments model seems to fit very well with the emphasis in social work on promoting user empowerment and self-determination (see, for instance, there is evidence of this on the use of direct payments to adults with learning disabilities (Holman and Collins, 1997). It does however mean dispensing with part of the service normally offered by social workers. In theory it allows the service user to purchase social care in much the same way that people purchase holidays, or TV sets or other things they want or need in life.

Of course the system is only empowering if service users are adequately safeguarded against exploitation by (for instance) relatives who might divert funds for other purposes. And it is only empowering if service users actually want to use it and do not feel that having to make their own care arrangements is one more burden. Direct payments will not be to every service user's taste and many service users would not want the additional worry and responsibility of, for instance, having to take on carers as their own employees. In much the same way, some entrepreneurially minded social workers might welcome their own budgets but others would feel that they would prefer others deal with financial matters and leave them to assess needs and identify ways of meeting them.

It is worth noting, incidentally, that while direct payments made by local authorities for community care is a relatively new idea, in fact state benefits paid to people with disabilities have been in effect a form of direct payment. These provide people with extra financial resources to meet their needs as they think fit: Disabled Living Allowances, Attendance Allowances, and Mobility Allowances. Eligibility for these is typically determined by medical and financial criteria.

Competing for resources

Social work assessments of need are integral to the resource allocation process. It is assessments, and how those assessments are presented, that determine how large a 'slice of the cake' is allocated to each service user in many situations. In some contexts there exist allocation panels to which social workers come to present their reports and argue the case of their respective service users, in other situations it will be an individual manager who decides between competing claims presented by social workers who have carried out assessments.

It is worth considering what sort of dynamic these sorts of mechanisms create within a social work agency. Social workers who have carried out assessments are often effectively bidding against one another to obtain access to a limited pool of resources. Inevitably practitioners learn to manipulate the system to maximise the benefits to the particular service users about whom they feel most strongly. As a result the bidding process is far from being a rational way of distributing resources. For instance, service users whose social workers are skilled performers or manipulators may win out over other clients, regardless of real need. What is more, the bidding process creates a strong temptation to exaggerate the needs of some service users to obtain resources for them.

This may be to their advantage in some respects, insofar as it may give them access to services that they otherwise would not have received but it may well be to their own considerable disadvantage in the long run if this means being labelled in some way. An extreme example of this would be if the risks to a child from a carer were exaggerated in order to obtain some resource. The parent gets the service at the expense of being labelled – on the record – a potential abuser. There is a very real danger that, in hard-pressed children and family services where cases are prioritised on the basis of risk, families may indeed end up getting unnecessarily labelled as 'child protection cases' because of this dynamic.

So a system in which social workers (or others such as outside agencies) compete for limited resources by pressing the case of their respective service users does have its dangers, particularly when it operates in a context where only 'at risk' cases are regarded as high enough priority to be eligible for service. It is therefore important for social workers to think about the principles that should underlie rational resource distribution so as to be able to try, as far as possible, to prevent those principles from being eroded by the exigencies of day to day practice.

ACTIVITY 5.3

Before continuing you may like to sketch out the principles under which you think limited resources should be allocated in a given social work context.

Philosophy of resource allocation

A reduction in home-help hours...and delays in admissions to residential homes...represent the fruits of resource decisions which have given to some while placing increased burdens on others. Decisions of such critical importance in people's lives require sound philosophical underpinning. Pragmatism is not enough.

Bamford, 1993: 34.

What should determine how time and other resources are allocated? The study of philosophy may seem a far cry from the messy, day to day realities we have been discussing, and yet, as Girling (1993) observes, in a discussion of resource allocation in the health care field, various philosophical assumptions do underlay the different ways that these decisions are made. He adds that clinicians and managers typically start from different philosophical bases. Clinicians tend to take a more deontological approach: the approach based on inherent duties and rights associated in particular with the 18th century German philosopher Immanuel Kant. Managers tend to take a more utilitarian approach: an approach based on a calculation of the benefits that will accrue from each possible course of action, an approach associated with the Scottish 18th century philosopher, David Hume. For a general discussion on the distinction between deonto-logical and utilitarian approaches see, for instance, Horne, 1999, Clark, 2000 or Banks, 2001):

...if the culture of management is informed by a theo-retical tradition at all, then its closest affinity is with utilitarianism. [But] the clinical culture on the other hand is much more comfortable with...deontological concerns. This may incidentally account for the apparent fact that managers and clinicians sometimes seem to inhabit different ethical universes.

Girling: 1993: 41–2.

An extreme example of the utilitarian approach that has been tried in the health care field is the concept of Quality Adjusted Life Years – or QALYs – which attempt to provide an objective scale for decision-making between different investment options, measuring returns in terms of the patients' life expectancy, adjusted for quality of life. In other words, if a given treatment or surgical procedure conferred an additional year of healthy life, then it could be said to confer one QALY. If it is conferred a year of life rated at 0.5 of full life quality, and then it confers half a QALY.

Using this (in theory) 'objective' measure of the benefits conferred by different procedures; it is then possible to compare the benefits of different ways of deploying resources. Table 5.1 shows the cost per QALY of different medical procedures (from: Ovretveit, 1998: 114).

Table 5.1   Cost per QALY

Intervention	Cost in £s per QALY
Hospital haemodialysis for kidney failure	19,000
Heart transplant	6,700
Hip replacement	1,030
Cholesterol-lowering diet programme	176

On the basis of the figures in Table 5.1, the most efficient use of resources is the cholesterol-lowering diet programme as every pound invested in it will be much more productive in terms of health benefits to patients, measured in QALYs, than any of the other procedures listed. On the other hand you may well argue, taking a rather more deontological approach, that anyone who is in imminent danger of dying should be entitled to every possible effort being made to save them, regardless of cost, and that society as a whole has a duty to try and save life regardless of cost.

To most people, the latter approach probably appears less cold and calculating, and therefore more attractive, than an approach based entirely on utilitarian calculation. But it does have a distinct downside. Concentrating resources on acute services means that preventative services end up being underfunded with the result that many people end up needing acute services that might not otherwise have done so. If more people went on cholesterol-lowering diets, after all, less people would need heart transplants.

Exactly the same dilemma exists in social work and social care, concerning the allocation of resources between costly acute services and less costly preventative services. What is more, we would suggest, the same philosophical gulf often exists in social work and social care between managers and front-line practitioners. A manager who says no to a given request for funding may feel they are doing their best to deploy limited resources to the maximum possible effect, but to a practitioner they may seem like a heartless bureaucrat, denying a service user their right to a better life.

Bamford (1993: 39) argues that social care provision could only be provided in a genuinely empowering way if service users were given an unambiguous legal right to a given level of service provision:

> *If there is a genuine desire to establish citizenship rights for the clients of personal social services, the stranglehold of professional discretion in determining eligibility has to be broken. Equity has to be translated into entitlement – a clear, publicly stated and legally enforceable entitlement to a given volume of service.*
> Bamford, 1993: 39.

But this is not the case at the moment. The NHS and Community Care Act 1990 gave a right to an assessment, not a right to a given level of service. The Children Act 1989 placed a duty on local authorities to assess the needs of children and their families and provide services, but it does not specify the level of service. You are therefore stuck with having to decide between competing claims.

Resources and intervention

Up to now we have been discussing the question of resource allocation (or, to call it by its blunter name: rationing) and its relationship to assessment. But resource considerations are equally unavoidable when making a care plan and considering what type of intervention to

make. In this area too it is impossible to separate out purely 'practice' decisions from resource decisions.

In a medical context for instance, it is obvious that, in a given case, the decision as to whether to perform, say, a heart transplant should be based not only on the condition of the patient but on consideration of the resources available. This includes the type of equipment available, the training of staff, the amount of aftercare that can be provided – and so on. It would be absurd to say 'This man needs a heart transplant and therefore that is what he must have,' and then to proceed without considering all these other questions. The chances of a successful outcome would vary from quite good to zero depending on the human and material resources to hand. Exactly the same is true of many kinds of social work interventions, though it isn't always quite as obvious.

Nevertheless in social work you will often encounter those who demand an intervention regardless of whether the resources are available to do it properly. In fact a social work intervention carried out without ensuring that the necessary resources are available could be considered irresponsible and unethical. We suggest that all social work interventions are likely to do some harm, so (as with surgical interventions or military ones) they are only justified if there are reasonable grounds for believing that the benefits would outweigh the harm. Realistic consideration of the resources available should properly be part of this calculation.

To give an instance: placing an 11-year-old child with an adoptive family is a high risk intervention (the risk of breakdown for an adoptive placement for a child at this age may be as high as 50% see PIU, 2000). Any decision about whether this is a suitable plan for a given child should take into account not only the child's needs and wishes, but also factors such as:

- Availability of suitable adoptive families.
- Availability of skilled long-term support to adoptive families.
- Availability of skilled intensive input in support of the child.

■ Commitment of agency to provide adequate funding to keep this service in place, if necessary until the child is 18.

If these things are not forthcoming, it might well be the case that this is simply not an appropriate plan for the child and that other arrangements might be preferable. There are those who might argue that every child has the 'right' to a permanent family, and that therefore, regardless of resource considerations, this should be the plan. Our point is that it is not appropriate – or ethical – to lay down fixed rules for practice unless a specific resource context is specified.

For instance, one criticism that can be made of the Laming Report into Victoria Climbié's death (Laming, 2003), is that Lord Laming criticises social services departments for not routinely interviewing every child in need referred to them. To interview separately every child in need referred to a social work agency – including those whose need was ostensibly purely a practical need for money or housing – might be desirable. But whether it could or should be made a universal requirement must surely depend on the amount of social work time that is available and on the competing claims being made on that social work time (Beckett, 2003a: 10). Would we want to insist on social workers separately interviewing every child in need referred to their agency if, for instance, this meant taking time away from child protection investigations, or from visiting children in the care system?

ACTIVITY 5.4

Can you think of instances of interventions which should not be attempted unless adequate resources were secured in advance?

Commentary

You will probably be able to think of other examples, but it seems to us that some interventions should not be attempted unless the person carrying them out has the necessary skills and training, and funding is secured to allow them to

bring the process to an appropriate conclusion. What is more they should not be carried out unless adequate support is available to the user of the service, and their carers, during the difficult period while the work is underway.

Time as a resource

While management of financial resources is, as we've seen, traditionally the province of social work managers, day to day time management is a task which all practitioners need to take on board. The daily business of juggling competing demands and deciding which to respond to, which to defer and which to decline to meet, may not seem to be the same kind of activity as (say) determining how to spend the financial budget, but it is in essence exactly the same task. Just as managers allocating funds will try to ensure that limited money is used to best possible effect, so the individual social worker, deciding how to use their own time, is trying to deploy a limited resource to best effect. All the same issues that we have been discussing about resource decisions in general occur here, as it were in microcosm. (How to respond to crises without squeezing out preventative work? Whether it is right to take a purely utilitarian view or whether there are some calls on social work time that have, in principle, some sort of absolute priority?) Indeed, even to describe this sort of decision-making as resource management 'in microcosm' is perhaps misleading, as the staff budget is the largest item in any social work agency's budget, so that effective use of staff time should be the single most important management priority.

However one of the problems that flow from the traditional management-practitioner split is that managers can be surprisingly indifferent to how staff actually spends their time. A social worker is given a 'case' but it is not usual for a 'budget' of time to be agreed for the social worker to deal with the case, in the same way that a budget of money would certainly need to be agreed. In fact as has been observed elsewhere, simple arithmetic places very severe restraints on what a social worker can do in a given week:

If a social worker has twenty cases, she has less than two hours per week to spend on all the visits, telephone calls, recording, travelling, completing forms, going to court and attending meetings that the case requires.
Beckett, 2003b: 241.

That social work time is just as much a limited resource as money is commonly forgotten. If social workers want to spend their agency's money in some new way then it is normal to ask where the money is going to come from and (if the budget is fixed) where savings are going to be made in order to make it available. But for some reason this sort of thinking process is often cast aside when it comes to the allocation of time. Additional tasks are given to people, who are already fully occupied, the unspoken assumption being that 'they will fit it in somehow'. This poor practice is the basis of our criticism of the Laming Report above. We would suggest that there is no merit in demanding that, for example, social worker agencies should routinely interview every child in need referred to them, unless the person making the demand can identify where the time is going to come from. Assuming that additional staff time is not going to be made available, the person making the demand needs to specify what tasks are going to be dropped in order to create time for this new one.

In particular it is worth noting that the principle, which we have already discussed under the heading 'Resources and Intervention', of not undertaking an intervention unless adequate resources are available, should apply with equal force to questions about time as it does to questions about funding (for example: funds to buy in services from external providers). In many areas of social work, extremely ambitious pieces of work are attempted, of which establishing a child in a new family is a good example. It is not realistic to expect such endeavours to work without a really substantial input of time on planning, negotiation and preparatory work with all parties.

Our suggestion that, just as one would normally want to negotiate a cash budget in advance before undertaking an ambitious new project, a 'time budget' should really be agreed between a social worker and their manager before they embark on complex, demanding and ambitious pieces of work of this kind. There are many projects which are unsustainable unless a reasonable amount of time is made available for them.

ACTIVITY 5.5

Can you think of other examples in your own experience of complex pieces of work which should not be undertaken unless an appropriate amount of time is made available?

Commentary

You will have thought of other examples, but the following are a few suggestions:

■ Helping a person with a learning disability to move from long-term institutional care to community living, a process which requires having to relearn long-established habits and expectations. (One of the authors recalls an encounter with a middle-aged mildly learning disabled man who looked back nostalgically to his days in an institution from which he had been discharged and effectively left to cope on his own: theoretically 'in the community' but in practice in very miserable isolation.)

■ Changing the functioning of a family which has, for several generations, been viewed by professional agencies as abusive or neglectful. (Some middle class users of private therapists think nothing of attending weekly sessions for years on end in order to resolve what may be, on the scale of things, relatively minor psychological problems: yet social workers, juggling a therapeutic role with several other roles, set themselves the task of radically changing family functioning in a few sessions.)

■ Working to change long-established patterns of behaviour such as drug addiction or sexually abusive behaviour.

Avoiding waste

If it is sensible for all levels of a social work agency to take some responsibility for the management of resources then it follows that front-line practitioners, as well as managers, should ensure that resources are not wasted. This means they are not being used in ways that are predictably unproductive, or in ways whose likely benefits are minimal in relation to the costs. Wasted resources are resources that are not being used for the benefit of service users. There are many ways in which resources – both in terms of social work time and in terms of money – are commonly wasted. For instance: an elaborate and costly assessment process is wasteful if the outcome appears to be a foregone conclusion, or if the recommendations flowing from it are not likely to be carried out. Equally this is the case if the possible options are very limited and a decision could be made between them on much more limited information. One might ask, for instance, whether the very substantial information-gathering exercise that is entailed in carrying out an assessment under the *Framework for the Assessment of Children in Need* (Department of Health, 2000) is always proportionate to the often quite limited interventions that flow from it?

As we have just discussed, many interventions are wasteful if they are not properly followed through to ensure that any change achieved is durable. (For example: sending a service user with a long history of family relationship problems on a six session anger management course and then closing their case.) Unless a realistic 'time budget' is made available to see through a task, many tasks would be better not undertaken at all, so that the time and money could be used to more effect in other ways and service users would not be set up to fail.

Completion of elaborate paperwork is wasteful if the paperwork is not actually going to be read or used. An interview with a service user may largely be a waste of time (and therefore of resources) if the social worker has not adequately prepared for it and is not clear what the purpose of the interview is.

Many meetings are wasteful if they have no clear purpose or if there is no mechanism whereby decisions made in the meeting can be effectively translated into action. (An hour's meeting attended by eight salaried employees takes, after all, eight hours of staff time: the equivalent of a whole day's work.)

ACTIVITY 5.6

In your own experience of social work what have been the main forms of waste that you have identified?

The concepts of economy, efficiency and effectiveness

We will return in Chapter 9 to the subject of the evaluation of social work practice in respect of assessment and intervention. There is an increasing emphasis on asking questions about the efficacy and performance of public services, including social work. Actually measuring the performance of public services is a complex matter, but among the criteria by which they are judged (as we will discuss in Chapter 9) are so-called 'three Es': economy, efficiency and effectiveness. Of these three, the first two both relate to the use of resources. *Economy,* in these terms, is a measure of the cost of inputs used. An organisation which is doing well on this measure will be one which obtains inputs of a given quality specification at the lowest possible cost. Consider a social work agency which is in the business of purchasing domiciliary care for elderly service users from independent providers. The agency will score well on measures of economy if it works hard to negotiate the cheapest possible rate and will score better than agencies which pay more for domiciliary care of the same specification.

Efficiency is the cost to the organisation of producing a given output. If the same outcome for a service user can be achieved in several different ways, then the most efficient way is the one that costs the least, whether the cost is measured in cash, or in time. Clearly any responsible social work agency should try to obtain the maximum benefits for its service users from whatever limited resources available and it follows that a responsible social work agency should try to be as efficient as possible. Pursuing efficiency is not just some bureaucratic notion: it is, or should be, an ethical requirement.

Having said this, though, we should also note that, it is often a false economy to try to do tasks in too little time, or with inadequate resources, because the input can achieve nothing at all, meaning that the expenditure is entirely wasted. Investing insufficient resources to successfully complete the task in hand may superficially look like saving resources but it is in fact *wasting* resources and is extremely inefficient. On the other hand proper investment by local and central government in social care services has the opportunity of producing greater efficiency in the longer term.

Chapter summary

In this chapter we have tried to introduce some ideas about resource management into the discussion about social work practice, both in relation to assessment and to intervention. We have argued that rationing of resources is often a key part of the social work task and that rationing per se is an inevitable part of social work not only in the public sector but also in the voluntary sector.

Resource issues tend to be set aside in discussion about social work practice. We noted that a form of 'splitting' can occur within social work agencies, as in other public services, where resource matters are in the hands of managers and casework decisions are in the hands of practi-tioners. This raised the question as to whether this sort of split is healthy for social work practice. We considered alternatives, including the seemingly radical alternative of 'direct payments' in which the service user is left to decide how to use resources allocated to their care.

We considered the dynamics of systems in which social workers are effectively competing with each other for limited resources for their clients and we have identified the distinct risk of negatively labelling service users which this creates. The philosophical underpinnings of resource allocation decisions have articulated the difference between utilitarian and deontological approaches. We looked at how choices about appropriate interventions are – or should be – influenced by the resources that are available to carry them out.

We noted that time is a resource and considered the importance of time management in social work. We considered how waste occurs in social work.

When evaluating social work agencies, the way that resources are used is an important measure. Efficiency – maximising the benefit to service users that is obtained from limited resources – is, or should be, an important aim for any social work agency, but pointed out also that many attempts to save resources can be counter-productive.

CHAPTER 6

Thresholds of Need and Risk

Introduction

One of the main tasks of a social worker carrying out assessments is to *discriminate*. Given that it is generally agreed that social work should strive to be *anti-discriminatory*, this sounds like an odd thing to say, but there is a difference between being discriminatory and being discriminating. Indeed, though both words refer to making distinctions, they are in some ways opposites. Being discriminatory means making bad judgements on the basis of irrational prejudice. The adjective 'discriminating' however refers to an ability to make fine judgements based on skill and knowledge. It would be *discriminatory* to exclude people of a particular ethnic group from receiving a service. It would be *discriminating* in a useful sense, however, to recognise that, either because of culture, or because of physical characteristics, or because of their different experiences in this society, people from different ethnic backgrounds may have different needs.

From the outset, a social worker dealing with a new case has to ask themselves, 'What kind of situation is this?' Clearly it is important not to label people, or to put people into pigeonholes – we all have our own unique biography and we can all change in ways that others would never be able to predict – but if a social worker is to be able to use their previous experience, and the experience of others, in order to decide what to do, they have to be able to tentatively make links and comparisons between one service user's case and another. To give an obvious example if we know that an elderly man has been diagnosed as suffering from Alzheimer's disease we should be careful not to think or act as if this label was the only important thing about him. If the diagnosis is correct it is useful information but it could be wrong and there are many symptoms consistent with Alzheimer's. If accurate it tells us that he is likely to suffer from poor short-term memory and may not be able to retain things that are said to him. It tells us that one of the things we need to look at is the extent of his difficulty with retaining and processing information and the impact this has on his everyday life.

More generally workers carrying out assessments have to make – or participate in – difficult decisions about the level of service users' needs in order to determine what kind of service they will receive. This happens in two ways. Firstly, as discussed in the previous two chapters, one of the functions of a social worker carrying out assessments is to assist with decisions about rationing: that is, decisions about how an agency can best and most fairly deploy its limited resources. This requires that service users' needs be categorised in terms of *eligibility*. (Is their level of need such as to make them eligible for a service and, if so, what level of service?) Secondly, in many contexts, it is necessary to categorise service users' circumstances in terms of *risk*. (Is this a high risk or a low risk case?) This is required not only to determine eligibility – though in circumstances of limited resources it can indeed be the case that only high risk cases are considered eligible for a service – but also to determine the *type* of response. In children and family social work, for instance, there is a distinction to be made between 'children in need' and 'children in need of protection' and the response to the two is different, the latter involving the social worker playing much more of what we have called a 'policing' role.

So there are thresholds of need and thresholds of risk. Assessing social workers may be assigned the task, in any given case, of determining which thresholds that case has crossed and which it has not. The remainder of this chapter will look at the issues this raises.

ACTIVITY 6.1

Before going on to look at thresholds of need, you might like to consider what kind of systems, in your experience, social work agencies use to decide whether or not someone referred to them is eligible for a service?

Commentary

As we discussed in the last chapter, any agency will have to set some limits on what it takes on. Large statutory agencies, with a high volume of work referred to them, may have quite formal systems (like the one we are about to discuss). These may involve tools such as charts or checklists which are used to determine the level of need against some sort of numerical scale. But this is not necessarily the case. Eligibility for service may be determined in less formal ways. For example a team may meet and go through referrals and arrive at a decision by discussing how much work they should take on, and which cases should be given priority. Or a team manager may make this decision alone, without using any formal framework. In such situations the basis on which priority is determined may be implicit rather than explicit: and even those making the decision might be hard-pressed to define precisely the criteria they are using.

Thresholds of need

Quite specific guidance is given by the government to local authorities as to how to go about determining whether adult services users are eligible for social care services. A document called *Fair Access to Care Services* (Department of Health, 2002) sets out how local authorities should draw up their eligibility criteria in order to allow a 'more consistent approach to eligibility and fairer access to care services across the country.' It sets out a framework for measuring eligibility which involves categorising cases into the following four bands; critical, substantial, moderate and low:

Critical

- When life is, or will be, threatened; and/or
- Significant health problems have developed or will develop; and/or
- There is, or will be, little or no choice and control over vital aspects of the immediate environment; and/or
- Serious abuse or neglect has occurred or will occur; and/or
- There is, or will be, an inability to carry out vital personal care or domestic routines; and/or
- Vital involvement in work, education or learning cannot or will not be sustained; and/or
- Vital social support systems and relationships cannot or will not be sustained; and/or
- Vital family and other social roles and responsibilities cannot or will not be undertaken.

Substantial

- When there is, or will be, only partial choice and control over the immediate environment; and/or
- Abuse or neglect has occurred or will occur; and/or
- There is, or will be, an inability to carry out the majority of personal care or domestic routines; and/or
- Involvement in many aspects of work, education or learning cannot or will not be sustained; and/or

■ The majority of social support systems and relationships cannot or will not be sustained; and/or

■ The majority of family and other social roles and responsibilities cannot or will not be undertaken.

Moderate

■ When there is, or will be, an inability to carry out several personal care or domestic routines; and/or

■ Involvement in several aspects of work, education or learning cannot or will not be sustained; and/or

■ Several social support systems and relationships cannot or will not be sustained; and/or

■ Several family and other social roles and responsibilities cannot or will not be undertaken.

Low

■ When there is, or will be, an inability to carry out one or two personal care or domestic routines; and/or

■ Involvement in one or two aspects of work, education or learning cannot or will not be sustained; and/or

■ One or two social support systems and relationships cannot or will not be sustained; and/or

■ One or two family and other social roles and responsibilities cannot or will not be undertaken.

Department of Health, 2002: 4–5.

The guidance does not, however, specify a particular level at which a service must be provided. The decision as to where this level should be set is acknowledged to be dependent on the level of resources available to the local authority concerned. But the guidance seeks to set down a way of categorising the level of need and prioritising cases:

In constructing and using their eligibility criteria, and also in determining eligibility for individuals, councils should prioritise needs that have immediate and longer-term critical consequences for independence

ahead of needs with substantial consequences. Similarly, needs that have substantial consequences should be placed before needs with moderate consequences; and so on.

Department of Health, 2002: 5, Para 17.

An eligibility threshold (or any other kind of threshold) requires a notional *scale*. The threshold of eligibility, then, is a line drawn *across* that scale. The government is choosing not to dictate the level at which the threshold of eligibility is drawn, but is defining the scale to be used. In theory, as a result of this guidance, every local authority should assign service users with the same level of need to the same level in the scale (that is: to 'critical', 'substantial', 'moderate' or 'low'). But it still remains open to one local authority to decide that it can only meet critical needs, for instance, while another local authority might decide that it has the resources to meet critical and substantial needs. And variations such as these do happen in practice. Suffolk County Council, for instance, states on its website, as at 13th June 2003, that it has 'made the cut off' (that is: set the threshold of eligibility) between moderate and low. By contrast the neighbouring county of Cambridgeshire states, on the same date, that 'to be eligible for our services, you must have needs at level 3 (substantial). Figure 6.1 illustrates this, showing the four levels of need defined by the government as four layers arranged in a pyramid (which is narrower at the top because a smaller number will have high care needs as compared to low care needs). The two eligibility thresholds A and B are drawn at the levels set by Cambridgeshire (A) and Suffolk (B) as of June 2003.

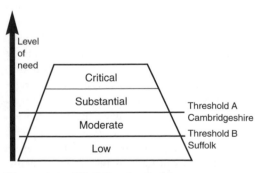

Figure 6.1 Eligibility thresholds

The business of collecting the information required to assign people to these various levels of need, which in turn will determine eligibility for a service, is discussed in *Fair Access to Care Services* under the heading *Principles of Assessment*. It does not specify what group of staff should carry out this task. In practice this mainly falls to people designated as care co-ordinators who are often, though not always, qualified social workers. 'It is important that the assessment is person-centred,' states the Department of Health (2002: 8), 'and for the evaluation of assessment information to lead to appropriate eligibility decisions and services that promotes independence.' We have argued in the two previous chapters that rationing is a key social work role. Here the guidance makes this explicit.

ACTIVITY 6.2

What advantages can you see to a standardised system such as the one we have just described as a way of determining which requests for services are met? And what difficulties can you see?

Commentary

You may have thought of others, but some of the advantages that strike us are:

■ By making local authorities have an explicit 'scale' and an explicit threshold, this system promotes 'transparency'. Service users can see how it works, where they have been placed on the scale and how this relates to the eligibility criterion set by the local authority in question. (As noted earlier, many local authorities make their eligibility criteria for adult services available on the internet as well as on paper.) If service users think they have been placed wrongly on the scale then they have the information they need to challenge the assessment. If service users think that the eligibility criterion is set too high then they have the information they need, as citizens, to lobby for it to change. The more informal systems which we mentioned in Activity 6.1 are less transparent and therefore harder to challenge.

■ Arguably, the existence of an explicit scale and an explicit threshold makes the system less 'subjective'. Since all staff involved in determining eligibility must work to the same scales and thresholds, this should mean more consistency and therefore a fairer system. A more informal system, where criteria are not made explicit, is more open to being shaped by the prejudices of those who administer it and therefore may be more in danger of being discriminatory.

Disadvantages that strike us are:

■ A fixed scale and a fixed threshold are rigid. It does not allow for subtleties and anomalies or for rare and unexpected situations. It limits the ability of staff to develop their own, perhaps more sophisticated ways of coming to decisions.

■ Such systems are in fact much more 'subjective' than at first sight they appear. For instance, the categories within the governments' four bands of risk include the following: 'there is, or will be, only partial choice and control over the immediate environment' (one of the categories within 'substantial need'), and 'there is, or will be, an inability to carry out several personal care or domestic routines' (one of the categories within 'moderate need'). One can imagine situations in which it would be a matter of opinion whether a person's disability placed them in the first or the second of these two categories – and yet (as we've seen) in some local authority areas this could make the difference to whether the service user gets a service or not. The system is far from immune to discriminatory prejudices creeping in and influencing the level of priority that a case is given.

■ Although the 'scale' as we have called it is (in theory) standardised across the country, the threshold is not. While this is the case, service users with the same level of need may or may not receive a service depending on the area where they live. When this occurs in respect of health care it is commonly described in the media as a 'postcode lottery' and is generally regarded as unfair.

Need and eligibility in children's services

The above scheme applies only to social care services for adults in the UK. The government has not laid down a comparable scheme for measuring eligibility in the case of services for children and families. But, as we discussed in the previous chapter, services to children in need and their families do also have to be rationed and in practice a major function of social workers taking referrals and undertaking initial assessments (Department of Health, 2000: 31, para 3.9) is to gather information that can be used for determining which cases should be a priority when limited resources are allocated. The concept of 'eligibility' – of a specifically defined threshold above which a service user becomes eligible for a service – is not such a feature in child care social work and is not, for instance, a topic covered in the *Framework for the Assessment of Children in Need and their Families* (Department of Health, 2000).

The difference may reflect the different political context in which child care services and those for adults operate. There appears to be a certain coyness about acknowledging that services for children are also rationed. However, since resources for children and families are no less finite than resources for adult care, essentially the same issues arise and you may like to consider whether services for children and families would benefit from a uniform national framework for assessing *level* of need such as exists for adults, or whether less formal (but also less transparent) methods are preferable.

Thresholds of risk

A person who is seriously at risk is also a person who is in need of help and it is therefore not surprising that eligibility criteria such as we have been discussing categorise those at most risk as having the highest priority for services. However in statutory social work a decision about the level of risk does not just determine whether or not a service is offered but also the *kind* of intervention. A mental health social worker making an assessment of a client under Section (2) of the 1983 Mental Health Act (see

Chapter 4) is not primarily trying to decide whether the service user should receive a service: very probably the service user will be eligible for a service whether or not the social worker decides to make a Section (2) application. The question that the social worker is addressing in this context is whether the service user should receive – or continue to receive – services on a voluntary basis, or whether the risk that the service user poses to themselves or others is sufficiently grave to merit compulsory detention for assessment. The social worker may not conceptualise it in this way, but you could say that we have a scale and a threshold again. This time, though, the scale is not level of need, but level of risk and the threshold is not a threshold of eligibility but the point at which the social worker feels that it is appropriate to move into 'policing' mode (to use the terminology of Chapter 4). This is illustrated by Figure 6.2.

As we mentioned earlier, in social work in the UK with children and families there is a crucial distinction between 'children in need' and 'children in need of protection', with local authorities having different duties and responsibilities in each case, defined respectively by Section (17) and Section (47) of the 1989 Children Act. Here again is a risk threshold which does not necessarily determine eligibility for a service (though there have been times and areas where only child protection case have been regarded as high enough priority to receive services) but does determine the *type* of service. Specifically it determines whether or not the agency should move into

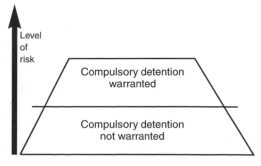

Figure 6.2   Risk thresholds

'policing' mode, the latter often necessitating the involvement of the actual police themselves in a joint investigation. This risk threshold could be represented in a diagram such as that in Figure 6.2.

Actually in child care social work, one could identify a number of *different* thresholds of this kind, including, for instance:

■ The threshold of risk above which the names of children are placed on the child protection register (*Working Together*, Department of Health, 1999: 55, paras 5.64 ff. We should emphasise that this is a multi-agency decision and not a decision made by social work agencies on their own).
■ The threshold at which care proceedings are initiated (Children Act Section 31).
■ The threshold at which use of an Emergency Protection Order (1989 Children Act, Sections 44–46) to remove children immediately from home is considered to be warranted.

In each of these instances, guidance and legislation specifies that the test as to whether the threshold conditions are met should be based on the concept of 'significant harm'. Here is paragraph 5.64 of *Working Together*, discussing how a decision on registration should be made by a child protection conference:

> *5.64 The conference should consider the following question when determining whether to register a child: Is the child at risk of significant harm?*
> *The test should be that either:*
> *The child can be shown to have suffered ill-treatment or impairment of health or development as a result of physical, emotional, or sexual abuse or neglect, and professional judgement is that further ill-treatment or impairment are likely: or*
> *Professional judgement, substantiated by the findings of enquiries in this individual case, or by research evidence, is that the child is likely to suffer ill-treatment or the impairment of health or development, as a result of physical, emotional, or sexual abuse or neglect;*
> *If the child is at continuing risk of significant harm, it will therefore be the case that safeguarding the child requires inter-agency help and intervention delivered through a formal child protection plan. It is also the*
> *role of the initial child protection conference to formulate the outline child protection plan, in as much detail as possible.*
>
> Department of Health, 1999: 55.

'Significant harm' is not defined – and actually could not really be defined, in such a precise way as to make it immune from different understandings and interpretations – but risk of significant harm is the basic criterion for registration, as it is for the making of orders under the 1989 Act.

Harm and risk

The quotation from *Working Together* just given included the phrase 'likely to suffer ill-treatment or the impairment of health or development'. This phrase encapsulates the two components that are contained within the idea of 'risk' (a topic which we discussed earlier in Chapter 3). If we are assessing the risk posed by a particular situation we are looking at:

■ The harm that may result (from whatever circumstance is being discussed).
■ The *likelihood* that this may occur.

Thus, although air crashes and train crashes do occur and can have fatal consequences, we do not describe air travel or train travel as high risk activities because the likelihood of a crash occurring is extremely low. It follows that when constructing a pyramid of risk as in Figure 6.2 situations are arranged from cases at the bottom where the harmful event is very unlikely to occur, to cases at the top where the event is very likely – or even almost certain – to occur. Although in reality it is never possible to be anything like as precise as this, Figure 6.3 illustrates this in a simplistic and idealised way for the sake of argument.

If we are carrying out a risk assessment in child protection (or in any other context), we are seeking to come to a conclusion of how likely a given set of harmful events are to occur in the absence of protective intervention. In child protection the set of harmful events we are trying to predict are the various kinds of 'significant harm' that a child may suffer. In an assessment under Section 2 of the Mental Health

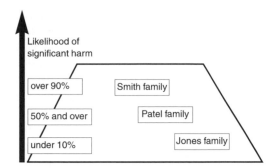

Figure 6.3   Likelihood of significant harm diagram

Act, the harmful events whose likelihood is being considered are the patient either harming themselves or others. In theory our assessments of particular cases should allow us to be able to place them approximately in terms of such events occurring, as illustrated by the Smith, Patel and Jones families in Figure 6.3.

ACTIVITY 6.3

What difficulties exist in practice with trying to arrange situations accurately against a scale of risk such as that in Figure 6.3? If these difficulties could be overcome and we could arrange cases against such a scale with confidence, what would remain the limitations of the scale as a decision-making tool?

Commentary

You may have identified any one of a number of difficulties, of which some may have been:

- Events such as 'significant harm' are not precisely defined.
- Although there is certainly research information to draw on, there is no 'precise science' to tell us what will be the consequences of any given circumstances.
- Human situations are extremely complex and it is never possible to know all the information.
- Every human situation is unique and therefore can only be compared in an approximate, tentative way with previous experience and research.

Even if, just for the sake of argument, you could come up with a precise figure – such as 65% – for the likelihood of a given event in a given situation this information has at least two limitations as a guide to action:

- If an event has a 65% likelihood of happening in a given situation, then it also has a 35% likelihood of not happening. Conversely even if an event has a 99% likelihood of not happening in a given situation, it still has a 1% chance of happening. In fact there is no such thing as a zero risk situation. Accurate data about the likelihood of risk helps us to reduce the possibilities of harm happening, but it does not allow us to eliminate the possibility of harmful events. (We will explore this further shortly.)
- Even if we have a very accurate scale, the question remains as to whereabouts on the scale to draw the threshold. Is a 5% risk of signficant harm sufficiently high to warrant (for instance) registration? Or should the line be drawn at 10%, or 20%, or 30%? The decision as to where to draw the threshold is a value judgement and therefore not a question which facts, however accurate, can answer. ('No amount of knowledge of what is the case can ever establish for us what we ought to do about it', Downrie and Telfer, 1980: 22.)

False negatives and false positives

The discussion so far may seem rather dry and theoretical, but we now come to a difficulty that creates very real problems for social work.

In the chart in Figure 6.3, the situations placed at the top of the pyramid are those where the harmful event (whatever it may be!) is thought to have an over 90% chance of happening. The situations placed at the bottom of the pyramid are those where this event is thought to have a less than 10% chance of happening. If the risk calculation is correct it follows that, if there was no intervention, and if events were allowed to take their course, the harmful event would actually happen in more than 90% of the cases at the top of the chart, but

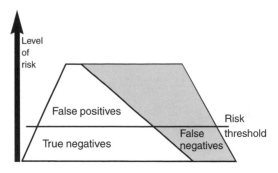

Figure 6.4   Predicted vs actual outcomes

there would be a small minority of cases where it would not happen. At the other end of the scale, the harmful event would also sometimes happen, but only in less than 10% of cases. We could represent this by Figure 6.4, in which the shaded area represents those cases where the harmful event would actually happen if there was no intervention. Since by definition the event is more likely for high risk cases and less likely for low risk cases, the shaded area gets progressively wider towards the top of the pyramid.

As we have already discussed, a risk threshold, like the eligibility thresholds that we looked at earlier, can be represented as a horizontal line drawn at a certain point on a vertical scale. The horizontal line across Figure 6.4 represents a risk threshold. Depending on the type of harmful event that we are discussing, this could be the threshold of risk at which a social worker feels that detention under the Mental Health is warranted, or the threshold of risk at which a child's name is placed on the child protection register.

What we want to point out is that, although most of the shaded area (representing cases where, if there was no protective intervention, the harmful event would actually occur) is above the threshold, there is also a substantial amount of white space above the line. Similarly, while most of the white space is below the threshold, there is also a small but significant amount of shaded area below the line. The shaded area below the line represents cases that are categorised as low risk but where a harmful event does actually occur. In other words they

are cases where, with hindsight, we would wish that we had taken protective action even though, *on the information available* we may have been quite correct to describe them as low risk. The white space above the line represents cases where protective action is indicated by whatever risk indicators we used to determine the level of risk, but where in fact, if protective action had not been taken, no harm would have occurred. What we are now discussing is the problem of false positives and false negatives: the false positives being represented by the white space above the threshold, the false negatives by the shaded area below it. (See Table 6.1).

Depending on the event in question, false negatives can be tragedies: a child left in the care of a parent in a situation deemed to be low risk but where the parent subsequently kills or abuses the child; a mentally ill person who an Approved Social Worker judges not to be 'sectionable' under the Mental Health Act but who goes on to (say) assault a member of the public and then commit suicide. Naturally such events are dreaded by social workers, as they are doubtless dreaded in any profession which has responsibilities for managing risks. But we need to be clear that when such events occur, they are not necessarily mistakes and do not necessarily reflect incompetence on the part of the social worker. Any calculated risk sometimes goes the 'wrong' way. Just because such events occur does not necessarily mean that those who assigned these cases to a low risk category were wrong.

To believe that, when something like this happens, it necessarily proves that a mistake has

Table 6.1   True and false positives and negatives

True positives	Situations identified as high risk where the harmful event actually occurs in the absence of protective intervention.
False positives	Situations identified as high risk where the harmful event actually would not occur even in the absence of protective intervention.
True negatives	Situations identified as low risk where no harmful event occurs.
False negatives	Situations identified as low risk, but where the harmful event does nevertheless occur.

been made, is in itself a serious error. It is known as the *hindsight fallacy*:

> If a decision involves risk, then even when one can demonstrate that one has chosen the unarguably optimal course of action, some proportion of the time the outcome will be suboptimal. It follows that a bad outcome in and of itself does not constitute evidence that the decision was mistaken. The hindsight fallacy is to assume that it does.
>
> Macdonald and Macdonald, 1999: 22.

This is not to say that actual mistakes cannot be made because of course they can. For example important pieces of evidence can be missed, or connections can fail to be made between pieces of evidence, resulting in cases being assigned to the wrong risk category. These are actual mistakes. But we should be careful to distinguish between risk indicators that should reasonably have been noticed in advance and those whose significance could not have reasonably been see without the benefit of hindsight.

False *positives* may be no less tragic in their consequences than false negatives: a child taken away from parents with whom they would actually have grown up quite happily, a person forcibly detained under the Mental Health Act, who would actually have been alright if left in their own home…But since we cannot know what *would* have happened if we had not intervened, false positives are relatively invisible as compared to false negatives. What *is* visible to all practitioners is that protective interventions in 'policing' mode are distressing to all concerned and should therefore be kept to a minimum.

Where to draw the line?

In child care social work, social workers have to deal with periodic exhortations to move thresholds in one direction or another, whether they be the threshold for initiating care proceedings or the threshold at which a child in need becomes a child in need of protection. The government's 'Refocussing' initiative, which followed the publication of *Child Protection: Messages from Research* (Department of Health, 1995), was an example of an attempt to push the latter threshold higher up the risk

scale. Behind these movements of the threshold lies awareness that both false positives and false negatives are undesirable. Unfortunately, however, there is a trade-off. If we move the risk threshold upwards we get more false negatives but *less* false positives. If we move it downwards on the other hand, we get less false positives, but more false negatives. You can see this in Figure 6.5. If the threshold is set at level A, there are far fewer false positives than at level B. As a result setting the threshold at A would result in fewer 'policing'-type protective interventions and the service would probably be experienced as more 'user-friendly' with more 'partnership' working and less coercion. The government's 'Refocussing' initiative was an attempt to set the 'child protection' threshold at a higher level with precisely this sort of aim. But the downside of setting the threshold at level A is that you get more false negatives. You can see that, with the line at level B, by contrast you get far less false negatives, but only at the cost of more false positives.

What we need to be aware of is the fact that wherever the threshold is drawn there will be some pros and some cons – some people that benefit, some that suffer. In terms of, say, the threshold at which an Emergency Protection Order is applied for, a high threshold of intervention means fewer false positives, fewer needless intrusions into family life, but more instances where abuse carries on when it could have been stopped. A low threshold of intervention means fewer false negatives, less cases 'slipping through the net', but more intrusion into family life of a very distressing kind.

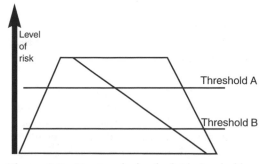

Figure 6.5   Varying the level of risk threshold

In the end, not only in Child Protection but in any field, there can be no objectively 'correct' place to draw the threshold, since any threshold is necessarily a compromise between competing benefits and disadvantages.

ACTIVITY 6.4

We have used the example of the threshold for the use of Emergency Protection Orders to demonstrate the pros and cons of setting thresholds higher or lower.

■ What would be the pros and cons of setting the threshold higher or lower in respect of Mental Health Act applications?
■ Going back to thresholds not of risk but of *need*, what would be the pros and cons of a local authority setting its eligibility threshold higher or lower up the scale of need?

Commentary

■ A high threshold for Mental Health Act applications would mean that compulsory admission under a section of the Act became relatively rare. This is desirable from a civil liberties point of view, since it reduces the number of people whose liberties are restricted against their wishes. It would also perhaps contribute to a more user-friendly service. On the other hand a lower threshold would reduce the number of false negatives: which in this context would mean people who were not 'sectioned' but who did actually go on to harm themselves or others, or to suffer distress that could otherwise have been avoided.
■ The same sort of dilemmas about setting thresholds apply to need and eligibility decisions as apply to risk. If the threshold of eligibility is set low, more people will become eligible for a service, but the available resources will be spread more thinly and less will be left for those who are in the most acute need. If the threshold is set high, by contrast, then those in the most acute need will benefit from better services but others will lose out.

Bureaucracy

The discussion in this chapter has revolved around the idea of looking at 'cases' – or situations – and placing them on a scale, whether that scale be one of 'need' or of 'risk'. But some might, with reason, object to thinking in this way. After all, what we have called 'cases' or 'situations' are in fact human beings, or groups of human beings, struggling with some aspect of life. One of the dangers of too much preoccupation with scales and charts and eligibility criteria (or with diagrams and theoretical abstractions such as those we have offered in this chapter) is that we forget that social work agencies are not machines for processing 'cases', but collections of people whose job is to try and help other people to get their needs met.

Fears about the dehumanising consequences of too much preoccupation with procedures and systems often lie behind the complaints that are frequently made by social workers about the excessive 'bureaucracy' involved in the job. Indeed such fears lie behind the negative connotations that the word 'bureaucracy' itself possesses both within and outside of social work. These fears are surely legitimate. We have all at some time or another been at the receiving end of organisations that treat us as a 'case' or a 'number' and do not deal with us as human beings.

The very idea of being able to measure a 'case' against some sort of 'scale' is perhaps in itself dehumanising. Arguably it presupposes the existence of some sort of body of 'objective' or 'scientific' expertise which is able, so to speak, to sit outside of human life and make measurements of it. Many writers about social work, especially those who are interested in 'postmodernist' ideas (for instance Parton and O'Byrne, 2000, Milner and O'Byrne, 2002 – or see Walker, 2001) would wish to challenge the validity of such a notion. For instance, Milner and O'Byrne, clearly see many merits in a narrative-based approach which looks at 'how service users can make meaning of their lives rather than be entered into stories by others' (Milner and O'Byrne, 2002: 153). Such an approach, they argue, encourages 'multiple perspectives' and acts 'to deconstruct stories of "expert" knowledge.'

These ideas represent important insights and important alternative ways of seeing the world. In a counselling/therapy context (using the term in the sense introduced in Chapter 4), such approaches are almost certainly preferable to a quasi-scientific approach which sets the therapist (or social worker) up as expert and the service user as recipient of this expertise. Nevertheless, there are many decisions in social work which require a yes or no answer. (Should this service user receive a slice of our agency's limited resources? Is the risk of harm posed by this situation so great as to merit the use of statutory powers to protect whoever is being placed at risk?) When answering such questions it simply is not practicable to respond to each new case as completely new and unique or to leave the decision to the service user. Equity and fairness *require* that we compare one case with another. Our responsibilities to protect the vulnerable *require* that we try and have a clear and consistent approach to assessing risk. For these kinds of tasks, we suggest, formal 'bureaucratic' structures actually have many advantages. Procedures, guidelines and clear lines of accountability do actually serve, among other purposes, the purpose of protecting service users against the whims, prejudices and arbitrary decisions of individuals. They provide some consistency and, potentially, some clarity about what can be expected, as we discussed in Activity 6.2.

Bureaucracy, in short, is not 'all bad'. As Paul du Gay points out in his book entitled *In Praise of Bureaucracy* (2000):

> The citizen who scoffs at the elaborate record keeping undertaken by government offices might well be equally annoyed should an official lose track of her affairs through relying on memory and telephone conversations. Similarly, the common complaint that government departments endlessly follow precedent might well lose its moral force if we find out that we have not received exactly the same treatment as our neighbour, friend or lover did in the same circumstances this time last year.
>
> du Gay, 2000: 1.

And he goes on to say that:

> ...while we may sometimes experience a sense of personal frustration in our dealings with state bureaux, we might learn to see such frustration as a largely inevitable by-product of the achievement of other objectives that we also value very highly: such as the desire to ensure fairness, justice and equality in the treatment of citizens – a crucial qualitative feature of modern government that we largely take for granted.
>
> du Gay, 2000: 2.

ACTIVITY 6.5

Think about the bureaucratic procedures and structures of a social work organisation you are familiar with. Consider:

■ What obstacles these procedures and structures place in the way of delivering a good service to the public?
■ What advantages these procedures and structures offer in terms of the service delivered to the public?

Commentary

Of course your answers will vary depending on the organisation you have in mind and on your own experience, but you may have come up with some of the following:

Obstacles:

■ Scope for initiative and imagination is restricted by rules.
■ Too much staff time spent on paperwork.
■ Decisions are slow in being made due to having to be passed up the hierarchy.
■ Service users are subjected to elaborate screening procedures and are passed between different members of staff.
■ Service users are made to feel 'small' and disempowered by the organisation.
■ Anomalies not anticipated by the procedures can create serious delays.

Advantages:

■ Consistency of service.
■ Fairness in terms of allocation of time and resources.

- ▇ Safeguards exist against dangerous or unprofessional practice by individuals.
- ▇ Speed: having set procedures for doing things saves workers from having to 'reinvent the wheel'.
- ▇ The organisation can be explicit about what it can and can't do – thus potentially empowering service users by providing them with the information they need to challenge the organisation's decisions.
- ▇ There is a clear line of accountability.

Chapter summary

In this chapter we have looked at what may seem, in some ways, a rather specialist subject: the setting of thresholds against notional scales of need and risk to determine eligibility for services or to determine the type of intervention. However we believe that these are questions which touch on many aspects of social work as it is practised on a daily basis, especially in the statutory services.

We began by looking at frameworks to determine eligibility for services on the basis of different levels of need, considering in particular the government's current guidelines on assessing eligibility for adult care services. We noted that these systems tended to be much more formalised in the adult care field than in child care social work, though in both fields there is a similar need to ration services.

Having introduced the concept of a threshold as a notional level on a scale of need, we then moved on to look at thresholds related to risk, such as the point at which an application under Section (2) of the Mental Health Act is warranted, or the point at which a child's name should be placed on the child protection register.

We discussed the concept of risk (discussed more fully in Chapter 3) and drew attention to the fact that risk has two components – harm and the probability that it will happen. Because risk is about probability not certainty, cases defined (by whatever measure) as high risk will include some cases where harm will not in fact happen and cases defined as low risk will include some cases where harm *will* in fact happen: these are false positives and false negatives. In human terms these translate into service users who receive a response that is not helpful and may cause harm, but we pointed out that when this happens it does not *necessarily* mean that a mistake has been made. We drew attention to the so-called *hindsight fallacy*.

We noted that, wherever one chooses to draw the line on the scale of risk between acceptable and unacceptable risks, there will be false negatives above it and false positives below it, but the proportion of the two will vary. Deciding where to put thresholds, we concluded, is a value based decision, not one that the facts themselves can settle for us.

In conclusion, recognising that much of this chapter has addressed processes and systems that many would see as 'bureaucratic', we considered the nature of bureaucracy. We observed that, while bureaucracy gets a bad press and can be rigid, oppressive and dehumanising, nevertheless bureaucratic systems can provide benefits too, including fairness, transparency and accountability.

Websites

Suffolk County Council: www.suffolkcc.gov.uk
Cambridgeshire County Council:
www.cambridgeshire.gov.uk

PART 3

Synthesising Practice

CHAPTER 7

Empowerment and Socially Inclusive Practice

Introduction

Assessment and intervention practice takes place in a context of personal or social needs mediated by factors such as eligibility criteria, legal obligation, priority and the quality and quantity of available resources in the short or long term. Social work is at the cutting edge of individuals', families' and communities' attempts to manage life challenges influenced by the effects of economic and social policy, welfare systems and their own internal make-up. The concept of empowerment and socially inclusive practice in social work can therefore be seen as self-evident or problematic.

It is self-evident if we perceive people and their problems as the product of an inequitable economic system that disenfranchises the weak, vulnerable, disabled or poor from equal participation and access to the resources produced by society. The task of social work is in this context, to work towards liberating service users and empowering them to gain access to those resources. If we conceive empowerment as problematic however, we might think that it is our job to reduce expectations and accept the prevailing economic paradigm that automatically excludes sections of society from equal participation. Social work in this context becomes modest in aim and seeks to help people manage with whatever provision is offered to support them.

These two versions of how empowerment can be considered are reflected in the literature

and characterised as a radical or conservative way of conceiving the social work task (Howe, 1994; Payne, 1997; Dominelli, 1998). These simplistic dichotomies are limited in their usefulness for the modern practitioner. A more helpful device in the context of empowering practice is to think whether in practising social work you are (Trevithick, 2000):

- Doing things to service users.
- Doing things for service users.
- Doing things with service users.

Here is an example of how to ensure your practice is dis-empowering – it is a caricature of bad practice developed by *Values into Action*, the national campaign with people who have learning difficulties. Reflect for a moment or two and ask yourself whether any of this actually happens more, or less often in your assessment and intervention practice:

- **Exclude non professionals**: this mustn't be done too obviously, so hold meetings at times and places which will be hopelessly inconvenient for friends and family. During working hours in a remote office with no bus service is best.
- **Intimidate advocates**: if anyone with a personal interest in the discussion still manages to attend, ensure that they feel too uncomfortable to speak freely. Hold meetings on professional territory where there are lots of symbols of professional

power, e.g. large desks, journals, and a good view of the staff car park.

- **Disempower the user**: don't risk the reputation of the service by excluding the user entirely (unless of course, they display challenging behaviours during the meetings, such as tearfulness or a tendency to disagree). Instead give them no time to prepare their own ideas about what kind of life they would like. Such thoughts are not helpful to sound practice.
- **Value all opinions**: the widest range of viewpoints is recommended. Ideally participants should be total strangers with no shared value system.
- **Keep the meeting short**: thirty minutes is quite long enough to plan the life of any service user. Ideally, ensure a prompt finish by either a) planning the meeting just before a union meeting on threatened staff cuts; or b) doing a batch of six assessments/reviews in one morning.
- **Stick to procedures**: use as many standard forms and checklists as possible, in different colours and using strange language. This has added benefit of giving people the feeling they are doing something really skilled and professional.
- **Be resource–driven**: whenever possible, ensure that needs are defined to match the resources available. Alternatively, identify a need for resources which are not available and under the control of another agency, so that everybody can just blame them.
- **Be objective**: always focus on needs, problems and deficiencies, and disregard any of the assets of the person or their community. Never, ever, dare to dream about people finding an escape from the service system to a life of freedom, dignity, and citizenship.

The term social inclusion has gained rapid acceptance within the social work lexicon at the beginning of the 21st century. It began to appear prominently in political discourse in the UK following the election of a Labour Government in 1997 which regarded social exclusion as an impediment to its vision of a more open and equal society concerned with social justice as well as economic progress (Walker, 2003). The concept of social exclusion has its origins in France in the 1970s where the idea of citizenship and social cohesion highlighted the plight of *Les exclus* who were relegated to the margins of society (Barry and Hallett, 1998; Pierson, 2002). The social policy aim therefore is to advance a socially inclusive social and health care policy enabling any and every citizen to enjoy the opportunities offered by late capitalist Britain and the European Economic Community in an increasingly economically globalised world. This should fit with an empowering social work practice.

Each individual regardless of class, race, culture, age, religion, disability or gender should find the traditional barriers to their advancement being dismantled so that nobody is excluded from sharing in the wealth and resources being offered at a time of sustained economic expansion. These political aspirations fit with the value base of social work which embodies anti-discriminatory practice, respect for persons, and equal opportunities for every citizen. However just as the earlier stages of capitalism resulted in new approaches to the social management of the disruption, impoverishment, and alienation of the social casualties of economic progress, so too are the late stages of capitalism (Leonard, 1997).

Social workers are among those in the front line faced with the consequences of the failure of this latest social policy aspiration and the raised expectations of people in need. Evidence suggests that the process of exclusion continued in the 1970s as rising levels of poverty began to be quantified. In the process a new role has evolved for statutory social work not so much as a provider of services or even as a therapeutic intervention but rather as a front-line service focused on the management of exclusion and rationing of scarce resources (Jones, 1997). This has always been an uncomfortable position for social workers who subscribe to an empowering model of practice that seeks to challenge social injustice.

The evidence confirms that the gap between rich and poor is widening, there are more children living in poverty, the prison population is at its highest recorded level, and disabled people are more likely to live in poverty or be unemployed than non-disabled people. Children from working class families are less likely to receive a further or higher education and black families are more likely to live in poor housing. There are however differences within these broad examples of social exclusion that need to be taken into account when you are assessing strengths, resources, and gaps in social networks where you are trying to help. For example, inner city deprivation, migration patterns, and poorer health outcomes are factors also associated with class and are therefore likely to affect any family in disadvantaged social circumstances.

Community practice and social development

The idea of community social work is based on the premise that most people's problems are sorted out within and between their existing local network of friends, relatives and neighbours. Social work has a role in seeking to reinforce and support those networks or helping to facilitate their growth where they have declined, as a protective and preventive strategy. Community practice therefore is *par excellence* the optimum intervention strategy for promoting social inclusion. It does not as is sometimes assumed, exclude work with individuals. The spectrum of activity includes (Smale et al., 2000):

Direct intervention: work carried out with individuals, families and local networks to tackle problems that directly affect them.
Indirect intervention: work with community groups and other professionals and agencies to tackle problems affecting a range of people.
Change agent activity: this seeks to change ways that people relate to each other that are responsible for social problems whether at individual, family or neighbourhood levels by reallocating resources.
Service delivery activity: providing services that help to maintain people in their own homes, to reduce risks to vulnerable people, and provide relief to parent and carers.

Community practice is not just about transforming neighbourhoods whether on a small or large scale but it can also enable personal change and growth in individuals through social action and the fostering of co-operative activity. The reverse of course is also true. Individual work such as that described earlier in this book that focuses on the internal problems of children and families can also contribute to wider social transformation in neighbourhoods. Defining precisely what community social work is can be difficult, it can mean almost what anyone wants it to mean from visiting lonely housebound people to organising a protest march to the Town Hall to lobby for improvements to neighbourhood services (Thompson, 2002; Adams et al., 2002).

With such broad definitional parameters it is not surprising to conclude that there is a shortage of reliable empirical data about social work assessment and intervention activity in this area of practice (Macdonald, 1999). The available evidence does suggest however, that it is community-oriented, pro-active initiatives that are helping to support families and individuals in need. A modern, psycho-social model offers the appropriate holistic perspective for social workers to engage with other professionals in the community, to work in partnership with families, and employ the personal relationship skills the majority aspire to use.

You may feel that community practice lacks a focus for your aspiration to facilitate neighbourhood development and empowering experiences for socially excluded people. Group work offers the optimum intervention in these circumstances whereby you together with other social workers or other staff, can engage in the extension of networks of carers, promotion of self-directed groups and the creation of new resources. Group work skills are distinctive but enshrine the core psycho-social base of social work practice and can incorporate elements of intervention skills we reviewed in Chapter 2.

Your decision to embark on a group work intervention as part of community practice should be on the basis that it is the best way of helping those people concerned, rather than because you want to try it or that it is cheaper than seeing people individually. Groups offer the opportunity to:

- Learn and test interpersonal skills.
- Provide a sense of belonging.
- Empower service users pressing for social change.
- Develop mutual support mechanisms.
- Exchange information and share experiences.

ACTIVITY 7.1

Consider the role of your agency in empowerment and socially inclusive practice. Do you recognise practices consistent with that role? List three changes to your practice that you can make and that aspire to empower service users.

Cultural competence

The concept of cultural competence has begun to emerge in the social science literature as a way of highlighting specific elements of a socially inclusive practice. Drawing together the elements of practice that can contribute towards a model of culturally competent care means it is possible to define this as a set of knowledge-based and interpersonal skills that allow individuals to understand, appreciate and work with individuals of cultures, other than their own. Five components have been identified (Kim, 1995) comprising culturally competent care:

- Awareness and acceptance of cultural differences.
- Capacity for cultural self-awareness.
- Understanding the dynamics of difference.
- Developing basic knowledge about the child's culture.
- Adapting practice skills to fit the cultural context of the child and family.

These are consistent with other work which critique the historical development of cross-cultural services and offer a model of service organisation and development designed to meet the needs of black and ethnic minority families (Moffic and Kinzie, 1996; Bhugra, 1999; Bhugra and Bahl, 1999). Ethnocentric and particularly Eurocentric explanations of emotional and psycho-social development are not inclusive enough to understand the development of diverse ethnic minority groups. Failure to understand the cultural background of service users can lead to unhelpful assessments, non-compliance, poor use of services, and alienation of the individual or family from the welfare system.

There is growing interest in the development of multi-disciplinary and interprofessional working in order to maximise the effectiveness of interventions to meet the diverse needs of multi-cultural societies and service users. The characteristics of such work apply in a framework familiar to social workers. It begins with assessment then proceeds through decision-making, planning, monitoring, evaluation, and finally to closure. It is argued that this common framework offers the optimum model for encouraging reflective practice to be at the core of contemporary social work (Walker, 2002). Reflective practice offers the opportunity to shift beyond functional analysis to making active links between the value base, policy-making process, and the variety of interventions conducted.

Combining reflective practice with culturally competent practice, social workers have the opportunity to make a major contribution towards responding to the social policy aspiration of inclusion and anti-oppressive practice. In so doing you can facilitate closer co-operation between professionals coming into contact with vulnerable service users on a shared agenda of challenging institutional and personal discrimination (Eber et al., 1996; VanDenBerg and Grealish, 1996; Sutton, 2000). One of the defining features of social work practice is the ability to work closely with other professionals and communities, often in a co-ordinating role or as a client advocate. This role in the context of work with a variety of problems and contexts is crucial at various points of the intervention process to ensure culturally competent practice.

Social workers using an anti-discriminatory, empowerment model of psycho-social practice are ideally placed to work with other professionals in multi-disciplinary contexts to enable the team to maintain a focus on culturally competent practice. For example, the increased demand for help from parents and children themselves suffering the effects of mental health problems has prompted policy initiatives to invest in and reconfigure child and adolescent mental health service provision. The aim is to make them more accessible and acceptable to all cultures by improving multi-agency working (House of Commons, 1997; Mental Health Foundation, 1999). However, in order to be effective all staff need to address the different belief systems and explanatory thinking behind psychological symptoms. Your social work skills and values are required to articulate these concepts in such teams. Combined with respectful consideration of indigenous healing practices within diverse populations this can optimise helping strategies.

Black and ethnic minority families

Inspection of social work services for black children and their families in Britain shows that despite years of rhetoric of anti-racist and anti-oppressive social work practice, assessments and care planning are still generally inadequate (DoH, 2000). The guidance suggests:

- Ensuring that services and staffing are monitored by ethnicity to ensure they are provided appropriately and equally.
- Involving ethnic minorities in planning and reviewing services.
- Training in anti-racist and anti-discriminatory practice.
- Investigating and monitoring complaints of racial discrimination or harassment.
- Explicit policies are in place for working with black families.

Social workers' skills in facilitating service user empowerment are indicated in any vision of the future shape of service provision (Walker, 2001). A psycho-social practice framework employing community social work and group work skills are also required to enable black families and young people to support each other and raise collective awareness of shared issues. Investigation of indigenous healing practices and beliefs provide a rich source of information to utilize in the helping process. Advocacy skills in which young people are encouraged to be supported and represented by advocates of their choice with a children's rights perspective, would help contribute to influencing current service provision (Ramon, 1999). A traditional psycho-social practice, that links the internal and external world of the client, augmented with culturally competent skills, can help meet the needs of socially excluded children and families.

Continual reflection and evaluation of practice is required to maintain an anti-racist socially inclusive practice. Recognising racial harassment as a child protection issue and as an indicator for subsequent potential mental health problems is evidence for example, of how you can translate policy generalisation into specific practice change. Social workers who make sure they take full account of a child's religion, racial, cultural and linguistic background in the decision making process are demonstrating the link between social policy and socially inclusive practice. Ensuring for example, that black children in residential care have access to advocates and positive role models can assist in challenging institutionally racist practice.

Anti racist and anti-oppressive social work practice will help develop strategies to overcome value judgements about the superiority of white British family culture and norms. Exploring the impact of white power and privileges in social work relationships with black people and drawing connections between racism and the social control elements of social work practice, is another example. Rejecting stereotypes of black and ethnic minority family structures and relationships will enable you to assess the rich cultural, linguistic and spiritual diversity of family life and permit the building of assessment and intervention practice that is not based on a deficit model judged against an Anglocentric norm.

ACTIVITY 7.2

What could you do personally to translate policy guidance into effective practice with black and ethnic minority families?

Commentary

Continual reflection and evaluation of your practice will enable you to maintain an anti-racist practice. Recognising racial harassment as a child protection issue is crucial as is making sure you take full account of a child's religion, racial, cultural and linguistic background in the decision-making process. Developing strategies to overcome value judgements about the superiority of white British family culture and norms requires continual checking of your assumptions about family life. You need to explore the impact of white power and privileges in your relationships with black people and draw connections between racism and the social control elements of social work practice. Rejecting stereotypes of black and ethnic minority family structures and relationships will enable you to assess the rich diversity of families and permit the building of an assessment not based on a deficit model judged against an Anglocentric norm. The more powerlessness is reinforced by services which deny felt experience and choice, and practitioners expect partnership without addressing the impact of powerlessness, the fewer users will be empowered (Braye and Preston-Shoot, 1995).

Disabled children and their families

There are a growing number of disabled children and young people living in the community who are socially excluded and need high levels of support. Partly this is because more of these children are surviving infancy, and partly because there is no longer the assumption that disabled children should be cared for in hospitals or other institutions. Lone parents with disabled children, families from ethnic minorities, and families caring for the most severely disabled children have the highest levels of unmet need, and live in the poorest conditions. A social model of disability rather than an impairment-specific model, can be useful in recognising the environmental barriers to disabled children that prevent them participating equally in society. This model emphasises the need to identify the way in which structures and institutions further disable people with disabilities so that these disabling structures can be challenged (Sharkey, 2000).

Disabled children with a severe disability want to know how to deal with the social and psychological challenges they face – including dealing with other family members, coping with their own negative feelings, and planning for the future. Families require relief and request a range of support including home-based sitting services, residential or family-based respite care, or long-term care from social services departments (Beresford et al., 1996). Needs change over time. For instance a family with an autistic child may want a graded range of services. In the early years they want information and support with their child's development. When the child is a bit older they need respite care. But when the children reach early teens research shows that about 60% of families want their child to be accommodated by the local authority (Oldman and Beresford 1998).

Lone parents with disabled children, families from ethnic minorities, and families caring for the most severely disabled children have the highest levels of unmet need, and live in the poorest conditions. The mental health needs of disabled children are often masked by a narrow focus on their disability through a medical, rather than social model of disability. Behaviour causing concern can often be ascribed to the physical or intellectual disability rather than a separate psychological need. Thoughtful assessment in these circumstances is crucial.

Under Part 3 of the Disability Discrimination Act 1995 social services and other service providers must not discriminate against disabled children by refusing to provide any service which is provided to other children, by providing a lower standard of service or offering a service on less favourable terms. From 2004 service providers will have to take reasonable measures to remove, alter, or provide reasonable means of avoiding physical features that make it impossible or unreasonably difficult for disabled children to use the services including when they are undertaking or contributing to assessments. This means access to services needs to be considered from the disabled child's perspective. A socially inclusive practice would link with local disabled children's networks and involve parents, carers and children in the planning and delivery of necessary changes.

The needs of deaf children like other disabled children are often overlooked or simply poorly understood. The medical model of disability ensures that the disability itself is the focus of attention rather than the disabling environment and attitudes of society. Very little research has been undertaken with this particularly socially excluded group to try to understand their emotional and psychological needs and the impact on them of their disability. Deaf culture needs to be taken into account if a socially inclusive practice is to be employed by social workers. Its principle characteristics are:

▪ Sharing a common language (BSL) for communication purposes.
▪ Social interaction choices.
▪ Identity issues.
▪ Historic understanding of discrimination.

Deaf BSL users view their deafness as a cultural identity; they are proud of their language and feel they belong to a linguistic minority group. They do not want their deafness to be cured and are more concerned about improved access to services, information and democracy. The Disability Rights Commission was established to act as a watchdog for implementation of the Disability Discrimination Act 1995. The commission would be a powerful ally to social workers seeking to ensure that the specific needs of deaf children and young people are not hindered by the lack of specific and appropriate services.

The low uptake of respite services by Asian parents with a disabled child are still perceived by some as evidence of the closed network of familial relationships within Asian culture, rather than evidence of the inaccessibility of existing

service provision. Sometimes this is a matter of proper translating services being unavailable but it can also represent a lack of effort from social workers and other social care professionals to understand the families they aspire to help. For example, some Asian families are reluctant to have daughters cared for by male carers, or they simply have little knowledge of the health and welfare system in Britain (Shah, 1992). Even when good translators are available they do not always manage to convey the subtleties of meaning related to feelings and cultural differences. Trying to distinguish the mental health needs of children and young people with a physical or learning disability is difficult enough for many professionals let alone for black families already disadvantaged and discriminated against.

ACTIVITY 7.3

In what ways do you think that guidance does not achieve its aims in relation to helping you meet the needs of disabled children and their families?

Commentary

The Carers and Disabled Children Act 2000 entitles all carers, including parent carers, to be assessed in their own right. But assessments and eligibility criteria seem to be less of a problem than a shortage of services to meet assessed needs. And a lack of flexibility within social services provision often means families having to adjust to fit whatever services are available – rather than services fitting their needs. The Children Act 1989 mirrors many of the provisions in the UN Convention on the Rights of the Child ostensibly promoting social inclusion. However local authorities have continued to locate the issue of exclusion within the disabled child rather than in the external social and environmental factors contributing to exclusion. This results in social services departments attempting to meet their obligations by locating care outside the disabled child's home, away from their families, and in ways that remove them from their communities (Morris, 1998).

Young offenders

According to recent figures there were 11,500 young people aged 15 to 20 in jail in England and Wales in 2000, of those 90% had a diagnosable mental health disorder, and many had substance abuse problems as well as personality disorders (Lyon et al., 2000). Young offenders are among the most socially excluded groups in society and the evidence suggests that imprisonment simply makes matters worse not better. Within two years of release, 75% will have been reconvicted and 47% will be back in jail (Social Exclusion Unit, 2002). If some of these young people become homeless or end up in insecure accommodation, they are between eight and 11 times more likely to develop mental health problems (Stephens, 2002).

Young offenders are three times as likely to have a mental health problem as other young people. Yet these problems are often neglected because there are no proper methods for screening and assessing mental health problems within the youth justice system (Farrington, 1996; Goodman and Scott, 1997; Royal College of Psychiatrists, 2002; Mental Health Foundation, 2002). Your assessment and intervention practice can make a huge difference to this vulnerable group of young people by:

- ▧ Challenging multi-agency decision-making meetings to consider alternatives to custodial sentences.
- ▧ Articulating the psychological and mental health needs of young offenders.
- ▧ Offering supportive interventions and diversionary activities to at risk young people.
- ▧ Combining and networking with like-minded staff from other agencies to offer group work or individual counselling to disaffected youth.

The evidence shows that more than 25% of young men and 41% of young women under 21 in prison had received treatment for mental health problems in the year before they were jailed (Lader et al., 1997). Once in the prison system, a lack of purposeful activity, long hours in cells, and a climate of brutality and bullying can reinforce negative attitudes and magnify underlying mental health problems. Prison is no place for young people. The risk of suicide is all too evident with frequent reports of suicide in young offenders' institutions. Even the most progressive regimes are inadequate to the task of meeting these already damaged individuals' needs for stability, certainty, care, and proper support to tackle their offending behaviour within a context of restorative justice and personal responsibility, backed up by therapeutic input.

Looked after children

Nearly 60,000 children were being looked after by local authorities for the year ending 2001. About 60% of these children had been abused or neglected with a further 10% coming from 'dysfunctional families' (DoH, 2001). Abuse of this nature can lead to self-harming behaviour, severe behavioural problems and depression. 38,400 of these children were in foster placements and 6,400 were in children's homes, yet foster carers and residential staff are among the least qualified and supported people left to manage sometimes extreme behaviour.

A recent research study emphasised the importance of a preventive approach with children in the public care system that are more likely to be excluded from school following emotional and behavioural difficulties (Fletcher-Campbell, 2001). Teacher training that fails to adequately prepare newly-qualified staff to respond to the mental health needs of pupils is considered to be a factor in the increased use of school exclusions (OFSTED, 1996). Social workers using a preventive approach could be helpful to teaching staff and organise collaborative work aimed at preventing difficult behaviour escalating. Unless the mental health needs of these children and young people are addressed as part of a strategy that effectively nurtures children's inclusion in school, the risk of deterioration is high. The risk factors for looked after children are probably the most extreme of any socially excluded group, they include (Richardson and Joughin, 2000):

- developmental delay
- school failure
- communication difficulty
- low self-esteem
- parent/carer conflict
- family breakdown
- rejection
- abuse
- parental mental illness
- alcohol/drug abuse
- poverty
- homelessness
- loss

Families with HIV/AIDS

The stress experienced by children and families infected with or affected by HIV is magnified by societal attitudes and prejudice about HIV/AIDS, and is a risk factor for the development of a range of problems. These are some of the psycho-social stressors that can contribute towards the social exclusion of these vulnerable families (Boyd-Franklin et al., 1995):

- **Stigma and fear of contagion**: this can produce alienation and rejection by peers of children with HIV/AIDS. Parents can lose employment or become homeless as a result of perceived risks.
- **Shame, guilt and anger**: the stigma can produce intense feelings of shame guilt and anger which are difficult to manage within the family system. Professionals may also blame drug abusing parents for causing their child's illness further reinforcing feelings of despair.
- **Secrecy and social isolation**: families often live in secrecy with their diagnosis and the associated stigma of homosexuality, drug abuse or prostitution. The consequent social isolation and rejection from extended family support systems can trigger depression, suicidal thoughts, and poor compliance with medical care.

Denial and fleeing medical facilities are not uncommon responses to a positive diagnosis particularly among adults with alcohol or other substance abuse habits. The emotional shock following a period of denial may be characterised by intense feelings of hysteria and anger followed by depressive symptoms, withdrawal and feelings of shame and guilt. Unless these feelings are managed and contained in a helping relationship they will affect the emotional temperature in the household and pose a further risk to the emotional and psychological health of children in the family. Social workers need to bear in mind that a simple referral about a child with behavioural difficulties could involve a child in the centre of an emotional whirlwind where stigma prevents the underlying cause being revealed.

Working with HIV infected children requires similar skills to working with any child or adolescent with added emphasis on issues of trust, time, loss, secrecy and bereavement. Understanding the child's conception of the illness is a crucial task. This can build on what the child or young person already understands about chronic illness causality in general. The key is in adapting knowledge and information to the developmental level the child is at in order for effective communication to take place. An important and difficult issue is the decision about whether and when to disclose the diagnosis to the child. Conflicts between family members and professionals can take place over this most sensitive issue, and affect the emotional state of the child. These principles are generally followed (Pollock and Boland, 1990):

- The truth is generally less threatening to a child than fear of the unknown.
- Information needs to be presented at a level that is developmentally appropriate for the child.
- Disclosure is a process not an event.

Refugees and asylum seekers

Refugee and asylum seeking people are among the most disadvantaged ethnic minority group for whom culturally competent practice is essential. Some are unaccompanied, and many affected by extreme circumstances might include those witnessing murder of parents or kin, dislocation from school and community, and severing of important friendships. Lack of extended family support, loss of home, and prolonged insecurity add to their sense of vulnerability. These experiences can trigger symptoms of post traumatic stress syndrome and a variety of mental health problems (Dwivedi, 2002).

Parents' coping strategies and overall resilience can be diminished in these trying circumstances, disrupting the self-regulatory patterns of comfort and family support usually available at times of stress. Your social work involvement needs to take a broad holistic and psycho-social approach to intervention and not overlook the need for careful assessment of mental health problems developing in adults and children, whilst responding to practical demands. If these are not tackled promptly these people may go on to develop serious and persistent difficulties which are harder, and more costly to resolve, in the long term.

The number of applications for asylum from unaccompanied under 18s almost trebled between 1997 and 2001 from 1,105 to 3,469. DoH figures indicate that there were 6,750 unaccompanied asylum seeking children supported by local authorities in 2001. Further evidence shows that many of these young people were accommodated and receiving a worse service than other children in need (Audit Commission, 2000). Very little research has been done to ascertain the needs of this group of children. However there is some evidence of the symptoms of post traumatic stress syndrome being present before they then experience the racist xenophobic abuse of individuals and institutions incapable of demonstrating humanitarian concern for their plight. This combination can shatter the most psychologically robust personality. It has been estimated that serious mental health disorders may be present in 40–50% of young refugees (Hodes, 1998).

Roma, Gypsy and Traveller children may be included in recent groups of asylum and refugee seeking families escaping ethnic 'cleansing' from the Balkan region of Central and Eastern Europe (Walker, 2003). These children and families have a long history of persecution and flight from discrimination. Roma, Gypsy and Traveller families who have for many years made their home in Britain are probably one of the most socially excluded groups of people living in Britain. Unemployment among Roma and Gypsies is in the region of 70%, while increasing numbers of children are failing to complete even a basic education (Save the Children, 2001). These factors particularly the lack of proper education, are risk factors for the development of psycho-social problems. The overall context of social exclusion means an absence of contact with preventive services or the positive interaction with peers necessary for developmental attainment.

Elements of socially inclusive practice

Social workers have to assess needs, evaluate risks and allocate resources in a way that is equitable as far as possible for a wide range of service users in various situations. Challenging oppression in relation to key issues such as poverty and social marginalisation that underpin interactions in social welfare requires a holistic approach to social change that tackles oppression at the personal, institutional and cultural levels (Dominelli, 2002). An empowering social work practice can contribute to the defence of marginalised people. A review of the elements that constitute a socially inclusive practice lists four core intervention skills necessary to build on an authentic social work practice that reflects your humanitarian values (Smale et al., 2000):

- social entrepreneurship
- reflection
- challenging
- reframing

Social entrepreneurship is the ability to initiate, lead and carry through problem-solving strategies in collaboration with other people in all kinds of social networks. Reflection is the worker's ability to pattern or make sense of information, in whatever form, including the impact of their own behaviour and that of the organisation on others. Challenging refers to the ability of staff to confront people effectively with their responsibilities, their problem-perpetuating/creating behaviours and their conflicting interests. Reframing is the worker's ability to help redefine circumstances in ways which lead towards problem resolution.

Social workers must counteract oppression, mobilise users' rights and promote choice, yet we have to act within organisational and legal structures which users experience as oppressive. Finding your way through this dilemma and reaching compromises, or discovering the potential for creative thinking and practice are the challenges and opportunities open to social workers committed to a socially inclusive practice. This means treating people as wholes, and as being in interaction with their environment, of respecting their understanding and interpretation of their experience, and seeing clients at the centre of what workers are doing (Payne, 1997). The unique psycho-social perspective of social work offers a vast reservoir of knowledge and skills to bring to bear on the multiple problems of socially excluded people.

Anti-racist practice

Anti-racist and anti-oppressive practices are repeatedly referred to in the social work literature and they have a long historical lineage as part of the social justice basis of modern practice. The concepts are backed up in codes of conduct, ethical guidance and occupational standards requiring services to meet the needs of diverse cultures and combat discrimination. They are part and parcel of what attracts many of us into social work in the first place. Translating good intentions is, however, harder than it might at first appear.

For example in the case of child care practice there is still a tendency for social workers to proceed with assessment on the basis that the mother is the main responsible carer with the father taking a minor role. Women are perceived therefore as responsible for any problems with their children and for their protection. You may feel that this reflects the reality especially in cases of single parenthood, or domestic violence

where fathers are absent or a threat. Anti-oppressive practice requires in these situations acknowledgement of the mother's predicament and multiple dilemmas. It requires an informed practice using feminist theory to evaluate the situation and seek every small opportunity to support the mother and engage the father.

A history of childhood mental health problems is strongly indicated in the risk factors for developing adult mental health problems. It is imperative therefore that the needs of all black and ethnic minority children vulnerable to mental health problems are addressed early and competently in order to prevent later problems. Your anti-racist work in multi-disciplinary ways as part of inter-agency groups' co-ordinating efforts to support the child and family through temporary or moderate difficulties could be critical. As specialist social workers you can support other staff in statutory or voluntary resources by offering risk assessment and interpretation of behaviour through the spectrum of child development theories adapted to take account of cultural diversity.

One of the central aims of anti-racist and anti-oppressive practice is to exclude the risk of misinterpretation or underplaying significant emotional and behavioural characteristics in black families. An understanding of the reluctance and resistance of black parents to consider a mental health explanation for their child's behaviour or emotional state is important when considering how to engage parents or carers from diverse cultural backgrounds in the process of support. It is equally important to make efforts to understand cultural explanations and belief systems around disturbed behaviour as part of risk assessment work. Respecting rather than challenging difference should be the starting point for finding ways of moving forward in partnership and co-operation. The dilemma in aspiring to practice in anti-oppressive ways is in balancing this respect with knowledge and evidence of the consequences of untreated emerging mental health problems.

The characteristics of non-Western societies such as collectivism, community and physical explanations for emotional problems are in contrast to Western concepts of individualism and psychological explanations (Bochner, 1994). The Western model of mental illness ignores the religious or spiritual aspects of the culture in which it is based. However, Eastern, African and Native American cultures tend to integrate them (Fernando, 2002). Spirituality and religion do not feature often in the social work literature, yet they can be critical components of a person's wellbeing, offering a source of strength and hope in trying circumstances. You need to address this dimension as part of the constellation of factors affecting black families, avoiding stereotyping, and bearing in mind the positive and sometimes negative impact spiritual or religious beliefs might have on their mental health.

Basing your practice on anti-oppressive principles is not a soft option, signing up to political correctness, or about being nice to black people. It is about how you define yourself as a social worker and your relationship to service users. A recent powerful contribution to the literature on this issue makes the point that you cannot bolt-on a bit of anti-oppressive practice, it has to be part and parcel of all your everyday practice as a contribution to tackling poverty, social justice, and the structural causes of inequality (Dominelli, 2002). This means articulating an anti-racist agenda in every possible context and challenging attempts to deny or avoid the issue.

This goes against theories of social work practice that advocate maintenance, therapeutically narrow, or a care management role for practitioners. Wherever you position yourself you will probably find you can occupy different roles at different times in your work regardless of your explicit intentions. This is because if you are client-centred then you will engage with them in partnership to help meet their needs to maintain them in their current circumstances, provide therapeutic input or offer care management if that is what they want. Doing this while actively embracing anti-racist principles is what will make the difference.

Disability, equality and social exclusion

Disability equality has established itself within the literature on social work practice and more broadly within theoretical debates about social inclusion. It is important therefore to consider some of the concepts attached to disability equality and how they can be translated into sound practice principles. A definition of disability that both encompasses the widest constituency of disabled people and the variety of disabilities they have, as well as the deepest understanding of the social construction of disability is a social model approach. This acknowledges that the lives of people with particular impairment labels or characteristics have the same value as the lives of people without that label. Although impairment may cause some disabled people pain and discomfort, what really disables is a socio-cultural system that does not recognise their right to genuinely equal treatment throughout the life course (Wolbring, 2001).

Within disability discourse there are complex arguments about the use of language and the meaning of terms such as social model that are instructive for you to acknowledge. Disabled critics of the social model suggest that this model's conceptualisation of disability as a structural/ material process makes possible the objectification of their oppression. This can reinforce definitions of disability related to normalcy and impairment, thereby individualising the experience of disability and undermining the structural aspects of discrimination (Corker, 1999).

Disability is a global issue. More than half a billion disabled people live in the world today – approximately one in ten of the population. This number is set to rise over the next 25 years (International Disability Foundation, 1998). Many more young disabled people are surviving into adulthood and old age, and more and more older people are living with impairments acquired later in life. At the same time, disabled people are empowering themselves to claim greater participation, integration, independence and equality.

Disabled people therefore aim not only to claim greater control over their individual lives, but also achieve greater influence over the social structures within which such lives are lived. It is impossible to disentangle the lived experience of disability from the context of disabling societies. Most disabled people encounter both disabling barriers and obstacles to scarce resources. Access to resources is biased against disabled women, children, and older people (Priestly, 2001).

Over the past 25 years disability has moved from the margins to the mainstream of the human rights agenda. This is a result of pressure from disabled people themselves organising locally, nationally, and internationally to influence the policy and practice of those seeking to deliver services and support. In 1975 the United Nations General Assembly made its first Declaration on the Rights of Disabled Persons. In 1981 the UN proclaimed the International Year of Disabled Persons and embarked upon a World Programme of Action. In 1985, the Universal Declaration of Human Rights was specifically extended to include disabled people. In 1992, the first International Day of Disabled Persons was inaugurated. In 1993 the UN introduced: *Rules on the Equalization of Opportunities for Disabled People (UN 1993)* that addressed participation in eight specific areas of life:

- accessibility
- education
- employment
- income maintenance and social security
- family life and personal integrity
- culture
- recreation and sports
- religion

Social model definitions of disability became mainstream, recognising that society creates a handicap when it fails to accommodate the diversity of all its members. The United Nations acknowledged that: 'People with disabilities often encounter attitudinal and environmental barriers that prevent their full, equal and active participation in society,' (UN, 1994). Current

government initiatives on standards in social care and health care such as SCIE and NICE, the NHS Plan, TOPSS, and clinical governance, are encouraging service providers to develop and promote best training and practice.

The practical expression of these aims is found, for example, in the white paper *Valuing People* which focuses on learning disability services but reflects all the issues in disability training. The emphasis throughout legislation and policy guidance is on the development of the health and social care workforce. This includes setting within the context of the governments' strategy of lifelong learning and training, a systems-wide approach, and partnership practice with disabled people.

Legislation and policy

The Chronically Sick and Disabled Persons Act 1970 was the first major piece of legislation attempting to strengthen the powers of local authorities in finding out and meeting the needs of disabled people. The Education Acts of 1944, 1976, and 1981 attempted to address the needs of disabled children for equal access to education. Over the past 20 years a number of attempts to introduce legislation in Parliament aimed at preventing discrimination and promoting the civil rights of disabled people, have been thwarted (Barnes 1991).

The most recent and significant legislative change to impact the disability agenda is the Human Rights Act 1998. This incorporates in to English Law all the conventions of the European Convention on Human Rights. Under the Act all public authorities have responsibilities to abide by basic rights and freedoms of the individual. Front-line staff working with disabled people should be trained on the implications of the Act for their standards of care.

Article 14 of the Act prohibits discrimination against disabled people in their enjoyment of the European Convention on Human Rights. This provides wide scope for disabled people to bring action under the Human Rights Act. More specific rights are provided under Article 2 which guarantees the right to life and will have a direct impact on the service disabled people can expect in the health system. Article 3 protects disabled people against inhuman or degrading treatment. This article affects social services community care provision.

Article 5 provides for the right to liberty. It is especially relevant to people with mental health difficulties who may be compulsorily detained and to other disabled people institutional or community care. Article 6 provides rights of due process in criminal and civil law. It imposes standards in the determination of social security disputes and complaints in the health service. Article 8 protects the right to private and family life and Article 12 the right to marry and found a family. These rights have widespread implications. For example, rights to fertility treatment; the sterilisation of young women with learning disabilities; the rights of severely disabled people to live independently; and rights of adoption are among the issues likely to arise.

The Disability Discrimination Act 1995 has been implemented incrementally since being placed on the statute book. Health and Social Care agencies as employers and as organisations providing services to the public have to make sure they are not discriminating against staff or service users. The particular elements of the law brought into force recently make it clear that service providers should now:

■ Amend policies, procedures and practices which make it impossible or unreasonably difficult for disabled people to use their services.
■ Provide extra help and services to help disabled people get access to their services.
■ Remove or alter physical barriers that prevent disabled people gaining access, or provide the service in an alternative way where reasonable.

According to a recent Social Services Inspectorate report (DoH, 2001) progress on Joint Investment Plans for welfare to work for disabled people is generally patchy. Eligibility criteria leading to an assessment for services generally make little reference to employment. Existing employment schemes tend to focus on people with learning disabilities or mental

health problems, with little attention given to physically disabled people or those with sensory impairments. The report states that what disabled people need is:

■ Effective co-ordination between agencies.
■ Recognition of their value and needs as a whole person.
■ Expert information and advice.
■ Physical access to services.
■ Guidance in making informed choices.
■ Local training and employment reflecting people's diversity.
■ Continuing support once in employment.

Independent living has become more of an option for disabled people as a result of the NHS Community Care Act 1990 and the subsequent introduction of direct payments in 1996. Social care practice has focused on independent living, generally defined as a disabled person living alone with support. Yet this may not be the same for young disabled people and is a complex issue for young black disabled people. A significant research project (Bignall and Butt, 2000) discovered that for young people the most important feature of independence was not living alone, but being able to make decisions, develop skills and do things themselves. For young black disabled people living apart from their families loneliness and pervasive racism were major issues. A number of existing disability groups either do not cater for young people or for black disabled people.

ACTIVITY 7.4

With a colleague at work discuss the ways in which your agency conceptualises disability, then measure this against the notion of a social model of disability. Consider placing this issue on the agenda of your next team meeting.

Globalisation and emancipatory practice

The term globalisation has begun to feature in the social work literature reflecting profound concerns about the shifts in the economic and social patterns of relationships between the richer industrialised countries and the poorer developing countries. It involves closer international economic integration prompted by the needs of capitalism, but also has demographic, social, cultural and psychological dimensions (Midgley, 2001). Consistent with the link between the social contexts of social work practice, it is therefore important to consider the global context in terms of the challenges for building empowering socially inclusive practice.

Critics of globalisation argue that its impact is to maintain unequal power relationships between the richer and poorer countries so that patterns of wealth and consumer consumption in Europe and North America can be sustained. This involves the exploitation of labour and other resources in poorer countries thereby preventing them achieving a diverse and equitable economic and social structure within which health and social welfare programmes can develop. In Britain the consequences of globalisation are being noticed in the way traditional social care systems are taking on the characteristics of business ethics and commercialism (Dominelli, 1998; Mishra, 1999). One of the side effects of this process is the standardisation and conformity required for consumer consumption patterns in order to maximise profit. The consequence is the steady and inexorable erosion of traditional markers of indigenous cultural identity combined with the elevation of global branding.

This critique of the latest phase of capitalist development echoes earlier concerns about the impact on economic growth and subsequent erosion of traditional government policies of full employment and social welfare (Corrigan and Leonard, 1978; Bailey and Brake, 1980). A failure to fully develop social welfare services, or to have them subjected to the gyrations of speculative global financial markets, invariably corrodes the quality and the depth of services designed to reach children and families in personal and culturally appropriate ways. This means that services are pared to the minimum, oriented towards crisis intervention and designed in the narrowest terms to conform to inflexible eligibility criteria that limit access. These features are inconsistent with empowering practice that aims to spread accessibility, improve acceptability and enrich social worker's creative potential to respond to a diverse society.

Dilemmas in trends towards cultural competence have been highlighted by reference to the practice of forced or arranged marriages and dowry, genital mutilation of children, and harsh physical punishments condoned by some societies (Midgley, 2001). These practices can be used to counter the argument for respecting ethnic and cultural diversity and support the notion of universal social work values as the basis for competent practice. Ethnic rivalries and the pride in national identity on which they are based also sit uneasily with culturally competent aspirations of international collaboration and mutual understanding.

However, rather than seek answers to these difficult issues in an introspective way, this emphasises the need for social workers and their professional representatives to reach out to the international social work community with service users, to continue to debate, discuss and strive for ways to discover solutions. We need to understand the impact such practices and the beliefs on which they are based are having on the mental health and emotional development of those families experiencing them.

Cultural competence has been defined as developing skills in assessing the cultural climate of an organisation and being able to practice in a strategic manner within it. It has also been broadened to include *any* context in which social workers practice in order to permit effective direct work at many levels (Baldwin, 2000; Fook, 2002). Whether at the strategic organisational level or the direct interpersonal level social workers can actively resist those pressures to conformity and routine practice that in often discreet and inconspicuous ways can undermine efforts to practise in empowering ways. The requirements of social justice demand vigilance and creativity in order to contribute towards an emancipatory practice that can liberate both social workers and service users from prescribed practice orthodoxies. Such practice is the antithesis of stereotyped, one-dimensional thinking and is characterised by (Leonard, 1994):

■ A commitment to standing alongside oppressed and impoverished populations.
■ The importance of dialogic relations between workers and service users.
■ Orientation towards the transformation of processes and structures that perpetuate domination and exploitation.

These characteristics are in harmony with socially inclusive practice. They do not imply that social workers should reject statutory practice for the voluntary sector, child care for community work, or psychodynamic theories for advocacy. These simplistic oppositional devices do not help social workers manage the complexities and dilemmas in seeking different practice orientations (Healy, 2002). The possibilities for creative practice within organisational constraints are there. They may be limited and subjected to pressures of time but in the personal relationship with service users, the rewards are unquantifiable for both worker and client. Even introducing a small change in practice can have a much larger disproportionate and beneficial impact.

The evidence from other European countries supports the need for social work to pay more attention to the social policy issue of social exclusion and how to build a practice that reflects that concern in practical ways. Emerging democracies in Eastern Europe are learning to take the best of traditional social work and combine it with community practices that address social development issues (Connely and Stubbs, 1997). The rise of ethnic nationalisms and increasing oppression of ethnic minorities, the dismantling of structures allowing gender equality, and the increasing inequalities generated by unemployment and poverty, are all illustrating the need for social work to emphasise a socially inclusive practice. The argument for a pan European paradigm of

social work based on social innovation is articulated by those who envisage social work being a more explicit part of social change and that in order to help our clients we have to engage with the social and political reality (Zavirsek, 1995).

Chapter summary

In this chapter we have reviewed the concept of empowerment and socially inclusive practice. The task of social work is in this context to work towards liberating service users and empowering them to gain access to those resources required to enable equal participation in society. The evidence confirms that the gap between rich and poor is widening, there are more children living in poverty, the prison population is at its highest recorded level, and disabled people are more likely to live in poverty or be unemployed than non-disabled people.

Children from working class families are less likely to receive a further or higher education and black families are more likely to live in poor housing. There is growing interest in the development of multi-disciplinary and interprofessional working in order to maximise the effectiveness of interventions to meet the diverse needs of multi-cultural societies and service users. Culturally competent practice is now an expectation in public service provision and is an expectation of modern social work practice.

The needs and problems faced by particular groups of excluded children and families have been identified. An empowering social work practice can contribute to the defence of such marginalised people. A review of the elements that constitute a socially inclusive practice lists four core intervention skills necessary to build on an authentic social work practice that reflects your humanitarian values – social entrepreneurship, reflection, challenging, and reframing. Anti-racist and anti-oppressive principles have been articulated in the context of the disability equality agenda.

CHAPTER 8

Integrating Methods, Skills and Values

Introduction

Social workers are informed by a wide range of social science theory in weighing up and making judgements about human difficulties. In developing a deeper understanding of people's difficulties in your assessment practice with a view to deciding on intervention, you can draw on a range of theories and methods. The skills and values that are part of your individual social work identity will influence, and be influenced, by these. Differing hypotheses result from viewing situations with the aid of these theories. This is healthy although it can be unhelpful if it leads to confusion and drift in your practice. At its best it can help guard against the temptation to claim a single truth in any situation. However you need to integrate all of these factors in order to practice in a coherent manner.

Forming alternative understandings and explanations is a good habit to acquire. However, judgements have to be made, will be demanded by managers and be expected in legal proceedings where they will be examined and tested. The most desirable practice is where an interpretation is helpful to both worker and client in developing solutions, and where it is rooted in values of respect and anti-oppressive practice. Maintaining a reflexive stance helps you consider the consequences of using particular theories and encouraging service users to develop their own theories about their situations. Also the notion of treating people as wholes, and as being in interaction with their environment is important.

Respecting their understanding and interpretation of their experience, and seeing clients at the centre of what workers are doing, all fit with the central principles of social work (Payne, 1997). You will need more than one model of assessment and intervention to enable you to meet the needs of all your clients – if not you will be like a plumber with only one spanner. Having a grasp of different models of practice should enable you with the client to select the most appropriate, and help you maintain a degree of open-mindedness. This process will enable you to plan your intervention by integrating and analysing information and forming a judgement in partnership with your client.

Integrating practice

We have reviewed the contemporary evidence for assessment and intervention practice, and in preceding chapters examined some of the dilemmas arising from the aims and aspirations expected within national occupational standards and other practice guidance. It is now important to consider ways of integrating the knowledge, skills and values required to analyse information and weigh its significance and priority. We also need to pay attention to considering how to demonstrate how an assessment leads to a set of concrete objectives for intervention. Working in partnership to negotiate and plan responses to assessed needs, risks, responsibilities, strengths and resources should form a significant part of the process of integration. These are some of the ways you can effectively generate and manage resources in practice and how to enable and support clients working with change.

Integrating knowledge, skills and values in analysing information and being able to weigh its significance and priority as a basis for effective planning is a demanding task. O'Sullivan (1999) suggests that sound planning will happen provided the following elements in the decision-making process are delineated:

■ **Being critically aware of and taking into account the decision-making contexts**: knowledge of legal requirements and agency procedures are critical ingredients of planning what is possible and permissible. Statutory duty has to be balanced against your endeavour to take a holistic perspective of the situation. Involving the client to the highest feasible level. There are four levels: being told; being consulted; being a partner; and being in control. A key skill is to fit the level of involvement to the nature of the particular planning situation.

■ **Consulting with all stakeholders**: there could be numerous stakeholders involved in your work with a particular service user. Some will have more systematic contact but only general knowledge about the client, they could be as valuable as someone with limited contact but who has specialised knowledge. A range of perceptions can either enhance the clarity in a situation and confirm your hypothesis, or produce a disparate and confusing picture which hinders rather than helps. Being clear in your thinking and aware of your emotions. A heightened element of self awareness is always useful. Over-reacting to a situation on the basis of tiredness, stress, the day of the week or simply false information need to be guarded against. Equally under-reacting to a risky situation because of feelings of pity, empathy, or over-optimism can contribute to an escalation of risk factors.

■ **Producing a well-reasoned frame of the decision situation that is consistent with the available information**: through framing processes you can shape the information into a picture of the situation, planning goals and a set of options. Listing key factors and considering the weight to give to each requires knowledge, experience, and the capacity for short and long-term predictions of the consequences of various interventions. Basing your course of action on a systematic appraisal of the options. The plan could be based on the principle that a statutory duty overrides the traumatic impact of the subsequent intervention. Alternatively which option is likely to provide the best outcome in the context of risk assessment and available supportive resources.

Strategies for integration

Learning arises as a result of the four-stage process of concrete experience; reflective observation; abstract conceptualisation; and active experimentation according to Thompson (2000). You can use this model to describe and facilitate the application of your knowledge and theory to practice. Guard against the false belief in theory-less practice. The skill is not whether – but how to use your theory to best effect. Being explicit about your knowledge base and resisting complacency about the values, ideas, and assumptions underpinning your practice will help.

Common sense is often invoked to justify conclusions. However this is another way of repeating dominant cultural values, and trying to avoid a more refined explanation for the thinking behind your judgement. Better to spend a little time on developing a critical perspective. Research-minded practice can help integrate theory and practice. It involves recognising the parallel between research activity and social work practice. A participative approach embodies this concept by blending creativity and rigour, and encouraging participants to share decisions, goal-setting, and the most desirable process to be followed.

The critical incident technique is a way of analysing a situation where strong emotions were raised in your practice and which interfered with your ability to function effectively then and in future. It involves reflecting on the incident and asking three questions: what happened; how would you account for this; what other conceptual frameworks could help understand this incident?

Developing a group approach for narrowing the gap between theory and practice can be very effective. It provides opportunities for mutual support within a team setting where critical exploration of ideas takes place in a safe environment. This approach promotes a sense of ownership and shared responsibility which can be empowering and facilitate continuous professional development.

Intuition versus analysis

Planning intervention in social work and the decision-making process includes thinking and feeling about the situation being addressed. But there is debate about whether intuitive or analytical thought is more suited to social work decisions. A contrast between these two distinct forms of thinking is drawn in the social work literature with the tendency to favour intuitive rather than analytical thinking, rejecting the latter as a technical, calculative approach not in harmony with social work values. As with many polarised debates the desire to simplify in order to heighten differences can obscure the valuable resources within each approach. It needs to be acknowledged that analysis is not inevitably technical, that intuition can be unreliable, but both can offer equally useful ways of thinking.

Intuition

Intuition has been variously described as the absence of analysis, the pinnacle of expertise, or the unconscious processing of data. This means that the basis for the consequent judgement is not made explicit at the time. It can be thought of as deciding in a relatively holistic way, without separating the decision situation into its various elements. This enables it to be a quick way of deciding by making use of limited infor-

mation – sensing patterns and filling in gaps. To be reliable and accurate, intuition needs to be based on expertise developed over time, but it has a fundamental drawback which stems from its implicit nature. This is that the reasons behind intuitive decisions are not readily available for comment and scrutiny, which is necessary for partnership practice.

Analysis

Analysis can be defined as a step by step, conscious, logically defensible process. There is deliberation over the different elements in a situation in a systematic and organised way. It can be thought of as using selected information in a precise way, whereas intuition uses all of the perceived information in an imprecise way. The strength of analysis is that it encourages openness about reasoning and so potentially holds your work open to scrutiny. The disadvantage in this approach is that it can induce misplaced faith in the ability to make predictions particularly in the increasing social work field of risk assessment.

Synthesis

Seeing intuition and analysis as opposites can obscure the potential compatibility and complementary nature of the approaches. Some social work planning decisions will require breaking down into their component parts and given careful consideration. But because this involves issues of uncertainty and values, intuition needs to be used within analysis in the making of judgements about the significance of information. Combining the explicitness of analysis with the skilled judgements of professional intuition offers you the advantages of each approach. When facilitating client decision-making or decisions in partnership, some degree of analysis will be helpful as it involves being explicit about the basis of choice.

Ethics and values

There are several sources of guidance for you in trying to juggle the variety of competing demands on your time and on the ethical dilemmas that contemporary social work practice presents you with. Trying to do this while seeking to integrate and synthesise all the different elements of practice is challenging. Clients, your agency management and professional principles all clamour for attention in your assessment and planning practice. There is a professional code (BASW, 2002) in which the expectations for professional practice are described and defined. There are your duties as prescribed in your job contract and based in part on legislative and practice guidance. Also there are the rights of service users that are being defined in the context of government health and social care policies informed by statutes such as the Human Rights Act 1998.

In all of these sources the ethics and values of social work practice are being indirectly put under the microscope and require careful examination if you are to achieve good practice standards and competencies. The ethics and values inherent in social work practice will help you navigate the sometimes turbulent waters where clients, your employer, the professional code and your personal position are all in conflict. Your duties as an employee and your obligations to service users will sometimes come into conflict causing angst and mixed feelings. It is important that you arrive at a position in which you can feel relatively at ease with your stance on a certain issue or with your practice decisions.

Assessment practice presents many situations where such conflicts can arise. For example over eligibility criteria for a particular service which you might regard as too restrictive and leaves clients vulnerable. Or in the case of needs assessment many social workers feel uneasy about conducting a full and comprehensive assessment of a person's situation that highlights many needs that cannot be met by their employing agency. The concept of identifying unmet need causes a great deal of difficulty in practice compared to the apparently innocuous administrative requirement to detail those unmet needs. Social workers are rightly sceptical about the claim that identification of such unmet need translates into effective data for future resource allocation.

The following summary of the different levels of duty inherent in your social work role can assist in positioning yourself in situations of ethical conflict (Banks, 1995):

- **Duties to users**: where you respect user's rights to make decisions, their rights to confidentiality, and to safeguard and promote the welfare of children. Guidance includes the professional code of ethics, agency policies, codes of practice law, public opinion and charters for user's rights.
- **Duties to the profession**: where you uphold the good name of social work by maintaining ethical and effective practice. Guidance here includes the professional code of ethics and guidance.
- **Duties to the agency**: where you follow the prescribed rules and procedures safeguarding the reputation of the agency. Guidance includes your job description, contract and agency policies and procedures.
- **Duties to society**: where you help maintain social order consistent with the responsibilities of social services departments or probation services as laid down in statute. Guidance includes the law, government guidance, and public opinion.

Is there a hierarchy of ethical practice in the context of these duties? The professional code of ethics is often quoted as the dominant source of guidance for your practice when you are faced with professional conflicts. In cases where agency policies contravene the professional code you may feel entitled to change or challenge those policies by refusing to comply with them. There can be no easy prescription or detailed guidance to cover every nuance within each unique situation you face. Each individual has to arrive at their own conclusion which will be decided by your own personal ethical code. Only you can make the decision to risk disciplinary proceedings from an employer or challenge practices inconsistent with your values by invoking grievance procedures backed by your trades union or BASW representative.

Probably the worst position is to feel disempowered, undervalued and forced into practices with which you fundamentally disagree yet carry on in a spirit of resentful collusion. This can corrode your sense of worth and undermine the humanitarian principles that brought you into social work practice. It results in low morale, routine practice, poor staff retention and recruitment that affect service quality and impacts on your relationship with service users. It is of course this relationship which is at the heart of professional practice and is the one aspect of service that clients consistently report valuing highly. In the wider context of increasingly managerialist styles of supervision in social work agencies where the needs of the bureaucracy seem to come before clients, it is little surprise that many social workers find their position untenable.

You may find a variety of answers to help you deal personally with these conflicts and impossible dilemmas. At times and in certain circumstances your position might change or as your career develops you may find your views changing on certain issues that were previously certain. It is likely that you might recognise the following strategies as options for dealing with these ethical challenges (Banks, 1995):

- **Defensive practice**: where you carry out to the letter agency duties and procedures. You perceive yourself as an official of the employing agency and find yourself referring clients to your managers or elected councillors when they complain about the level of service. You are aware that you have separated out your duties to your agency and your personal values, with the latter being subsumed to the agency rules.
- **Reflective practice**: where you recognise more actively the ethical dilemmas in practice and their roots in social inequalities. You are perhaps more confident about your own values, how to put them into practice and integrate them. This enables you to reflect, learn from practice and take risks. It also makes you more likely to challenge agency procedures and advocate on behalf of service users.

Social work skills

Separating out the distinctive skills of assessment and intervention is difficult and as we have seen already there are a plethora of methods, models and a variety of distinctions in their underpinning practice philosophies. The following summary is intended as a guide to help illuminate your way through the available material and provide a framework for integration within which your own personal values and ethical social work identity can flourish (Trevithick, 2000):

- **Information-gathering**: one of the major criticisms of contemporary assessment practice is the vast amount of time spent on assessment and in particular information-gathering. There could almost be an inverse relationship between the quantity of information gathered and the quality of the assessment. More in this case seems to be less. It is however understandable as a symptom of defensive practice and the needs of the bureaucracy rather than what might be in the best interests of the client. It is also tempting to think that a vital piece of information needs to be found in order to provide a significant clue that can aid analysis. It is probably better to learn to judge what information is relevant in particular situations – but without descending into robotic routinised practice.
- **Communication**: the bedrock of social work practice often taken for granted within the compassionate, caring instincts of your desire to help. Communication is a two-way process, it is as much about listening and observing as it is about talking. It includes non-verbal gesture, posture, tone of voice and the interactive nature of the assessment process. Recording and writing skills are part and parcel of everyday practice and these are almost an art in themselves. It is crucial to think about the impact your case notes might have on another worker or a service user who requests access to information held about them. Inspections frequently highlight the poor quality of case note recordings so it

is important to spend time improving your skills in this area.

■ **Analysis**: involves identifying the key elements of a situation and recognising significant patterns and interrelationships (Thompson and Thompson, 2002). The trouble is two workers might recognise different patterns in the same piece of work, or the pattern may be a result of the way assessment is carried out rather than inherent within the information. Systems theory could help you here because of its attention to circular reflexive patterns in family's, groups and institutions. Analysis calls for a process of weighing the significance of the elements of an assessment and forming a judgement based on valid evidence to support it.

■ **Planning**: can take place in a variety of contexts such as formal meetings, case conferences, supervision etc. It also occurs within the helping relationship with your clients. It may not be expressed as such overtly but during the assessment process the service user will be indicating what they hope to achieve or where they want to be at some point in the future with your assistance. Whereas in formal professional meetings the overt function is to draw up a plan, there may be a covert agenda about relationships, responsibilities and resources. The skill is in recognising these subtle interactions and placing their significance in your own strategic aims. Having a degree of imagination will help, so will having the capacity to stand back and see the bigger picture and being able to articulate your views in an authoritative way.

■ **Partnership**: the fundamental skill in all social work practice but essential to assessment and intervention. Not an equal partnership because this is not possible given the power differential and ultimate statutory responsibility underpinning your role, but a partnership in the sense that your client's views are taken seriously, recorded and properly acknowledged. Partnership includes having the capacity to engage with some people who are so overwhelmed or distressed by their circumstances that their aggressive, violent behaviour or feelings make it extremely hard work. Recognising that much of what is aimed at you is not personal and is a product of neglect, fear or abuse can help you maintain a professional stance. Also, taking on board the service user's perception can be done without deceiving them into thinking they can dictate terms.

ACTIVITY 8.1

Spend ten minutes thinking about the constraints on planning intervention in social work. Discuss your findings with a colleague or supervisor and consider the strategies you might use for managing.

Commentary

Your findings might include the excessive demands placed on you combined with diminished resources and increased expectation for accountability and efficiency. You have less time to think with more complex situations to deal with. There is pressure to narrow the scope of the assessment and work in the short term to purchase or commission services from sources with variable quality. You might feel constrained to think narrowly, to resort to routine practice yet the diversity of modern life challenges simplified eligibility and pro-forma guidelines. There may be a feeling of being expected to know everything and therefore to specialize in a particular area or client group. However this obscures the generic knowledge base in social work that transcends client group specialisms and minimises broader concepts of social welfare, practice methodology, human growth and development, anti-racist, and anti-oppressive practice.

Your strategies for managing might include reflection and self-awareness techniques to develop stress management skills. Supervision and consultation are central to this. Thinking big and acting small. This means keeping in mind the broader picture of the social and economic context of people's lives and the personal consequences which you may be able to help with. Without being pessimistic or underestimating service users' capacity you may find having small attainable goals which can be sustained and built on more useful than expecting dramatic shifts in people's situations.

The practice context

An illustration of the potential for integrating methods, skills and values can be found in the practice context example of child and family social work. Here we can detect a potential distinction between the specialised area of family therapy intervention with the more diffuse and broadly defined practice of family support. Family support can be defined as self-help or volunteer help with little statutory involvement, or it can mean a continuum of advice, support, and specialist help geared to provide early preventive intervention. The intervention can be directed at individual parents, couples, the child, the whole family, or in groups. It can consist of individual counselling, psychotherapy, group work, advice and information, or the provision of practical help. Within the mix of interventions are the hallmarks of the family therapy paradigm that assumes problems are interpersonal.

The status and perception of preventive family support work can be usefully conceptualised using a three-stage model identifying different levels of intervention (Hardiker, 1995). The primary level offers universally available services that can strengthen family functioning provided by a mix of state welfare providers and parent education services often organised by voluntary organisations. The secondary level provides services targeted on families in early difficulties such as relationship counselling for couples, informal family centres, and home visiting schemes by voluntary agencies to help families with young children.

At the third, or tertiary level, work with families can include those who are suffering severe difficulties and on the threshold of care proceedings characterised by intensive work either by the statutory or voluntary sector to prevent family breakdown.

Services geared towards the needs of specific age groups of children or young people, or adults can determine the type of help offered and whether it is perceived as family or individual support (Walker, 2001). This becomes particularly important in the area of child and adolescent mental health for example, where the initial assessment of the presenting problem could be formulated on an individual or family basis. Social workers trained in family therapy are particularly alert to the potential for scapegoat individual children within family systems functioning in negative and punitive ways. Family therapy has evolved into definitions as simple as offering a view of problems as interpersonal rather than individual (Dallos and Draper, 2000). Or, as comprehensive as Gorell-Barnes (1998) who describes the activities as:

- Encompassing a philosophy of relational events.
- Methods of description between people and their social context.
- A relational approach to work with families.
- A variety of therapeutic methods.

Some of the literature on family support describes ways of helping families (Sutton, 1999; Hill, 1999; Pinkerton et al., 2000). They provide the following common characteristics:

- Using listening skills.
- Getting alongside families.
- Emphasising collaboration.
- Developing cultural awareness.
- Gathering information.
- Recognising positives in the situation.

An examination of these terms quickly shows similarities with skills considered important for family therapy accreditation, even though different vocabulary is employed. How far support or therapy directly address the social context, or succeed in doing so is a moot point. The debate about the fit between family therapy practice and its application in social policy contexts has generated thoughtful contributions (Reimers and Treacher, 1995; Sveaass and Reichelt, 2001). The most recent focus on the socio-political discourse generated around refugees and asylum seekers, and how these meta-contexts invariably intrude on the therapeutic encounter.

Families from areas of conflict will encounter family therapy or family support services, particularly when the effects of trauma manifest in child behaviour problems. Without an active engagement with the social policy context that portrays these families as objects of pity or welfare scroungers, therapists and support staff can limit their helping potential. It could be argued that family support services by their very nature, would be oriented more towards this social policy context, and are created to specifically address issues raised within it.

But they may be missing important 'therapeutic' opportunities that are masked by too narrow a focus on human rights, legal, or welfare benefit tasks. On the other hand, family therapists employing an inflexible therapeutic model, and concentrating on the inter-familial beliefs, behaviour and patterns of communication, might be missing an important 'social' dimension to the family's experience and neglecting to find culturally competent ways of engaging them. The use of interpreters adds yet another complication. The important point is that your practice is not being too tightly prescribed as you move between various roles in your contact with families. You can therefore integrate the most useful parts of a family therapy intervention and combine it with broad family support measures. Your practice is more whole and families benefit from multi-skilled practitioners.

Social workers have the opportunity to employ communication and relationship skills in direct family support work which they traditionally find rewarding and which service users find more acceptable than intrusive, investigative risk assessment. Your role in multi-agency assessment and planning becomes significant in this context where several perceptions can be expressed, based on diverse evidence and different levels of professional anxiety. Managing these processes with individuals or groups in planning meetings, case conferences, or case reviews, require advanced negotiation and decision-making skills which are the hallmarks of integrated practice.

The renaissance of family support in Britain is currently perceived as an alternative to child protection, rather than part of a connected architecture of resources to be activated as different needs emerge. Therefore the policy to develop indirect voluntary provision of family support services in Britain can be better seen as a symptom of, rather than solution to, retrenchment in family support offered by professional social workers. The literature on social work in Europe acknowledges the dilemmas in seeking a common professional social work identity, and family support practice which can simultaneously value autonomy in each member country (Shardlow and Payne, 1998; Adams et al., 2002). This illustrates at a meta-level the complexities in trying to integrate all the elements making up modern social work practice.

Participatory practice

One of the key characteristics of contemporary social work services is the partnership approach to work with service users mentioned in Chapter 3. This is enshrined in practice guidance and codes of ethics. It involves a process of negotiation with families about the venue for work, and the choice of practice methods particularly during the assessment process. It is important to make distinctions about the different levels of partnership possible in your intervention as you begin to integrate your practice. The assessing social worker rarely meets with an individual on a truly voluntary basis therefore the experience is characterised by unequal power relations with decisions requiring professional judgement. However it is crucial to differentiate between making a judgement and being judgemental. The former requires facing up to the challenge of responsibility in order to be helpful, while the latter involves prejudice, blaming, and a closed mind.

Participatory practice has become embedded along with empowerment in social work practice to the extent that there is little debate about whether this is always an appropriate strategy and whether service users have said they desire this approach. Participation is normally thought of as a process where the key stakeholders in a service co-operate in defining how the service should be designed and delivered. This can happen in an individual or an organisational context. Parents may negotiate with a service for the best course of action to take in the interests of their child. Or people who use services may represent other service users' opinions in an organisational forum.

Research by Barnardo's concluded that of the parents who used their services none came with the intention of becoming a partner (Daines et al., 1990). Staff interviewed saw participatory practice as a strategy to empower users and build services around their views. Users on the other hand, saw participation embodied in the friendliness, accessibility and helpfulness of staff. Other research highlights the challenges in working in partnership with absent parents of children in long-term care. In these situations social workers have to contribute to planning on the basis of several conflicting issues and make a judgement about the viability of a partnership approach and how far to risk further harm to the child:

■ The importance of promoting contact with parents, relatives, community and culture.
■ The failings of the care system to enable children to reach their potential and fully meet their needs.
■ The importance of birth families and the value of different attachments in helping children form their identity.
■ In conflict-laden situations parents have often been passively hindered by inadequate resources, inaccurate information, or changes of social worker.
■ The potentially destructive effects of persistent abandonment, rejection or neglect from a parent failing to maintain arranged contact.

One means of working in partnership is by conferring rights such as the approach adopted by the disability movement and which is often linked to discussions about citizenship. This is further defined as participation and has been summarised by Mullender and Ward (1991):

■ All people have skills, understanding and ability.
■ People have rights to be heard, to participate, to choose, to define problems and action.
■ People's problems are complex and social oppression is a contributory factor.
■ People acting collectively are powerful.
■ Methods of work must be non-elitist and non-oppressive.

In this form of practice you have to assess needs, evaluate risks and allocate resources in a way that is as equitable as possible for a wide range of people in various situations. Here are some common pitfalls experienced in attempting to achieve a balanced assessment as a basis for planning your intervention (Thompson, 1995; Milner and O'Byrne, 1998):

■ **Selective attention**: research shows that while striving for objectivity we commonly weigh some evidence from assessments more heavily than others. It is easy to develop a mental checklist of factors considered important or relevant thereby excluding other potentially valuable information. First impressions tend to stick and these are invariably negative when clients are in crisis or not coping. This makes it hard to perceive strengths and can lead to an attempt to compensate by being unrealistically optimistic about a service user's ability to change.
■ **Stereotyping**: this can lead to compartmentalising people into ready-made classification rather than working hard to see the uniqueness in a person. The skill is being able to generalise to some extent about client groups and use broad parameters to ensure equitable service, but to avoid crude stereotyping which denies individuality. Superficial adherence to social work values and anti-discriminatory practice will not equip you to resist stereotyping. Research has shown that social workers for example describe challenges to their decisions as 'manipulative' (Davis and Ellis, 1995).

■ **Attributional bias**: research shows that we attribute successes to our own efforts and our failures to events outside ourselves. However we judge other people oppositely. This is called attribution bias. It is an attempt to make sense of situations so that we can exert some control over and influence events. But this can lead to victim-blaming and in social work intervention results in a tendency to locate the problem within the individual rather than their social circumstances. This concept also helps explain the notion of learned helplessness with people who are depressed and who behave passively towards social workers.

■ **Sensory distortions**: the most obvious sensory distortion in personal perception is the effect of physical appearance on judgements. Attractive people are usually ascribed positive personality traits whereas someone smelling of stale urine is not likely to be assessed as having strength of character. Clients in stressful or crisis situations with raised voices or disorganised thinking are going to affect your perception of their personality – however much you intellectually understand the context of their behaviour.

ACTIVITY 8.2

Think about yourself and events that have made an impact on you in your past. Consider situations where you felt vulnerable, desperate or in need. Think about how those present or concerned about you may have perceived you and the situation you were in. What sort of judgements were they making about you? Did they see someone with strengths or just weaknesses?

Commentary

In recalling your own personal past you may now be able to see how those around you were influenced by your behaviour and feelings to the extent where they were restricting their assessment of you and drawing stereotypical

conclusions. At the time, or now in retrospect you may feel a sense of injustice at how limited this perception of you was, and how it reinforced your sense of failure or vulnerability, if it persisted. Timing is as always crucial. It may be inappropriate to start identifying strengths in someone too early in your work in case it is interpreted by them as a signal of your impatience or punitive beliefs about pulling themselves together.

On the other hand dwelling on deficits may further push the client into a state of helplessness and despair. A good guide as always is your own feelings – these will be connected to how the service user is feeling, so by practising the habit of interrogating your own feelings you will begin to sense how the client is. For example you might feel angry with the client during a piece of work with them so instead of making yourself feel guilty about this another way of dealing with the feeling of anger is to see it as transference from the client. By openly acknowledging this with them and offering an interpretation of their anger you may open up an avenue of exploration that can help them at a deeper level.

This technique is sometimes misconstrued as amateur psychoanalysis or mystification, but actually it is based on simple humanitarian concepts and the real feelings generated during the helping process. It is also more liberating for service users to gain some insight into themselves as a step towards recovery and self-determination rather than allowing your embarrassment or timidity to prevent them from moving on in their lives.

Multi-disciplinary and inter-agency working

Partnership practice is not restricted to how you work with service users but also how you follow best practice guidance in relationships with other agencies. Government and professional expectations are for more integrated and therefore effective joint working across professional boundaries in community care, children and families, and mental health contexts. Research shows there are still barriers to effective working which have a negative impact on clients and hinder integrated practice. These include:

■ financial constraints
■ differing organisational and managerial structures
■ different priorities

Joint working can be improved and is influenced by intentional approaches as well as informal evolutionary factors. The intentional approach may formalise joint working arrangements but these can neglect the more personal and creative aspects of partnership. Embedding such approaches can take a long time, constrain opportunities into restrictive prescriptions, and result in relatively unresponsive mechanisms. An evolving approach, on the other hand, allows for informal networking but can become over-reliant on key personalities and historical associations. Charismatic individuals may be highly effective in the short term but prove impossible to replace and leave a void behind them, when they leave. A combination of formal and informal strategies can optimise the conditions for effective joint working by:

■ Joint planning meetings.
■ Creation of joint posts.
■ Development of joint strategy.
■ Individual initiatives.
■ Shared goals and vision.
■ Track record of joint working.

Interprofessional or multi-disciplinary care are contemporary terms often used synonymously to mean joint working between staff from different professional backgrounds. Staff may work in the same team location or operate from separate uni-professional teams. Within the same agency they may represent different disciplines or client groups. In whatever configuration joint working has always been recommended as the best way of delivering coherent and effective care in health and social work practice. Every social or health care textbook features injunctions for closer working between agencies, better communi-

cation, and clear lines of accountability. Absence of these elements of practice is usually highlighted in all-too frequent inquiries into deaths involving child abuse, mental health, or social care situations. Government practice guidance emphasises these ideas in slick managerialist terms and appeals to systems-level co-ordination, enhanced procedures, and strategic planning. Translating these ideas into practice skills is more difficult than rhetorical slogans.

There have been attempts to identify some key common skill and knowledge elements that inform work with children and young people for example (Tucker et al., 1999). The conclusions are that different workers from different professional contexts can share a common perception of what needs to be understood about a child or young person's life in order to intervene effectively. These can be transferred to all client groups through:

■ The social and environmental context.
■ Gender, class, ethnicity, disability.
■ Articulating a human rights perspective.
■ Recognising the individual characteristics of all people.
■ Developing reflective practice.

These are recognisable as consistent with social work practice knowledge and skills; however they are operationalised in different legal and organisational contexts where problems arise in trying to foster better inter-agency working. Staff in whatever agency context are hampered and hindered to some extent by the constraints of budgets, resource limits and service specifications. One way of mitigating these factors is to promote more joint education and training opportunities and to foster moves towards shared professional qualifications.

Social workers are often reminded of their pivotal role in multi-disciplinary working and the core skills of social work practice are cited as a major asset in helping achieve better interprofessional work (Parsloe, 1999; Smale et al., 2001; Adams et al., 2002). The care manager role has perhaps institutionalised this concept where social workers are employed to organise and monitor care plans using a variety of other agency staff, often in multi-disciplinary settings. In other situations you may be directly or indirectly involved in work in which your contribution, *however small*, could make a big difference to a successful outcome. In the context of child and family work for example, the social work role is crucial in the following circumstances:

■ As child and family workers involved in assessment.
■ As convenors of inter-agency planning meetings.
■ At case conferences involving child protection concerns.
■ In long-term care planning and reviews.
■ In the formal care management role.
■ As contributors to multi-disciplinary intervention.
■ In young offender teams.
■ As referrers to specialist and community resources.

In whatever context of practice you need to examine the complex web of agencies and staff available to contribute to the needs of your clients. This offers an opportunity to reflect on the potential for success, spot potential areas of professional disagreement or confusion, and clarify the social work contribution. The unique professional profile of social work embodying psycho-social principles, and a social model of human growth and development, find expression in the values enshrined in the latest social work code of ethics. Together with national occupational standards they offer a powerful intellectual *corpus* to bring to inter-professional and multi-disciplinary work (BASW, 2002).

The challenges in working together

The range of staff involved in the delivery of health and social care services is broad and the potential for disagreement, confusion or poor communication is high. The benefits of working together cannot be overstated but this should not happen at the expense of proper professional debate that sometimes can be difficult. However, before considering the diversity of professional and voluntary backgrounds engaged in this work, it is worth remembering that parents/carers provide over 90% of the care of their children. They are the people who will be in most contact with the child or young person at the centre of concern. Therefore they must be seen as partners with whom an appropriate alliance is formed, even in the face of profound disagreements about the way forward.

There is growing interest in the further development of interprofessional and multi-disciplinary working in order to maximise the effectiveness of interventions to meet the diverse needs of multi-cultural societies and service users (Magrab et al., 1997; Oberheumer, 1998; Tucker et al., 1999). The evidence suggests there are cost-benefit advantages if duplication of tasks can be avoided, relationships between staff are improved and there is more opportunity to maintain the client at the centre of attention rather than the needs of the various organisations.

Other professionals do not experience the same level or the same type of supervision that permits reflective practice and the opportunity for stress management and exploration of strategies for coping with difference. The tradition in social work of such supervision is constantly under pressure by managerialist prescriptions for brief, task-centred working practices, risk assessment and prioritisation of caseloads. However, supervision that enables a worker to understand and learn from the interactive processes experienced during work is a valuable tool to encourage you to reflect on practice that can be emotionally draining.

Some social workers may find the experience unsettling while others will draw immense comfort from it. Both will benefit and have their practice enhanced as a result. In multi-disciplinary and interprofessional contexts a culture of such enlightened supervision for all staff can create a rich climate for professional growth and improved quality of service to service users. The evidence suggests there is an appetite to incorporate this social work model of supervision into the new multi-disciplinary teams that are becoming more common in health and social care (Debell and Walker, 2002).

Social workers bring a distinctive contribution to interprofessional and multi-disciplinary work. Effective multi-disciplinary team working or inter-agency working requires the notion of power to be addressed and shared more equally between staff. It also requires power to be shared by more participative practices with service users and the community being served. Your skills in advocacy and empowerment are therefore crucial in making this happen. We also bring a concept of oppression and how discriminatory social contexts can blight the lives of children and families. This wider social and political perspective can raise awareness among other staff and inform and enrich the intervention practice of other professionals (Middleton, 1997).

ACTIVITY 8.3

The case study below gives an example where partnership appears fraught with difficulties and may appear unachievable. You have just been allocated this case. Think about how you would try to work in partnership with the family, taking into account the concerns of other professionals.

Father (Michael) age 45, is unemployed.
Mother (Susan) age 32, left the family six months ago, current whereabouts are unknown.
Daughter (Anne) age 11, is at a special school for children with learning difficulties.
Son (Adam) age six, attends primary school.
Twins (Steve and Linda) age 38 months, Steve is brain damaged and Linda has a hole in her heart. Both have developmental delays.

The case was transferred from another local authority and has been dealt with on a duty basis. The father, Michael, has been unco-operative with many agencies concerned about his children. He has been rude, hostile and racially abusive. Hospital appointments for the twins have been missed and your concerns have been increasing over time. Adam and Anne bed wet

and both have missed a lot of schooling. Michael feels there is nothing much wrong with them and focuses his attention mostly on the twins. He feels that professionals are exaggerating and he is determined to care for his family on his own.

The following questions might help in your planning:

■ What are your feelings about working with members of this particular family?
■ What are your anxieties about this case?
■ How would you handle Michael's anger?
■ How would you propose to share your concerns about the children with Michael?
■ What strategies would you hope to develop to work in partnership with the family?

Commentary

Reflecting on your feelings may produce elements of fear, disapproval, and frustration. Or perhaps you might be aware of a certain admiration for Michael's tenacity and self-sufficiency. You may feel protective towards the children and angry that Michael is not putting their needs first. As a black worker you may want to discuss whether you should be allocated this case given his racist language, on the other hand you may feel quite challenged to work with him.

Your main anxieties may come from Michael's lack of co-operation and from concerns about the children's needs being neglected. The long-term consequences of this on their development, together with the impact on Michael of soldiering on heighten your concerns. Michael's anger could be explored to tease out the cause and help him manage it more usefully. Is it due to his wife's exit? Being perceived as an inadequate parent? Professional interference? His feelings of helplessness and his own needs being eclipsed?

Being open and honest with Michael about your concerns for the children is important but tricky. If you are less open you are likely to be disempowering Michael by not sharing the same information about the reasons for your involvement. So the issue is *how* you share your concerns and whether you achieve this in a supportive manner, avoiding being patronising or accusatory.

You might find joint working with a colleague helpful in managing Michael's anger and protecting your own safety.

Arranging a multi-agency case conference might be useful for planning and using resources and offers a chance to share concerns and measure the level against other perspectives. You might find it useful to explore the family's wider network as a possible source of support. Thought also need to be given to the significance for the children of Susan and her absence. You might think about the use of a contract with Michael. This could set out the purposes of involvement and what is possible or not in terms of support, help and resources. It could give Michael space to outline his concerns, need and goals.

As part of the planning work, it might be helpful to list the needs of each child in the family, any concerns, and identify areas of agreement and disagreement between yourself and Michael. You may decide that Michael cannot be worked with and that legal intervention is the only way to secure the children's welfare. If this is the case, it is important that such a judgement is soundly based on evidence from other professionals, research, and only comes after all possibilities for engagement have been explored.

Imagine you have a supervision session arranged with your team leader. Supervision is part of a consultation and thinking process. Explore with your team leader, peer group, tutor or a colleague, some of the issues that have arisen when considering how to work in partnership with service users described above or in practice. This might include managing your own feelings, dilemmas and conflicts. You can also consider the challenges in trying to work in an anti-discriminatory way in partnership with other professionals and colleagues.

Supervision is a good opportunity to explore issues and feelings that you are uncertain or unconfident about. It gives you space and time to think and work through issues raised. You may find the questions below useful in helping you identify areas for further exploration, self-development and awareness:

- What particular dilemmas does partnership present for me?
- What are the advantages and disadvantages of working in partnership with clients?
- Do I find it easy or difficult to be open and honest with service users about my concerns?
- What strategies do I need to develop to handle difficult feelings?

Advocacy

Advocacy is associated with a rights-based approach to planning intervention and arises from recognition that social work has not always empowered service users. It is at its simplest about speaking up for or acting on behalf of another person. The aim of advocacy is to make sure the client's voice is heard; to make sure the person gets the services they need; and to make sure the client knows their rights so they can work towards getting what they are entitled to. It should be part of your integrated practice knowledge and skills.

Key principles:

- The service user's voice and views are paramount.
- Good advocacy leaves the person more able to do it themselves.
- Advocacy should help people to make informed choices.
- Ensuring the user feels in control of the process and trusts the advocate.
- Advising, assisting and supporting – not pressurising or persuading.

It is important to make the distinction between the role of care manager and advocate. The social worker as care manager may be intervening for the needs of the service user in negotiations about services to be provided, but they have also to make judgements about what they think is needed in the client's best interests. Direct payments are an example where budgets can be controlled by service users to select provision, but a social worker still assesses need and makes a judgement about the ability of a person to manage that budget. An advocate on the other hand can maintain their focus on representing the views of the client.

There are three main types of advocacy:

- **Citizen advocacy**: works on a one to one basis where usually volunteers act on behalf of those who require services. The citizen advocate primarily performs an instrumental role which can focus on welfare benefits problems or negotiating a care plan. There is also an expressive role which involves meeting emotional needs, befriending and providing support.
- **Self advocacy**: involves training and group support to help people learn skills and gain emotional strength to advocate for them. It is also about personal and political needs focusing on participation in all areas of service planning and delivery. The aim is not just to improve services but to improve the status of service users. Self advocacy has the important function of facilitating collective action as well as making it easier for individuals to be assertive.
- **Group advocacy**: brings people together with similar interests, so that they can operate as a group to represent their shared interests. Similar to self advocacy, the aim is to influence service delivery decisions and to reframe how certain problems or groups of clients are perceived by professionals. Group advocacy may be part of campaigning organisations operating in the voluntary sector. People with learning difficulties and mental health problems have been in the forefront of group advocacy as they have responded to depersonalised and institutional services failing to meet their needs.

A practical example of advocacy work is in enabling service users to access 'direct payments' with which they can engage in self-care planning. Using a social model theory you could concentrate on identifying the way in which structures and institutions further disable people with disabilities, and then set about challenging these structures. Your accountability to your agency and legal responsibilities will however create a tension in trying to authentically fulfil the requirements for effective advocacy practice enshrined in these points (Bateman, 2000):

- Always act in the client's best interest.
- Always act in accordance with the client's wishes and instructions.
- Keep the client properly informed.
- Carry out instructions with diligence and competence.
- Act impartially and offer frank independent advice.
- Maintain rules of confidentiality.

The skill is in making provision for the person's abilities and circumstances to begin to change as they are released from a disempowered position, rather than continuing to assess them in the here and now. This developmental perspective requires a certain amount of judgement and assumptions about the impact such a liberating intervention could have. It also assumes a degree of support to enable the transition from disempowered to empowered with a tapering of input and the inevitable feelings of dependency.

ACTIVITY 8.4

Think about some recent practice you have been involved in and reflect back on whether there were elements of advocacy in your work, or if not how you might evaluate whether your approach encompasses principles of advocacy.

Commentary

The following questions might be useful in helping decide whether and how you might incorporate an advocacy approach in your social work practice. How do service users have a say in these areas, what is the evidence their contribution is valued, and what helps or hinders advocacy? Look at the following and decide how far and how much service users are involved in these activities:

- Collecting and sharing information.
- Meeting the training needs of staff and service users.
- Policy-making and planning.
- Implementing policy and running the service.

Providing service users with resources to enable them to meet and discuss policy and practice issues is evidence of a genuine effort to engage and facilitate empowering strategies. Training in committee skills is required to help demystify official ways of working unfamiliar to those on the outside of the power system. It is very important to support and sustain people who may falter, feel nervous and appear ready to withdraw at the earliest obstacle to their participation. Try to resist assuming this proves they are not capable, instead build confidence and have a strategy in place to deal with anxieties about competence.

The smallest detail can make a big difference. For example remember to invite a user group to send a representative rather than submit to the temptation to select someone of your choice with whom you feel comfortable. It is probably better to invite more than one person because an individual can easily feel outnumbered in a meeting full of professionals. Two people can support each other and give each other confidence in speaking. It is also important to pay them to attend, and offensive to expect them to attend regularly as the only unpaid people in a roomful of salaried professionals.

Integrated practice

The volume of material to consider when seeking to assess, plan and intervene in social work can often feel overwhelming. The number of central government legislative and practice guidelines, research reports, agency priorities and procedures is awesome. Together with books like this crammed full of information – some of it contradictory, can present you with too many choices. It might make the task of putting it all together seem impossible. However there are some basis principles that can be useful as a quick reference point and a broad guide

within which you can add particular concepts or specialist areas of practice theory and knowledge.

One of these is the foundational qualities of effective helping, which have been identified as (Lishman, 1998):

- genuineness
- warmth
- acceptance
- encouragement
- approval
- empathy
- responsiveness
- sensitivity

Another is to cultivate a professional perspective that locates your practice in an organisational context. This can help make sense of the contradictions and impossible dilemmas that seem to present themselves to you frequently. The contemporary organisational context of social work practice is commented upon as producing a mechanistic, soulless practice that is driven by the demands not of service users but of the bureaucracies we work in and the political process in late capitalist societies. This results in an undermining of your expertise and judgement and a prioritisation of mechanistic practices in assessment work leading to form-filling routinised practices. These are not welcomed by clients or social workers as they disempower people, constrain choices and leave precious room for creative practice.

Political ideologies of the government dictate to a large extent the parameters of professional practice. These dictate the way that decisions are made about resource allocation and funding of health and social care programmes. Your skills in understanding this context to your practice can enable you to find ways of using it to the advantage of your clients. Seeking allies in specific practice interest groups or trades union activity or professional associations can help reduce any isolation you feel and help share strategies for overcoming bureaucratic obstacles to sound ethical practice. Part of the process of understanding the organisational context is to appreciate that resources are finite and boundaries to your practice have to be drawn. The key is whether you can feel satisfied that this is done with your co-operation and contribution consistent with service user participation or whether it is an imposed, artificial limit based on inequitable socially unjust imperatives.

Service user involvement

Integrating your commitment to service user empowerment and participatory practice in a meaningful way rather than a vaguely expressed desire to do something means challenging and reflecting on the way you practice on a daily basis. The difficulty is to ensure that service user involvement becomes a practical and routine activity that is absorbed into the very fabric of your social work practice. One way of helping you navigate through this potentially difficult task is the approach recommended below which uses the four concepts of inclusion, diversity, impact and location (Beresford and Croft, 1992):

- **Inclusion**: participatory ways of working are favoured by service users and groups representing them. This does not mean reducing the role of other stakeholders but adding another element to the process of service improvement. You need to be aware that there are two versions of user involvement. One is the managerialist or consumerist approach that focuses on the service system and obtains service users input to inform provision. The second is a more egalitarian approach that puts service users lives at the centre of the process of involvement. In other words improving service users' lives is what matters most.
- **Diversity**: initiatives for user involvement must challenge rather than mirror prevailing social exclusions and discrimination. They should ensure that people are involved on an equal basis, which means offering particular support to those most marginalised and excluded, or who have difficulty communicating in writing or verbally. This means making sure that proper access and enough

support is available to enable everybody to contribute.
- **Impact**: enabling service user involvement in the design, delivery and monitoring of services is of little help unless there is a demonstrable difference to the lives of service users. The most effective basis for service user involvement is the provision of adequate and secure resources for independent user controlled organisations. More democratic and empowering approaches to participation are required that change the balance of power so that service users are directly involved in the decision-making process.
- **Location**: service user organisations have begun to prioritise areas where they feel they can make the most difference. These include professional practice where service users are involved in discussion and negotiation that influences practice development. Training is another area where service users can be involved directly with students on pre- and post-qualifying courses, the design of curricula, and assessment of student practice. Involvement in policy development can be another way whereby service users' views can be collated and integrated into policy formulation. Finally, service users have much to offer in terms of research, evaluation and monitoring of service provision. But this means challenging the prevailing orthodoxy in research methodologies and the hierarchy of knowledge and the evidence base so that users' views are afforded equal status.

Recording and record keeping

Recording and record keeping are probably the least addressed task faced by social workers in whatever practice context yet they consistently appear in critical comments from joint inspections and public enquiries into deaths of clients. They can be perceived as routine mundane tasks and afforded little priority in the busy schedule of most practitioners. Yet they are a potentially rich source of information not just for the sake of recording facts but for their analytical and interpretative value.

Training manuals and staff development opportunities will emphasise the importance of accuracy in case recording and you will be advised to distinguish facts from opinion. Access to files for service users in the Data Protection Act 1984 and the Access to Personal Files Act 1990 provide a powerful incentive to make sure that what you commit to official records can be justified by evidence and open to scrutiny. In the spirit of partnership practice you should be routinely offering clients opportunities to witness what you have written about them and enabling their perceptions, comments and disagreements to be recorded equally.

However the conclusion is still that recording is a bureaucratic exercise designed to meet service specifications or agency requirements. Ostensibly they are expected to be clear, precise and understandable to a range of people including other agency staff, managers, and service users. In practice case notes can be either so brief and perfunctory or so long and meandering to be both lacking in utility and satisfying no-one. Depending on your practice context you might be encouraged to more or less record client contact and decisions or record process interviews for therapeutic evaluation of the casework relationship. The optimum is to incorporate both so that service user records can be accessed by others in order to maintain continuity, measure your intervention progress and evaluate the effectiveness of your work.

The value in this activity is that clients can feel a real sense of empowerment if you facilitate access in terms of their rights to examine files kept on them, rather than conveying a sense of reluctance and unimportance. Records can be an incredibly important documentation of a young person's life story that will at some stage in their life prove invaluable as they look back to make sense of circumstances and events. Great care should therefore be taken to ensure that material is accurate and contains positive as well as negative information (Macdonald, 1999).

Endings, closure and doubt

While there are a multitude of books in social work and health care on the subject of loss and bereavement, there is a contrasting dearth of literature on the subject of case closure and the ending of social work input. It is important in the context of assessment and intervention practice that you have an awareness of the potency of ending contact with a service user and the range of feelings generated at this crucial time. Understanding these feelings of loss can help your future practice as well as the current issues for your client. For example you might have planned to end contact at a point in time or after completion of certain tasks, yet find events take over and thwart your planning.

This can be the result of workload management decisions, service user choice, resource limitations, you or the client leaving the area, or other agency influences. Each reason for premature or planned ending can bring a variety of feelings and issues to the surface. Proper reflective attention to these can be helpful in terms of developing professional practice as well as offering service users a platform to express frustration, anger, happiness or confusion. You may feel guilty about leaving a client or placing them in residential care despite having a rational, evidence-based justification. Feelings of uncertainty and confusion are not weakness and shedding a tear is not unprofessional. These are quite normal and better out than in – especially in a supervisory context where they can be processed in a supportive way. A model of ending incorporating the following elements is suggested (Coulshed, 1991):

- A discussion in the first meeting that help will not go on for ever.
- Use the experience of ending to confirm what the client has gained.
- Employ a fixed time limit where possible.
- Giving the client certain objectives to achieve in the ending phase of work.
- Explore a person's feelings about the forthcoming ending.
- Introduce a new worker and facilitate expressions of anger or resentment.
- Help the person construct a natural helping network within their community.
- Explore your own feelings and show the client they will be remembered.

- In some contexts a ritual ending and exchange of gifts might be appropriate.
- Write a closing record together.

Chapter summary

In this chapter we have considered how to plan intervention on the basis of the assessment you have conducted and how to integrate knowledge, skills and values. We also paid attention to considering how to demonstrate how an assessment leads to a set of concrete objectives for intervention. Working in partnership to negotiate and plan responses to assessed needs, risks, responsibilities, strengths and resources should form a significant part of the process of integration.

Working in partnership to negotiate and plan responses has been discussed in order to identify and utilise strengths and resources of service users. Planning intervention in social work and the decision-making process includes thinking and feeling about the situation being addressed. But there is debate about whether intuitive or analytical thought is more suited to social work decisions. A contrast between these two distinct forms of thinking is drawn in the social work literature with the tendency to favour intuitive rather than analytical thinking, rejecting the latter as a technical, calculative approach not in harmony with social work values.

We argued that one of the key characteristics of contemporary social work services is the partnership approach to work with service users. This is enshrined in practice guidance and codes of ethics. It involves a process of negotiation with families about the venue for work, and the choice of practice methods particularly during the assessment process. It is important to make distinctions about the different levels of partnership possible in your intervention as you begin to integrate your practice.

Interprofessional or multi disciplinary care are contemporary terms often used synonymously to mean joint working between staff from different professional backgrounds. Staff may work in the same team location or operate from separate uni-professional teams. Within the same agency they may represent different disciplines or client groups. In whatever configuration joint working has always been recommended as the best way of delivering coherent and effective care in health and social work practice.

We acknowledged that integrating your commitment to service user empowerment and participatory practice in a meaningful way rather than a vaguely expressed desire to do something, means challenging and reflecting on the way you practice on a daily basis. The difficulty is to ensure that service user involvement becomes a practical and routine activity that is absorbed into the very fabric of your social work practice. We have examined the skills and resources necessary for effective decision-making in the context of inter-agency working, considered the role of advocacy as an empowering approach, and concluded with a discussion of the process of change and the implications for each stakeholder in the change process.

CHAPTER 9

Evaluation and Evidence-based Practice

Introduction

The importance of evaluation and the evidence base that informs our practice cannot be overstated. It has now been given extra weight in the context of health and social care service delivery with the creation of the National Institute for Clinical Excellence and the Social Care Institute for Excellence. Both aspire to drive the government's agenda for modernisation of local government and health and welfare services, leading to better efficiency and effectiveness. In practical terms you may seek to draw upon research evidence in order to inform the decision-making process during assessment and intervention. For example, you may seek to understand more about the effects of long-term residential care on young people to argue in favour of placing a child in foster care or for adoption. Or you may need to argue for the removal of a child from an abusing parent on the basis of evidence of the risks and consequences of abuse. More than ever before you are going to have to base your judgements on the best available evidence combined with sound theoretical principles.

Considering the idea of evaluating social work can take us into several different areas of exploration. One is the methodological arena where debate and discussion centre around what form the evaluation should take – typically revolving around arguments about the merits of quantitative and qualitative evaluative methods. Social workers are caricatured as obsessed with the qualitative methodologies, preferring to hear the voice of the service user and regarding statistical quantitative research as unfeeling and mechanistic. You may indeed have an aversion to mathematical techniques and research employing what appear to be obscure methodologies for presenting significant data. However you will find that both complement each other and power is added to the weight of your arguments that are based on such mixed research. Hard facts about gaps in service provision or the needs of certain clients can be brought to life with personal testimony and verbatim comments derived from qualitative research with real people.

Another area of interest might be to define what we mean by evaluation, and discuss whether this is an appropriate use of our time. Different methods of evaluation require different evidence and therefore produce different results – even though they are examining the same thing. There can be a sense that research is done by academics that have the time, resources and motivation whereas practitioners have no time for such activity but depend on the results to help inform practice. This feeds the artificial divide between research and practice and fosters resentment and frustration in equal measures for all concerned. Nevertheless attempts to bridge this gap and present research in meaningful and accessible ways to busy social workers continue, so that influence can be achieved at various levels from the ground level of practice to the strategic policy level.

We might consider the question of the usefulness of evaluation – what is it for and how will it be used? Here there are a raft of issues connected to the use of resources and in the public sector the inevitable constraints on resources employed in the service of social work clients. As a busy practitioner you might wonder what the point of evaluation is if it does not lead to more resources or enable the conclusions of the evaluation to be put into effect. You might cynically feel that evaluation is invariably going to lead to disruption in working practices and further disempowers you and the service users to whom you personally feel accountable. Are measures used by evaluators practical or relevant to your social work practice for instance?

Many are based on audit and clinical outcome measurement designed for clinical controlled environments, rather than the messy, sometimes chaotic and uncertain environment of our clients. It is also useful to consider what we mean by social work when seeking to evaluate it. This might seem a redundant question if we consider the variety of tasks, processes and factors involved in work with a family, group or single client that all go into the casework file. We might wonder whether it is possible or even feasible to consider measuring and quantifying something as ephemeral as social work. Isolating the myriad of factors influencing a family from beginning of work to case closure, and seeking to identify those that can be proven to have made the most effective impact is a challenge. Much research activity is focused on the outcomes of particular interventions. Two ways of categorising outcomes can be considered (Cheetham et al., 1992):

■ **Service based outcomes**: outcomes of a particular service to identify the nature, extent, and quality of what is provided.
■ **Client based outcomes**: outcomes for service users to identify the effects of a particular provision on its recipients.

So perhaps it is better to think about how the concept of evaluation can be introduced into working practices as a way of bolstering reflective practice and professional development

to the benefit of our service users. This chapter therefore aims to demonstrate how evaluation can be useful, practical and meaningful to the busy social work practitioner.

Evaluation involves the collection, analysis and interpretation of data bearing on the individual's or organisation's goals and programme objectives. Evaluation usually attempts to measure the extent to which certain outcomes can be correlated with inputs. These quantifiable indicators of performance can provide evidence of the extent to which specified targets are being met. The culture of evaluation in public services became prominent in the last decades of the 20th century as social and economic changes introduced privatised services, welfare cutbacks, and a mixed economy of care in which recipients of services were misleadingly defined as consumers.

In attempting to match resources and services to service users' expectations and perceived needs, social workers are faced with increasing and more complex demands to improve efficiency and effectiveness. Central to all this is the concept of quality assurance which demands a commitment to the pursuit of a high standard of services. Policy statements setting out performance indicators in all areas of social work practice stress the essential role of monitoring and evaluation. You need to know what these terms mean, how they are used, and how you can engage positively with them.

Types of evaluation

It is a useful start to think about evaluation and distinguishing between subjective and objective approaches. Subjective evaluation concentrates on gauging how clients have experienced what you and your agency have offered them. Objective evaluation involves identifying particular objectives in the work and then deciding whether or not these have been achieved.

ACTIVITY 9.1

Imagine that your agency has been criticised for the way it evaluates its services. Your job is to devise a more explicit way of doing this. You are about to make a brief presentation of your initial thoughts on how evaluation might be improved. Think about how you might use subjective and objective evaluation in your work.

Commentary

Subjective evaluation could be carried out either through discussion or through some form of questionnaire, either in the company of a social worker or not. Or you might also wish to think about how, in devising a questionnaire, you could focus on partnership and empowerment by:

■ Asking specific questions on degree of involvement, for example whether the client felt they were properly listened to.
■ Working together with the service user to make sure the questionnaire reflected their agenda.
■ Looking at whether the outcome of intervention was satisfactory, and if not how it could be done differently.
■ Tackling issues of power and discrimination such as asking particular questions related to the service user's needs as a black person, lesbian or gay, woman or someone with a disability.

With objective evaluation your objectives will depend on your particular work setting. The important point is that they are clearly measurable such as:

■ Removal from the child protection register, or return home.
■ A young person finding accommodation or a job.
■ Finding an adoptive family.
■ Maintaining an older person in their own home.
■ Improving a child's school attendance.
■ Helping a person avoid readmission to psychiatric hospital.

Central to the ideas of efficiency and effectiveness within evaluation is the concept of quality assurance. Judgements as to whether

services are up to the standard expected have traditionally been based on whether the right amount of care was being provided rather than the quality of care. The question 'Are we doing things right?' has been supplemented by the question 'Are we doing the right things?' Below are some of the approaches to determining the quality of care.

Inspection

Since the NHS and Community Care Act 1990 inspection units were created within social service departments separate from the day to day management function of monitoring residential provision. Currently a new system of inspection is being inaugurated which completely separates inspection from those providing residential care. Apart from the physical environment in these homes inspectors should elicit the views of residents and staff. The limitations of this approach are:

■ In depth understanding is constrained due to the volume of work to be carried out and the limited contact with everyone concerned.
■ It is difficult to be objective when you are working for the same authority responsible for running the home.
■ Inspectors will invariably come with their own perceptions and values and may not be able to involve service users or staff as fully as they should.

Reviews

The idea of a review is that an organisation should prepare its plans on a regular basis and that progress towards the achievement of objectives and targets set out in those plans should be subjected to scrutiny. These plans are submitted to central government in accordance with guidelines laid down as part of overall strategic planning. This macro level has its parallel with the micro level of your work with clients. The limitations of reviews are:

■ Organisational reviews relate to whether the plan is being conformed to usually in terms of budget and efficiency. These issues can take precedence over questions of appropriateness and acceptability.

■ Service user representatives may be consulted during the process of devising plans but they are primarily the domain of senior management staff.

■ The views and expectations of field staff, carers and clients, are not paramount despite rhetoric in mission statements avowing to empower users.

Performance assessment

Central government has begun to issue guidance in the form of national comparative data from many local authorities and social care organisations to judge particular aspects of performance. The white paper *Modernising Social Services* (DoH, 1999) set out new arrangements to assess the performance of each council within the wider Best Value regime that requires local authorities to achieve improved cost effectiveness. These have been translated into targets for services to attain – for example the number of children on the child protection register, or the number of home care organisers per head of population. Local authorities are awarded star ratings on a range of performance measures. This framework is designed to improve services that people receive by:

■ Helping councils develop their own performance management arrangements.

■ Ensuring that corporate management and political scrutiny promotes better social services that contribute to community wellbeing.

■ Ensuring that councils work effectively with the NHS to address joint health and social care policy and service delivery issues.

■ Assessing councils' progress in implementing government policies for social care.

■ Identifying and promoting best practice.

■ Identifying councils that are performing poorly and ensuring they take action to improve.

They are criticised as crude measures that do not adequately reflect the individual characteristics of different parts of the country, and the levels of need within them. Little account seems to be taken of the differences and distinctions between inner city deprived neighbourhoods, leafy suburbs, or remote rural communities. These misleading measures do not adequately reflect subtle changes and improvements that might disproportionately impact on the quality of service user's lives but do not show up in broad statistical data. The issue of resources is notably absent from the above list. Their limitations are:

■ Although they aim to improve standards of care the preparation of performance indicators does not involve the intended beneficiaries.

■ Their quantitative nature stresses procedures and outcomes rather than effectiveness and acceptability.

■ Their compilation presupposes that local authorities have uniform, accurate, and comprehensive comparable information systems.

■ They take little account of variations in the priority given by different authorities to aspects of their care services.

Some of the key indicators used to measure performance include:

■ Information on education, employment and training for care leavers.

■ Placement stability for looked after children in the short term and longer term.

■ The percentage of children looked after in foster placements or placed for adoption.

■ The percentage of children on the child protection registers.

Satisfaction surveys

The collection of qualitative, highly personal data offers another perspective on the issue of service planning and evaluation of provision. Asking clients what they think of current services seems straightforward, and there are procedures publicised that offer the public an avenue to pursue grievances or register compliments. However satisfaction surveys cannot counterbalance the organisations' attempts to determine performance. The danger is that the act of conducting a survey can be seen as an end in itself. Unless such surveys are backed up with action plans and a set of measurable improvements based on them they can end up being viewed as at best tokenistic and at worse deeply patronising. Further limitations are:

- They often assume that the person asked has knowledge of alternative provision.
- Satisfaction may not tell much about the quality of the service since the client may be starting from a low expectation.
- Data derived from questionnaires is limited when alternatives such as case studies, personal diaries or group interviews could yield richer information.

How to evaluate

Many social workers tend to avoid evaluation or to interpret it in such a way that it comes to mean a brief retrospective review of a piece of work or an initiative. You may also hold the view that your agency has to collect so much performance-related information for the government that anything that appears to detract from work with service users and your primary responsibilities has to be avoided. However, accountable practice demands that public services need to justify what they do and find useful ways of demonstrating this.

An action evaluation model has been developed in Bradford (Fawcett, 2000) which is based on a partnership between the University, Social Services Department, and the Health Trust aimed at demystifying the evaluation process and providing staff with the tools and support to conduct evaluations. Action evaluations take place in the workplace, and focus on areas viewed as important by those involved with the findings feeding into the services being studied. These are the main characteristics:

- **Outline the current situation**: collect baseline information and establish the service's overall aims and objectives. This can

include quantitative data such as the numbers using a service, and qualitative data such as details of service users' experiences.

- **Specify available resources, overall aim and objectives**: any project or initiative is likely to have a number of objectives but it is important to be specific about them and what the broad overall purpose of the activity is.
- **Link goals to specific objectives**: identifying the desired outcomes or goals enable you to work backwards through any intermediary stages in the process. This helps to provide progress indicators and how goals can be achieved.
- **Detail why the agreed objectives and goals were decided upon**: no evaluation goes strictly according to plan therefore it is important to record how goals were established. A record needs to be kept of the reasoning behind the aims, and any deviation clearly stated and made transparent. This information needs to be easily retrievable so it can be used to explain why goals have changed.
- **Monitor and review the activity**: information from all stakeholders can be collated including recommendations for changing or improving the service. Activity related to goals can be appraised, and evidence of progress summarised. It is important to document how and why progress was made and what obstacles were encountered. This data can be fed back to service purchasers and planners reflecting an inclusive, bottom-up approach to evaluation.

ACTIVITY 9.2

Locate the latest evaluation of your service from your manager or the research and information section of your agency. See whether you can work out the methodology employed and whether the results have or have not influenced working practices.

Evaluating in practice

Reviews of the literature on empirical evaluations of family support, provide evidence of the problematic nature of evaluation in this core area of social work activity. Family support constitutes a great deal of social work practice whether it is in the context of work with children and families, elderly people or people with mental health problems. The studies demonstrate that services yielded mixed results and acknowledged that natural, developmental changes have the potential to be mistakenly attributed to effects due to the service. Intervention programmes tend to focus on a single outcome as a measure of success such as changes in a child's behaviour. Taking into account other dimensions such as improved parent/child interactions or better use of community resources could be more useful (Rossi, 1992; Gardner, 1998; Franklin and Madge, 2000).

Effectiveness studies have tended to neglect the views of service users and especially children as independent evaluators (Kent and Read, 1998; Laws et al., 1999). Equally, in studies attempting to validate service user evaluation, a trend towards positive bias has been identified in child and adolescent services particularly where treatment is continuing (Polowczyk, 1993). Social workers seeking to measure or gauge the impact of their work face a difficult challenge particularly in the context of the drive to evidence-based practice. Traditional scientific research based methods are usually beyond the capacity of field social workers who are just about managing their caseloads and the day to day administration involved.

Even some of the most well-resourced professionals with time and advanced research skills cannot lay claim to levels of efficacy when there are so many variables affecting the outcomes for people with complex problems. The traditional randomised control trial may not provide a comprehensive assessment of outcome or represent accurately what actually happens in practice (Barton, 1999). This is considered to be the required standard for evaluating a specific treatment or intervention by randomly allocating the intervention to half a group of clients. The results of the intervention with this group are compared to the results of those who received no treatment or a different type. Ethical questions are raised in the case of people in distress and the withholding of potentially beneficial intervention. However without getting bogged down in methodological quandaries or inhibiting yourself from participating in valid research, you can incorporate the concepts of effectiveness and evaluation in ways consistent with your professional ethics and values and in the best interests of your clients.

The social work dilemma

In a climate of public sector financial constraints that impose strict guidelines on the use of resources and requiring demonstrable outcomes for practice, social workers are invariably pulled in different directions. On the one hand there are the familiar overtures to work systematically in a focused manner within budget limits, while on the other hand there are highly vulnerable dependent clients who we are told should have needs-led services. This implies that there is no conflict between resource limitations and service user needs, when of course there is. Experienced staff knows that in some cases long-term support is the only option for some of the most damaged and disadvantaged clients, yet service managers impose artificial limits to the length of time spent on these cases.

We all know that a case closed prematurely will likely reappear in due course and probably be much harder to work. This is particularly the case when clients have experienced losses, neglect and lack of care in their history which are being reproduced in their relationship with their social worker. Finding a way out of this dilemma is one of the modern challenges to professional ethical practice. The task is all the harder because there is not a reliable robust evidence base to call upon to justify a particular plan of intervention. Social workers seeking evidence-based practice using therapeutic skills and techniques will find the literature on evaluation in this field is rather less than helpful.

There is for example a historical legacy of reluctance among psychotherapists to employ quantitative empirical methods to investigate the effectiveness of their practice. This is partly because therapists have tended to prefer demonstrating results using case study descriptions to support their particular theoretical model. It is also because they have not been trained in these methodologies and are more comfortable with the qualitative research that emphasises the more intangible elements of the subtle processes at work during the therapeutic experience (Target, 1998; Cowie, 1999). If you are trying to implement therapeutic work with a service user this makes it harder to justify your approach. The question of reliability and validity of the research methodology has a bearing on the status of the therapeutic effectiveness.

Reliability chiefly is about whether the same person was assessed on a different day or location, or by another researcher, the result would be similar or different. Validity refers to whether the research is telling you what you think it is – in other words whether what a service users says about how they are, is accurate. These concepts of reliability and validity matter because of the tendency of quantitative research to interpret and generalise from the findings, thereby influencing choice of treatment or intervention. Research is used to justify investment in social work organisation and methods with practitioners left feeling buffeted by changes imposed on their practice and cynical about the underlying rationale.

It is not hard to understand that social work practitioners trained to take account of the social and environmental context of service users lives, also use this to take account of the financial pressures influencing their practice. These pressures are not based on rational evidence-based research methods about effective interventions but on resource constraints. This is the heart of our dilemma in contemporary social work – how to deliver effective services within artificial limits to practice. But rather than descend into brutal cynicism or negative practice we can learn to use the principles of evaluation and effectiveness to our and our clients' advantage. There are ways of using the available research evidence base and combining it with partici-

patory partnership practice to ensure that the arguments for better quality resources and cost effectiveness are articulated.

The old adage about prevention being better than cure has a weight and enduring simplicity that can resonate in the minds of service managers or budget controllers. It is almost impossible to prove that a certain intervention definitely prevented something else from happening, but governments and social policy experts have generated expensive intervention programmes on this basis. For example the multi-million pound Sure Start programme launched early in this century was based on the untested assumption that such a huge programme would prevent later anti-social, educational, and health problems in the future with a generation of disadvantaged children. It is therefore part of received wisdom that investment of this nature helps.

Reflective and reflexive practice

Contemporary social work literature contains references to reflective practice as well as reflexive practice and it would be unsurprising if practitioners were confused by these terms. They are close in spelling, sound and in meaning but are actually different. They are important because they are linked closely to the concept of evaluation and how to move forward in professional practice from the dilemmas described above. Reflective practice was first considered as early as the 1930s as an active persistent and careful consideration of any belief or supposed form of knowledge in the light of the grounds that support it and the further conclusions to which it tends. This definition was applied to the context of professional practice by later writers who argued that reflective practice consisted of reflection in action or thinking while doing, and reflection on action which occurs after an incident takes place. Reflective practice therefore encompasses the need for a useful outcome to the reflective process that will lead to a change in practice.

Reflection in assessment and intervention practice is crucial because of the need for you to make sense of a lot of information – written, verbal, emotional, including the impact your own working practices on service users and other people connected to them. Reflective practice is the antithesis of standardised routine practice prescribed by increasingly bureaucratic organisations. It is essential that you maintain a critical, independent stance that enables you to respond pro-actively to diverse situations and meet professional standards of practice because of (Smale et al., 2000):

■ The often complex conflicts of interest involved in the nature of social problems.
■ The unique mix of skills, resources, experience, strengths, weaknesses and gaps involved, particularly where some people's behaviour is defined as 'the problem'.
■ The need to understand and unravel the complexities of relationships that perpetuate social problems through self-defeating strategies and mutually defeating interactions: the need for maintenance of the marginal position of the worker.
■ The frequent necessity for an 'exchange model' of relationship to achieve effective and lasting change.
■ The risk that procedures, guidelines, the worker's own behaviour and that of their organisation can contribute to and perpetuate the problems which the worker is intending to resolve.
■ The need to identify and respond to unintended and unforeseen consequences of social interventions.

Reflexive practice is derived from the term reflexivity which gained currency in contemporary debates about the need to conduct research that did not depend on notions of universality and objectivity in social research. Reflexivity is recommended as a critical practice for social research and social work practice that flows from it (Alvesson and Skoldberg, 2000; Pels, 2000). Critical practice is regarded as a challenge to the orthodoxy and contested notions of realism. These debates are connected to broader discussion of the merits of post-modernism which try to consider the best ways of finding out the effects and impact

that social work practices have in new ways that challenge the classic models of quantitative research (May, 2002; Walker, 2001). In this context reflexive practice means that you can embrace evaluation from a sceptical position about reality and certainty, whilst working hard to ensure the process of evaluation is culturally competent and conscious of the power relationships between service user and social worker.

Reflexivity suggests that we interrogate previously taken for granted assumptions, it contends that knowledge does not have fixed stable meanings but that it is made rather than revealed thanks to research effort (Taylor and White, 2000). Empowering social work practice can be described and defined as we try to do in this book but actually explaining how it is applied in practice requires reflexivity. Reflective practice assumes that you can become more skilled at applying child developmental theories to your practice for example, whereas reflexivity takes this further and questions whether this is possible.

These debates may seem obscure or irrelevant to your practice, but they find expression in practical ways that have a large impact on the type of social work you can do. The increasing emphasis in strategic planning, government guidance and occupational standards is, as we have noted elsewhere in this book, on risk assessment, risk analysis or risk management. These can be considered as a reaction to the post-modern project of deconstructing orthodox theories and rejecting expert discourses with uncertainty and multiple explanations for social phenomena. It is possible to suggest that the resulting anxiety and lack of guidance naturally produce attempts by organisations and individuals to exert control and authority (Parton, 1994; Dean, 1997). Anxiety can flourish where there is an intellectual vacuum or no eligibility criteria for your service, procedure manuals, mission statements or assessment matrixes to signpost your interventions.

Without these anchors of stability in the turmoil of clients sometimes chaotic, disorganised, and painful lives, you may feel more overwhelmed or driven by the meandering directionless process of a service user's family process. However, if you are sceptical about risk assessment and understand the limitations of contemporary evaluation practice, how can you begin to scrutinise your practice in ways that satisfy intellectual as well as ethical considerations? An empowering and emancipatory social work practice that liberates both client and worker from their mutually helpless positions combined with inner self-knowledge is a powerful prospect. This offers a practical and achievable solution to the dilemmas described above whilst preserving the heart of the value base of social work practice.

ACTIVITY 9.3

Spend a few minutes reflecting on what you have read so far in this chapter. Now begin to jot down some notes to begin to construct an integrated model of evaluation that embraces methodological rigour with the value base of social work.

Commentary

An integrated evaluative model of social work prioritises the task of understanding the experience of the service user whilst preserving the importance of explanatory power in a context of a plurality of social interpretations that embrace a range of explanations. Within this model discriminatory processes can be exposed and resisted while participatory and partnership approaches given legitimacy. It also reminds us of the crucial importance of supervision and the capacity to gain insight into our own feelings and reactions to the distressing circumstances of our clients. Not the supervision of administrative management but the much more valuable supervision based on the psycho-social mandate of social work practitioners that links the inner with the outer worlds. Its characteristics are:

■ Offers a both/and rather than either/or position.

■ Conserves what is useful and practical.
■ Tolerates inconsistency and the messiness of lived experience.
■ Bears uncertainty and challenges complacency.
■ Accepts that change is continuous while research is static.

The sheer range and quantity of research material available and, thanks to the internet, quickly accessible, is both a blessing and a curse. It is a testimony to the desire of professionals to seek answers to important questions and to find the best way of helping service users. Nobody wants to miss the chance to work more effectively and to the highest possible standard. However the consequence of such a wealth of evidence is that you may find you only have time to concentrate on what is called propositional and process knowledge. The first relates to substantive knowledge related to a discrete area of work, the second relates to material intended to promote skill development (Eraut, 1994). Both can restrict your vision whilst appearing to offer certainty and exactness in specialist areas of work.

One of the dangers in having an uncritical view of evidence-based practice is that you are put in the position of a technician whose task is to apply knowledge created elsewhere rather than in assessing its suitability, relevance and utility in particular practice situations (Taylor and White, 2000). Practitioners often lament the way theory is neatly described and fluently illustrated in social work text books when they contrast this with the imperfection and messiness of daily practice. The gap between theory and practice can feel extremely wide with the consequence that you might be tempted to describe your practice as eclectic, when in fact it is some way from the proper definition of a conscious choice in the selection of methods of work. This can be the case when you feel that your practice is being driven by a reaction to events rather than directed by a planned course of action.

Evaluation and the evidence base

We have examined how different methods of evaluation can produce different types of evidence, and proponents of particular methodologies vigorously advocate the merits of their approach. We might find an agnostic position helps in this situation. In other words remain sceptical of all who claim superiority or privilege for a particular evaluation model. Another way of conceptualising this is to value all contributions to the debate about validity and reliability in research findings. An open approach to methodology is recommended (Fuller, 1996). Perhaps the most useful attitude to adopt is that of a flexible, inquisitive mind on this subject, rather than become wedded to a particular methodology and ruling anything else out. The evidence suggests there is no certainty in any of them and if you are consistent in your client-centred social work practice, then you will strive to find the evidence that best meets your clients' needs and optimises the opportunities for empowering practice.

The key in all of this is to satisfy yourself that you have competently examined the available evidence that can support your choice of intervention. This is good professional practice and will be required in complex work involving legal proceedings where your work will be scrutinised, for example. It will also be helpful in supervision where your actions can be justified and where some degree of planning is essential. As we noted earlier, this is also where you can properly hypothesise about the expected outcomes to intervention and the probability of such outcomes occurring. However, working with service users places all of these aspirations in a context where despite the evidence and your advocacy of a particular intervention, the client may not co-operate. As we are often reminded, we then have to adapt, negotiate and compromise within the helping relationship that is the bedrock of psycho-social practice (Frost, 2002).

A creative evaluation practice that seeks to be empowering for you and your clients is one that puts the service user at the centre of the process. This means abandoning the illusion of expert-led evaluation or at least putting it into perspective. Clients can be brought into the evaluation process and indeed enabled to undertake the evaluation themselves with you acting as facilitator. This probably requires more initial effort in terms of training, and support but has long-term benefits in terms of producing more authentic results that reflect the agenda of service users themselves rather than a management or bureaucratic exercise in rationing and restricting access to services. Establishing clear and effective liaison is the means to ensuring people are informed and able to contribute more effectively.

Methods of evaluation should be adapted to the size and nature of the organisation or service being evaluated. Often a mixture of quantitative and qualitative methods can produce breadth and richness in the data. As many stakeholders as possible need to be involved or at least invited to participate in the proposed evaluation. Bringing as many people in at the planning stage is not only evidence of an inclusive approach but it can provide talent, resources and skills previously hidden because of the restrictions imposed by prescribed roles. Dissemination of the conclusions of an evaluation is a crucial part of the process. Reports can be spread widely and published as papers or parts of academic books, or they can be restricted to managers and key decision-makers. A creative practice requires you to ensure that results are used by service users to impact upon policy and practice as part of critical reflective practice (Frost, 2002)

Thus the relationship between the evidence base and social work practice is not as straightforward as some would propose. The task is to fashion an evaluation methodology that can manage some of the contradictions and dilemmas we have already identified without permitting these to impede your progress towards identifying an informed basis for your actions. In recent years considerable effort has been made by researchers to overcome the obstacles to identifying good practice in social work. The following is a selection of work we can use to illustrate how evaluation can inform practice without prejudicing your commitment to client-centred empowering practice.

Research methods

The following are a sample of research methods that could be employed in social work contexts.

This is not an exhaustive list but they are included to give you an impression of the common formats you might encounter in your work, or in the literature that seeks to inform your practice. It is very important therefore that you understand the way research is organised and the limitations of various designs (Macdonald and Roberts, 1995):

- **Randomised controlled trials**: as mentioned above the randomised controlled trial (RCT), is the method favoured particularly in medical and clinical situations where a high degree of control can be used to try to minimise bias or reliability. By randomly allocating a procedure or intervention the chances of introducing bias into the selection of service users to receive the intervention is reduced. Other external sources of bias such as age, gender, class are discounted by this method because these factors will be equally affecting those clients receiving the intervention and those who are not. However, the RCT cannot help when interpretation of the results occurs because the specific intervention could be affected by other factors such as the characteristics of the practitioner. Or in the case of a group intervention any differences could be due to the specific dynamics of a particular group – however randomly constructed.

- **Quasi-experimental study**: ethical considerations and other factors may mean it is not practical or desirable to evaluate effectiveness by denying one client group a service received by another through a RCT. In order to try to measure the impact of a new or different intervention it is crucial however to try to ensure that alternatives are designed, analysed and interpreted in ways that maximise our knowledge of what works. A common way of doing this is to arrange a study that has the benefit of a control group of service users who continue to receive the standard intervention to a problem, but to compare them with a similar group who receive a new intervention.

- **Non-experimental study**: research designs within this category are evaluated interventions but without a random allocation or any matching of groups for comparative purposes. Results based on studies using these designs are considered to be suggestive rather than conclusive. They can be used as indicators of where further evaluative research might be useful, or when combined with several studies with similar results, their significance can be enhanced.

- **Client opinion study**: these provide valuable information and insights into how service users experience interventions. They offer opportunities to listen to the clients' opinion and perceptions of service provision, what effects and outcomes are produced, and what impact your work has had on service user's behaviour or patterns of change. Social workers will feel a natural attraction to this form of evaluation as it fits with client-centred practices and advocacy and empowerment concepts. Recent research into service user opinion consistently demonstrates appreciation of social work support but equally consistently rarely shows clients understand what social workers are attempting to achieve and how they expect to do it.

- **Survey**: this is an important research method that while it may not enable evaluation of practice effectiveness does provide valuable data about the prevalence of particular phenomena. The value of this type of research is that it can mitigate the effects of our assumptions about service user groups we work with constantly. They can be a safeguard against stereotyping and routine practices derived from failing to notice changes in client populations. In social work, quantitative surveys of large or discrete populations can remind us of the existence of clients who despite negative indicators of child abuse, risk, or anti-social problems, nevertheless do not become delinquent or damage themselves or their children. They can remind us that it is as important to understand why some people manage to survive personal problems compared to similar people who suffer repetitive crises. Surveys are also useful in attempts to measure the impact of policy initiatives.

■ **Cohort study**: this is another sort of survey in which it can be possible to identify factors that have a demonstrable effect. They are especially valuable in determining which kinds of preventive activity are more likely to produce a beneficial effect. Health and social data can be collected from a group or cohort of older people, mentally ill people or children sharing similar characteristics. The research then tracks these people and at regular intervals collects data from them over time. Cohort studies can give some indication of the effects of new social policies introduced by government with the intention of improving service user's lives in some way. They can also permit some predictions about likely problems and challenges to be faced by other service user groups.

What works in practice?

We reviewed some findings related to practice interventions in Chapter 2 to indicate the potential for your selection of practice based on certain theoretical assumptions. Now we can take this further by examining some of the most recent evidence about effectiveness in a selection of practice contexts. It is important to acknowledge that often these individual methods and approaches take place in a context of other variables very likely to affect the process and outcome of the work. Most research studies acknowledge these limitations to their findings but this should not detract from examining them and adapting them to your particular practice context. These are intended as an indicative resource to help guide your choice of working practice in child care within your agency resource constraints (Reimers and Treacher, 1995; Macdonald and Roberts, 1995; Alderson et al., 1996; Beresford et al., 1996).

Behavioural and cognitive-behavioural ways of working with clients where child abuse has occurred or is at risk offer the most convincing evidence of effectiveness. In particular parent training programmes that endeavour to improve parents' capacity to manage and understand their children's behaviour generally show positive results. The following strategies are at the heart of most parent training programmes:

■ Emphasising the importance of the maintenance of ground rules and boundaries of acceptable family behaviour, so that children have a growing appreciation of a plan against which to assess their own behaviour.
■ Helping parents to gain an understanding of what they can expect from their children in order to acquire a reasonable level of awareness.
■ Teaching parents to give clear, rather than mixed messages to their children.
■ Training in managing children's behaviour with appropriate rewards for reinforcing desired behaviour and strategies for dealing with unwanted behaviour.

Anger control is a strategy aimed at preventing parents reaching the point where a cycle of poor interaction escalates to a point where anger is expressed violently and physically against a child. It is based on cognitive-behavioural work aiming to:

■ Teach the parent when to identify the early signs of their levels of anger building, and the typical scenarios where it is more likely to get out of control. The key is to teach recognition and prediction of events before they begin to develop.
■ Teaching the parent once they have achieved recognition to learn alternative strategies and coping mechanisms such as for example, engaging in an alternative activity, learning to relax by deep breathing, or changing the way they think about the situation.

Multi-systemic family therapy based on classic systems thinking combined with cognitive-behavioural techniques evidences statistically significant improvement in parent mental health problems, overall stress, and the severity of identified problems in cases of child abuse and neglect. Family therapy in general has its appeal for social workers who are often expected to work with families where children have been identified as in need or on the child protection register. As with much work with children and families in general it is hard to locate methodologically robust meta-analyses that meet the criteria to offer definitive conclusions on effectiveness. In particular studies reflecting service users' perceptions are still too rare in the research literature. Nevertheless, given the maxim that any therapy is better than no therapy, and in a climate of resource shortages and waiting lists for specialist therapeutic agencies, social workers can offer something that may well make a difference. Not all social workers are registered family therapists but the skills and techniques are available to be employed as family support as much as psychodynamic or task-centred approaches. The characteristics of family therapy work are:

- Viewing the family as a constantly interacting system.
- Avoiding colluding with individual blaming strategies.
- Reframing problems in ways that offer families positive solutions.
- Using the concept of circular causality to explain the pattern of relationships.
- Actively working to change the way the family system, rather than any individual functions.
- Prescribing tasks and rituals to engage the whole family in problem-solving activity.

An example of a recent research project in the field of mental health illustrates the importance of seeking service users' perceptions of the service they are experiencing. An active outreach team was established with the aim of engaging a group of people who traditionally found it hard to accept help. The researcher spent time with service users using a qualitative methodology that placed them at the centre of the research process.

The innovative outreach project was found to be achieving its aims because (Graley-Wetherell and Morgan, 2001):

- Staff were spending more time with clients.
- Service users felt respected and listened to.
- Service users felt their social lives had improved.
- Cash benefits had increased and helped improve mental wellbeing.

Another example of recent research addressing the needs of elderly people illustrates how innovative and creative thinking can enable older people to remain in their own homes (McClatchey et al., 2001). Elderly people with dementia are likely to remain in their own homes longer and in much greater numbers than previously. This means social workers in community care contexts will be under pressure to manage the specific needs of this client group. The research team in this study discovered that specialist housing agencies with the capacity to make adaptations and improvements to elderly people's homes can help sustain them for longer. However the home improvement agencies were unable and unwilling to assess the cognitive ability of the elderly people they were assisting. The implications of this research were that social workers working with home improvement agencies could sustain elderly people with dementia in their own homes for longer, rather than precipitate an unwanted admission to residential care. To do this social workers need to think beyond resource-led assessment and intervention and explore other more creative possibilities.

Comparing practice interventions

An examination of the characteristics of models of assessment, analysis of methods of support, and evaluation of measures of effectiveness provides us with a good example of the intervention choices facing you in typical child care, community care or mental health social work. The following permits some comparisons to be drawn between family therapy and family support interventions and how they best meet the needs of families. The family therapy literature tends to be limited on the subject of proactive community involvement and a social dimension to practice, beyond rhetorical injunctions to address oppressive and discriminatory contexts of lived experience in codes of conduct and ethical guidance. Family therapists have largely failed to integrate a thorough social policy perspective with their theoretical paradigms by remaining disconnected from the communities they aspire to help.

These criticisms rely on a rather narrow and impatiently explicit concept of social action. It may be that the subtle and more implicit benefits of family therapy practice are not visible to conventional research methodologies. The concept of more collaborative, client-centred, community oriented practice in family therapy is echoed in some contemporary writings (Reimers and Treacher, 1995; Anderson, 1997; Anderson, 2001). They have a robust historical pedigree (Bell, 1961; Minuchin, 1974). Feminist family therapists have contributed important thinking regarding one of the most important social contexts of family therapy practice – that of gender which is not inconsistent with the aims of staff working in family support (Perelberg and Miller, 1990). Relatively new literature is responding to earlier criticisms about family therapy's notorious resistance to tackle issues of culture, race, and sexuality (Lau, 1986; McGoldrick et al., 1982; Hardy and Laszloffy, 1994).

Studies into the effectiveness of family support or family therapy evidence the micro and macro level of intervention context and the subtle interaction between both levels (Estrada and Pinsof, 1995; Hill, 1999). Apart from registering success with the external parent-child relationship, findings suggest impact at the internal intra-psychic relationships. The concept of the shaman illustrates this when describing the therapist as a figure who intervenes at the junction between different orders of reality – the physiological, psychological, and social. A broad repertoire of therapeutic modalities including cognitive, behavioural, systemic, psycho-dynamic, solution-focused approaches have demonstrated positive outcome in a range of presenting problems in a variety of specialist, statutory, or voluntary, community settings (Carr, 2000).

A review of the literature on empirical evaluations of family support services yielded mixed results and conceded that the disparate number of variables affecting outcome, makes it difficult to isolate the particular impact of such an intervention (Rossi, 1992). Other research notes that family support programmes tend to focus on single outcome measures related to a child's behaviour, rather than taking into account other dimensions such as parent/child interaction or use of community resources (Gardner, 1998). A review of consumer studies of family therapy concluded that the importance of the relationship aspects of therapy were crucial as far as service users were concerned (Reimers and Treacher, 1995). Active elements such as advice giving need to be combined with reflective and supportive elements as is the case in family support work. The concepts of family therapy and family support are therefore not as incompatible as might at first appear.

Family support provides individual, parent, couple, and group work interventions to children and families referred because of concerns about the emotional and behavioural development of children. Evidence from similar initiatives suggested that family support could provide valuable help to socially excluded children and families (Arcelus et al., 1999). The multi-faceted approach to assessment common to both family therapy and family support interventions is consistent with the recently introduced *Framework for the Assessment of Children in Need* which requires professionals working with children to expand the focus of their assessments in order to improve decision-making (DoH, 2000). This framework also explicitly acknowledges environmental factors and the wider social context in the analysis of children and family difficulties.

The aim of this government policy guidance is to try to move away from the much criticised intrusive and inspectorial style of assessment of families where there were concerns about the welfare of children. Practitioners are required to make comprehensive assessments of all the variables affecting the functioning of the family not relying on a narrow focus on any one of the three key assessment areas: parenting, environment, or child development. The model of assessment has all the characteristics of a psycho-social, holistic, and participative approach, maintaining the focus towards intervention that is appropriate, accessible, and acceptable to children and parents.

Change and the practice evidence base

Central to an empowering socially inclusive approach in social work is finding out whether the work has, on the basis of reliable evidence, contributed towards the process of change. Change can be considered as something that is endless, constant and inevitable. How it is perceived and experienced by service users is crucial (Walker, 2003). Various models of intervention permit change stemming from within the psyche of the person to physical changes in their environment and abilities. There are changes imposed on certain clients compulsorily and those that are accepted voluntarily – either of which may lead to long-term benefits for them or their kin. Change is often thought of as something initiated by a social worker in a linear cause and effect process. But it can be useful to think about it in a more circular or reflexive pattern. How much did you change during the course of an intervention? What impact did the client have on you and how did this affect your thinking and behaviour? Indeed most of the change may occur within you as you find out more over time about a person and their circumstances compared to the first encounter.

Change is connected to difference but every stakeholder in the change process has a unique perception of what counts as difference. Pointing out differences to a person might be experienced as empowering but it might equally provoke feelings of fear or anxiety. A minimum amount of help might produce significant changes and equally a substantial amount of intervention results in no change or a worsening of circumstances. Where you choose to look for change may not be where other professionals or the service user is looking. Change can therefore be liberating or constraining, it can generate enlightenment or promote feelings of anger, loss and bereavement. Maintaining a degree of professional optimism with realism and managing uncertainty with a modest and respectful approach offers you the potential for being a useful resource to your clients.

Seven stages of change have been described which serve as a useful tool for social workers trying to evaluate their practice and assess the effectiveness of the chosen intervention with an individual service user (Rogers, 1957). The stages can be used with the child, young person or adult, or parent or carer, to include them in the process of insight development and self-reflection:

- Stage 1: Communication is about external events.
- Stage 2: Expression flows more freely.
- Stage 3: Describes personal reactions to external events.
- Stage 4: Descriptions of feelings and personal experiences.
- Stage 5: Present feelings are expressed.
- Stage 6: A flow of feeling which has a life of its own.
- Stage 7: A series of felt senses connecting different aspects of an issue.

The need to expand and refine the evidence base of social work practice in order to demonstrate effectiveness is more important than ever especially in times when the welfare state is contracting and the pressure to find cost-effective solutions is strong. The growing problem requires a concerted effort from all agencies in contact with service users to understand the services they are providing and finding out better ways of measuring success. Three key factors have been identified in defining and explaining why evidence-based practice is not an option, but a necessity (Sheldon and Chilvers, 2000):

- **Conscientiousness**: this means a constant vigilance to monitor and review social work practice and to maintain service user welfare as paramount. It entails keeping up to date with new developments and a commitment to further professional understanding of human growth and development and social problems.
- **Explicitness**: this means working in an open and honest way with clients based on reliable evidence of what works and what is understood to be effective. The principle of explicitness demands a review of the

available options with clients based upon thorough assessment of their problems.

■ **Judiciousness**: this means the exercise of sound, prudent, sensible, judgement. Potential risks arising from some, or no intervention either in cases or policies, should be thoroughly assessed and evaluated in the knowledge that not all eventualities can be predicted.

The drive to encourage a research-minded profession in order to improve practice standards and accountability is however in danger of producing a confusion of research studies varying in quality and methodological rigour yet producing potentially useful data hidden within the quantity being produced. Practitioner research in social work is being encouraged as a means of influencing policy, management and practice using evaluative concepts moulded by service user expectations (Fuller, 1996). It is possible to contribute to good quality effectiveness and evaluation studies by working in partnership with your clients to ensure their perspectives are at the heart of this activity. Practice is constantly evolving as society changes and the lives of our clients are influenced by multiple factors beyond their and our control. Maintaining an open mind and a receptive attitude to new learning is important so that we continue to think about (Thompson and Thompson, 2002):

■ What we are doing?
■ Why we are doing it?
■ Are we doing it well?
■ What we can learn from doing it?

The potential for evidence-based practice to enhance the quality of work and the satisfaction of service users is huge. The history of research and evaluation in social work is patchy and reflects deep ambivalence in practitioners and managers about the nature of the task. However, as the profession develops with the change to a degree level qualification, the establishment of a workforce regulatory council and a national body for collating good practice examples, the importance of good quality, reliable information

on which to base practice can not be overstated. The development of evidence-based practice therefore depends on the following (Davies et al., 2000):

■ The generation of good quality data concerning effectiveness.
■ A workforce able critically to appraise evidence and contribute to the process of systematic reviews of research findings.
■ The dissemination of data or research syntheses in a readily accessible form to professionals, managers, policy makers and to service users – a methodological and technical challenge.
■ A work and policy environment that facilitates rather than impedes the development of practices that reflect best evidence.

Your role as a professional social worker includes that of researcher and within that term there are three elements that need to be integrated in order for you to contribute to the knowledge base of social work practice. As a research consumer you need to know how to locate and use research findings, test their reliability and translate them into specific and appropriate interventions. As a knowledge creator and disseminator you will be involved in the production of research findings as part of a proper professional role in participating in systematic efforts to determine effective practice methods. Disseminating the findings can involve a simple written description circulated to team or agency colleagues or submitted to a magazine or journal so that as many social workers as possible can access the results. As a contributing partner in research you can join with others and take responsibility for a specific part of the research process. Collaborative working like this can feel less stressful, be more manageable and ultimately be more powerful.

Chapter summary

We have discussed how in attempting to match resources and services to service users expectations and perceived needs, social workers are faced with increasing and more complex demands to improve efficiency and effectiveness. Central to all this is the concept of quality assurance which demands a commitment to the pursuit of a high standard of services. Policy statements setting out performance indicators in all areas of social work practice stress the essential role of monitoring and evaluation. You need to know what these terms mean, how they are used, and how you can engage positively with them.

Subjective and objective evaluations are two general ways of thinking about the types of evaluation you might consider. Specific examples include – satisfaction surveys, inspections, joint reviews, performance assessment. They are aimed at measuring quantitative data such as numbers of cases worked or numbers of admissions to residential care. Or they aim to gain qualitative data – the voices and experiences from the service users' perspective.

We suggested that a useful framework to consider applying in your evaluation practice includes collecting baseline information and establishing the service's overall aims and objectives. Specify available resources, overall aim and objectives. Link goals to specific objectives by identifying the desired outcomes or goals enable you to work backwards through any intermediary stages in the process. Detail why the agreed objectives and goals were decided upon. No evaluation goes strictly according to plan; therefore it is important to record how goals were established. Collate information from all stakeholders including recommendations for changing or improving the service.

Reflective practice as part of evaluation in social work encompasses the need for a useful outcome to the reflective process that will lead to a change in practice. Reflexivity suggests that we interrogate previously taken for granted assumptions, it contends that knowledge does not have fixed stable meanings but that it is made rather than revealed thanks to research effort. Research methods that could be employed in social work contexts include: randomised controlled trials, quasi-experimental studies, non-experimental studies, client opinion studies, surveys, and a cohort studies. Probably the most attractive to practising social workers is the service user oriented research that seeks to articulate their experiences and requirements from the personal social services.

Further Reading

Adams, R., Dominelli, L. and Payne, M. (2002) *Critical Practice in Social Work*. Basingstoke: Palgrave Macmillan.

Ahmad, B. (1990) *Black Perspectives in Social Work*. Birmingham:Venture Press.

Alderson, P. et al. (1996) *What Works? Effective Social Interventions in Child Welfare*. Barkingside: Barnardo's.

Alvesson, M. and Skoldberg, K. (2000) *Reflexive Methodology: New Vistas for Qualitative Research*. London: Sage.

Arcelus, J., Bellerby, T. and Vostanis, V. (1999) A mental health service for young people in the care of the local authority. *Clinical Child Psychology and Psychiatry*. 4: 2, 233–245.

Audit Commission (2000) *Half Way Home: An Analysis of the Variations in the Cost of Supporting Asylum Seekers*. London: Audit Commission.

Bagley, C. and Mallick, K. (1995) Negative Self Perception and Components of Stress in Canadian, British and Hong Kong Adolescents. *Perceptual Motor Skills*. 81: 123–7.

Bagley, C. and Mallick, K. (2000) How Adolescents Perceive Their Emotional Life, Behaviour, and Self-Esteem in Relation to Family Stressors: A Six-Culture Study. In: Singh, N., Leung, J. and Singh, A. *International Perspectives on Child and Adolescent Mental Health*. Oxford: Elsevier.

Baldwin, M. (2000) *Care Management and Community Care*. Aldershot: Ashgate.

Bamford, T. (1993) Rationing: A Philosophy of Care. In Allen, I. (1993) *Rationing of Health and Social Care*. London: Policy Services Institute.

Bandura, A. (1986) *Social Foundations of Thought and Action: A Social Cognitive Perspective*. New Jersey: Prentice-Hall.

Banks, S. (1995) *Ethics and Values in Social Work*. Basingstoke: Macmillan.

Banks, S. (2001) *Ethics and Values in Social Work*. 2nd edn, Basingstoke: Palgrave.

Barnes, C. (1991). *Disabled People in Britain and Discrimination*. London: Hurst.

Barnes, C. and Mercer, G. (1997) *Doing Disability Research*. Leeds: The Disability Press.

Barnes, H., Thornton, P. and Maynard, S. (1998) *Disabled People and Employment: A Review of Research and Development Work*. Bristol: Policy Press.

Barnes, M., McGuire, J., Stein, A. and Rosenberg, W. (1997) Evidence Based Medicine and Child Mental Health Services. *Children and Society*. 11: 89–96.

Barry, M. and Hallett, C. (1998) *Social Exclusion and Social Work*. Lyme Regis: Russell House Publishing.

Barton, J. (1999) Child and Adolescent Psychiatry. In: Hill, M. (Ed.) *Effective Ways of Working with Children and their Families*. London: Jessica Kingsley.

BASW (2002) *Code of Ethics for Social Workers*. Birmingham: BASW.

Bateman, N. (2000) *Advocacy Skills for Health and Social Care Professionals*. London: Jessica Kingsley.

Beales, D., Denham, M. and Tulloch, A. (Eds.) (1998) *Community Care of Older People*. Oxford: Radcliffe Medical Press.

Beckett, C. (2003a) Dear Lord Laming. *Professional Social Work*. April, p10.

Beckett, C. (2003b) *Child Protection: An Introduction*. London: Sage.

Beckett, C. and Wrighton, E. (2000) What Matters to Me is Not What You're Talking About: Maintaining the Social Model of Disability in Public Private Negotiations. *Disability and Society*. 15: 7, 991–9.

Bennett, G. and Kingston, P. (1993) *Elder Abuse: Concepts, Theories and Interventions*. London: Chapman Hall.

Beresford, B. et al. (1996) *What Works in Services for Families With a Disabled Child?* Barkingside: Barnardos.

Beresford, P. and Croft, S. (1993) *Citizen Involvement: A Practical Guide for Change*. Basingstoke: Macmillan.

Berridge, D. (1997) *Foster Care: A Research Review*. London: HMSO.

Bewley, C. and Glendinning, C. (1994) *Involving Disabled People in Community Care Planning*. York: Joseph Rowntree Foundation.

Bignall, T. and Butt, J. (200) *Between Ambition and Achievement: Young Black Disabled Peoples Views and Experiences of Independence*. Bristol: Policy Press.

Bochner, S. (1994) Cross-Cultural Differences in The Self-Concept: A Test of Hofstede's Individualism/Collectivism Distinction. *Journal of Cross-Cultural Psychology*. 2: 273–83.

Boyd-Franklin, N. (Ed.) (1995) *Children, Families and HIV/AIDS*. Hove, Brunner Routledge.

Bradshaw, J. (1972) The Concept of Human Need. *New Society*. 30.3.72

Braye, S. and Preston-Shoot, M. (1995) *Empowering Practice in Social Care*. Buckingham: Open University Press.

Braye, S. and Preston-Shoot, M. (1997) *Practising Social Work Law*. 2nd edn. London: Macmillan.

Brearley, C. P. (1982) *Risks and Social Work*. London: Routledge.

Bughra, D. and Bahl, V. (1999) *Ethnicity: An Agenda for Mental Health*. London: Gaskill.

Caplan, G. (1964) *Principles of Preventive Psychiatry*. London: Basic Books.

Carpenter, J. and Sbaraini, S. (1997) *Choice, Implementation and Dignity: Involving Users and Carers in Care Management in Mental Health*. Bristol: Policy Press.

Carr, A. (Ed.) (2000) What works for children and adolescents? A critical review of Psychological Interventions with Children, Adolescents and their Families. London: Routledge.

Cheetham, J. et al. (1992) *Evaluating Social Work Effectiveness*. Buckingham: Open University Press.

Clark, C. L. (2000) *Social Work Ethics: Politics, Principles and Practice*. Basingstoke: Macmillan.

Clarke, J., Gewirtz, S. and McLaughlin, E. (2000) *New Managerialism, New Welfare*. London: Sage.

Clarke, N. (2001) The Impact of In-Service Training Within Social Services. *British Journal of Social Work*. 31: 757–74.

Compton, B. and Galaway, B. (1999) *Social Work Processes*. 6th edn. Pacific Grove: Brooks/Cole Publishing.

Connelly, N. and Stubbs, P. (1997) *Trends in Social Work and Social Work Education Across Europe*. London: NISW.

Connor, A. (1993) *Monitoring and Evaluation Made Easy*. London: HMSO.

Corby, B., Millar, M. and Pope, A. (2002) Out of the Frame. *Community Care*. Sept. 40–1.

Corker, M. (1999) New Disability Discourse, The Principle of Optimization and Social Change. In Corker, M. and French, S. (Eds.) *Disability Discourse*. Buckingham: Open University Press.

Corrigan, P. and Leonard, P. (1978) *Social Work under Capitalism*. London: Macmillan.

Coulshed, V. and Orme, J. (1998) *Social Work Practice: An Introduction*. Basingstoke: Macmillan.

Cowie, H. (1999) Counselling Psychology in the UK: The Interface between Practice and

Research. *The European Journal of Psychotherapy, Counselling and Health*. 2: 1, 69–80.

Daines, R., Lyon, K. and Parsloe, P. (1990) *Aiming for Partnership*. London: Barnardo's.

Dallos, R. and Draper, R. (2000) *An Introduction to Family Therapy*. Buckingham: Open University Press.

Davies, H., Nutley, S. and Smith, P. (2000) *What Works: Evidence Based Policy and Practice in Public Services*. Bristol: Policy Press.

Davies, M. (Ed.) (1997) *The Blackwell Companion to Social Work*. London: Blackwell.

Davis, A. (1996) Risk Work in Mental Health. In Kemshall, H. and Pritchard, J. (Eds.) *Good Practice in Risk Assessment and Management*. London: Jessica Kingsley.

Davis, A. and Ellis, K. (1995) Enforced Altruism or Community Care. In Hugman, R. and Smith, D. (Eds.) *Ethical Issues in Social Work*. London: Routledge.

Davis, A., Ellis, K. and Rummery, B. (1997) *Access to Assessment: Perspectives of Practitioners, Disabled People, and Carers*. Bristol: Policy Press.

Davis, J., Rendell, P. and Sims, D. (1999) The Joint Practitioner: A New Concept in Professional Training. *Journal of Interprofessional Care*. 13: 4, 395–404.

Dean, M. (1997) Sociology after Society. In Owen, D. (Ed.) *Sociology after Postmodernism*. London: Sage.

Debell, D. and Walker, S. (2002) *Norfolk Family Support Teams Final Evaluation Report*. Chelmsford: APU Centre for Research in Health and Social Care.

Doel, M. and Marsh, P. (1992) *Task-Centred Social Work*. Aldershot: Ashgate.

DoH (1988) *Protecting Children: A Guide for Social Workers Undertaking a Comprehensive Assessment*. London: HMSO.

DoH (1995) *Child Protection: Messages From Research*. London: HMSO.

DoH (1996) *Community Care (Direct Payments) Act, 1996: Policy and Practice Guidance*. London: Stationery Office.

DoH (1996) *National Commission of Inquiry into Child Protection*. London: HMSO.

DoH (1997). *Developing Partnerships in Mental Health*. London: HMSO.

DoH (1998) *Disabled Children: Directions for Their Future Care*. London: HMSO.

DoH (1999) *Modernising Social Services*. London: DoH.

DoH (1999) *Working Together to Safeguard Children*. London: Stationery Office.

DoH (2000) *Framework for the Assessment of Children in Need and Their Families*. London: HMSO.

DoH (2000) *The Children Act Report (1995–1999)*. London: HMSO.

DoH (2001) *Making It Work: Inspection of Welfare to Work for Disabled People*. London: HMSO.

DoH (2002) *Fair Access to Care Services: Guidance on Eligibility Criteria for Adult Social Care*. London: DoH.

DoH/SSI (1991) *Care Management and Assessment. Practitioners Guide to The NHS and Community Care Act 1990*. London: HMSO.

DoH/SSI (1996) *Caring for People at Home Part 2-Inspection Arrangements for Assessment and Delivery of Home Care*. London: HMSO.

DoH/SSI (1997a) *At Home with Dementia: Inspection of Services for Older People with Dementia in the Community*. London: HMSO.

DoH/SSI (1997b) *Responding to Families in Need*. London: HMSO.

DoH/SSI (1997c) *The Cornerstone of Care: Care Planning for Older People*. London: HMSO.

DoH/SSI (1998) *They Look After Their Own Don't They? Inspection of Community Care Services for Black and Ethnic Minority People*. London: HMSO.

DoH/SSI (2000) *A Quality Strategy for Social Care*. London: HMSO.

DoH/SSO (2000) Excellence not Excuses: Inspection of Services for Ethnic Minority and Families. London: HMSO.

Dominelli, L. (1996) Deprofessionalising Social Work: Equal Opportunities, Competencies, and Postmodernism. *British Journal of Social Work*. 26: 2, 153–75.

Dominelli, L. (1997) *Anti-Racist Social Work*. London: Macmillan/BASW.

Dominelli, L. (1998) Globalisation and Gender Relations in Social Work. In Lesnik, B. (Ed.)

Countering Discrimination in Social Work. Aldershot: Ashgate.

Dominelli, L. (2002) *Anti-Oppressive Social Work Theory and Practice.* Basingstoke: Palgrave Macmillan.

Downrie, R. S. and Telfer, E. (1980) *Caring and Curing: A Philosophy of Medicine and Social Work.* London: Methuen.

du Gay, P. (2000) *In Praise of Bureaucracy.* London: Sage.

Durlak, J. and Wells, A. (1997) Primary Prevention Mental Health Programs for Children and Adolescents: A Meta-analytic Review. *American Journal of Community Psychology.* 25: 2, 115–52.

Eastman, M. (Ed.) (1994) *Old Age Abuse: A New Perspective.* London: Chapman and Hall.

Eber, L., Osuch, R. and Reddit, C. (1996) School based applications of the wraparound process: Early results on service provision and student outcomes. *Journal of Child and Family Studies.* 5: 83–99.

Eraut, M. (1994) *Developing Professional Knowledge and Competence.* London: Falmer Press.

Estrada, A. V. and Pinsoff, W. M. (1995) The Effectiveness Family Therapies for Selected Behavioural Disorders in Childhood. *Journal of Marital and Family Therapy.* 21: 403–40.

Farrington, D. (1996) *Understanding and Preventing Youth Crime.* York: Joseph Rowntree Foundation.

Fawcett, B. (2000) Look Listen and Learn. *Community Care.* July 27. 24–5.

Fletcher-Campbell, F. (2001) Issues of Exclusion: Evidence from Three Recent Research Studies. *Support for Learning.* 17: 1, 19–22.

Fook, J. (2002) *Social Work: Critical Theory and Practice.* London: Sage.

Franklin, A. and Madge, N. (2000) *In Our View.* London: NCB.

Flynn, N. (1997) *Public Sector Management.* 3rd edn. Hemel Hempstead: Prentice-Hall.

Foucault, M. (1977) *The Archaeology of Knowledge.* London: Tavistock.

Frost, N. (2002) Evaluating Practice. In Adams, R., Dominelli, L. and Payne, M. (Eds.)

Critical Practice in Social Work: Basingstoke: Palgrave Macmillan.

Fuller, R. (1996) Evaluating Social Work Effectiveness: A Pragmatic Approach. In Alderson, P. et al. (Eds.) *What Works? Effective Social Interventions in Child Welfare.* Barkingside: Barnardo's.

Fuller, R. and Petch, A. (1995) *Practitioner Research: The Reflexive Social Worker.* Buckingham: Open University Press.

Gardner, R. (1998) *Family Support: A practitioners guide.* Birmingham: Venture Press.

Gibson-Cline, J. (Ed.) (1996) *Adolescence: From Crisis to Coping.* London: Butterworth-Heinemann.

Girling, J. (1993) Who gets what – and why? Ethical Frameworks for Managers. In Allen, I. (1993) *Rationing of Health and Social Care.* London: Policy Services Institute.

Goodman, R. and Scott, S. (1997) *Child Psychiatry.* Oxford: Blackwell Science.

Gorell-Barnes, G. (1998) *Family Therapy in Changing Times.* Basingstoke: Macmillan.

Graley-Wetherell, R. and Morgan, S. (2001) *Active Outreach: An Independent Service User Evaluation of a Model of Assertive Outreach Practice.* London: Sainsbury Centre for Mental Health.

Hardiker, P. (1995) *The Social Policy Contexts of Services to Prevent Unstable Family Life.* York: Joseph Rowntree Foundation.

Harding, T. and Beresford, P. (Eds.) (1996) *The Standards We Expect: What Service Users and Carers Want From Social Services Workers.* London: NISW.

Hardy, K. V. and Laszloffy, T. A. (1992) Training Racially Sensitive Family Therapists. *Families in Society.* 73: 364–70.

Haynes, K. and Holmes, K. (1994) Invitation to Social Work, New York, Longman.

Healy, K. (2002) *Social Work Practices: Contemporary Perspectives on Change.* London: Sage.

Henderson, P. and Thomas, D. (1987) *Skills in Neighbourhood Work.* London: Allen and Unwin.

Hill, M. (1999) *Effective Ways of Working With Children and their Families.* London: Jessica Kingsley.

Hodes, M. (1998) *Refugee Children*. London: HARP.

Hogg, M. A. and Abrams, D. (1988) *Social Identification: A Social Psychology of Intergroup Relations and Group Processes*. London: Routledge.

Holman, A. and Collins, J. (1997) *Funding Freedom: Direct Payments for People with Learning Difficulties*. London: VIA.

Holman, B. (1983) *Resourceful Friends: Skills in Community Social Work*. London: Children's Society.

Horne, M. (1999) *Values in Social Work*. 2nd edn, Aldershot: Ashgate Arena.

Horwath, J. (2002) Maintaining a Focus on the Child? *Child Abuse Review*. 11: 195–213.

House of Commons (1997) Child and Adolescent Mental Health Services. Health Committee. London: HMSO.

Howe, D. (1987) *An Introduction to Social Work Theory*. Aldershot: Gower.

Howe, D. (1994) Modernity, Post Modernity and Social Work. *British Journal of Social Work*. 24: 513–32.

Howe, G. (1999) *Mental Health Assessments*. London: Jessica Kingsley.

International Disability Foundation (1998) *World Disability Report*. Geneva: IDF.

Jack, R. and Walker, S. (2000) *Social Work Assessment and Intervention*. Cambridge: APU.

Jones, C. (1997) Poverty. In Davies, M. (Ed.) *The Blackwell Companion to Social Work*. Oxford: Blackwell.

Kashani, J. and Allan, W. (1998) *The Impact of Family Violence on Children and Adolescents*. London: Sage.

Kelley, D. and Warr, B. (Eds) (1992) *Quality Counts: Achieving Quality in Social Care Service*. London: Whiting and Birch.

Kent, H. and Read, J. (1998) Measuring Consumer Participation in Mental Health Services. *International Journal of Social Psychiatry*. 44: 4, 295–310.

Knapp, M. and Scott, S. (1998) *Lifetime Costs of Conduct Disorder*. London: Mind.

Lader, et al. (1997) *Psychiatric Morbidity Among Young Offenders in England and Wales*. London: DoH.

Laing, R. D. (1976) *Facts of Life*. London: Allen Lane.

Lau, A. (1986) Family Therapy Across Cultures. In: J. L. Cox (Ed.) *Transcultural Psychiatry*. London: Croom Helm.

Laws, S., Armitt, D., Metzendort, W., Percival, P. and Reisel, J. (1999) *Time to Listen: Young Peoples Experiences of Mental Health Services*. London: Save the Children.

Leonard, P. (1997) *Postmodern Welfare: Reconstructing an Emancipatory Project*. London: Sage.

Lishman, J. (1998) Personal and Professional Development. In Adams et al. (Eds.) *Social Work: Themes, Issues and Critical Debates*. London: Macmillan.

Lord Laming (2003) *The Victoria Climbié Inquiry: Report of an Inquiry*. London: Stationery Office.

Lyon, J., Dennison, C. and Wilson, A. (2000) Tell them so they listen: Messages from young people in custody. Home Office Research Study 201. London: HMSO.

Macdonald, A. (1999) *Understanding Community Care*. Basingstoke: Macmillan.

Macdonald, G. and Roberts, H. (1995) *What Works in the Early Years?* Barkingside: Barnardos.

Macdonald, K. and Macdonald, G. (1999) Perceptions of Risk. In Parsloe, P. (Ed.) *Risk Assessment in Social Work and Social Care*, London: Jessica Kingsley.

Magrab, P., Evans, P. and Hurrell, P. (1997) Integrated services for children and youth at risk: an international study of multi-disciplinary training. *Journal of Interprofessional Care*. 11: 1, 99–108.

Martin, G. et al. (1995) Adolescent Suicide, Depression and Family Dysfunction'. *Acta Psychiatrica Scandinavica*. 92: 336–44

May, T. (Ed.) (2002) *Qualitative Research in Action*. London: Sage.

McCaffrey, T. (1998) The Pain of Managing. In Foster, A. and Zagier Roberts, V. (Eds.) (1998) *Managing Mental Health in the Community*. London: Routledge.

McClatchey, T., Means, R. and Morbey, H. (2001) *Housing Adaptations and Improvements for People With Dementia: Developing The Role of Home Improvement Agencies:* Bristol: University of The West of England.

McGoldrick, M. et al. (1982) *Ethnicity and Family Therapy.* Guilford Press.

McIntyre, D. (1982) On the possibility of 'radical' social work: a 'radical' dissent. *Contemporary Social Work Education.* 5: 3, 191–208.

McLennan, G. (1996) Post-Marxism and the Four Sins of Modernist Theorizing. *New Left Review.* 218: 53–75.

McReadie, C. (1995) *Elder Abuse: Update on Research.* London: Institute of Gerontology, Kings College London.

Mental Health Foundation (1999) The Big Picture: Promoting Children and Young People's Mental Health. London: MHF.

Mental Health Foundation (2002) The Mental Health Needs of Young Offenders. London: MHF.

Middleton, L. (1997) *The Art of Assessment.* Birmingham: Venture Press.

Midgley, J. (2001) Issues in International Social Work: Resolving Critical Debates in the Profession. *Journal of Social Work.* 1: 1, 21–25.

Milne, A. (2002) *Teach Yourself Counselling.* Abingdon: Teach Yourself.

Milner, J. and O'Byrne, P. (1998) *Assessment in Social Work.* Basingstoke: Macmillan.

Mishra, R. (1990) *The Welfare State in a Capitalist Society.* London: Harvester Wheatsheaf.

Moffic, S. A. and Kinzie, J. D. (1996) The History and Future of Cross Cultural Psychiatric Services. *Community Mental Health Journal.* 32: 6, 581–92.

Morris, J. (1998) *Accessing Human Rights: Disabled Children and the Children Act.* Barkingside: Barnardos.

Mullender, A. and Ward, D. (1991) *Self Directed Group work: Users Take Action for Empowerment.* London: Whiting and Birch.

NISW (1982) *Social Workers: Their Role and Tasks.* London: NISW.

Nolan, M. Caldock, K. (1996) Assessment: Identifying the Barriers to Good Practice. *Health and Social Care in the Community.* 4: 2, 77–85.

O'Hagan, K. (1996) *Competence in Social Work Practice: A Practical Guide for Professionals.* London: Jessica Kingsley.

O'Sullivan, T. (1999) *Decision Making in Social Work.* London: Macmillan.

Oberhuemer, P. (1998) A European Perspective on Early Years Training. In Abbott, L. and Pugh, G. (Eds.) *Training to Work in the Early Years.* Buckingham: Open University Press.

OFSTED (1996) Exclusion From Secondary Schools 1995–1996. London: HMSO.

Oldman, C. and Beresford, B. (1998) *Disabled Children and Their Families.* York: Joseph Rowntree Foundation.

Oliver, M. (1996) *Understanding Disability: From Theory to Practice.* London: Macmillan.

Oliver, M. and Sapey, B. (1999) *Social Work With Disabled People.* Basingstoke: Macmillan.

Ovretveit, J. (1998) *Evaluating Health Interventions.* Buckingham: Open University Press.

Owivedi, K. N. (Ed.) (2002) Meeting the Needs of Ethnic Minority Children. London: Jessica Kingsley.

Parsloe, P. (Ed.) (1999) *Risk Assessment in Social Care.* London: Jessica Kingsley.

Parton, N. (1991) *Governing the Family.* Basingstoke: Macmillan.

Parton, N. (1994) The Nature of Social Work Under Conditions of (Post) Modernity. *Social Work and Social Science Review.* 5: 2, 93–112.

Parton, N. and O'Byrne, P. (2000) *Constructive Social Work.* London: Macmillan.

Parton, N. and O'Byrne, P. (2000) *Constructive Social Work: Towards a New Practice.* Basingstoke: Macmillan.

Payne, M. (1997) *Modern Social Work Theory.* 2nd edn, Basingstoke: Macmillan.

Pearce, J. B. (1999) Collaboration between the NHS and Social Services in the Provision of Child and Adolescent Mental Health Services: A Personal View. *Child Psychology and Psychiatry Review.* 4: 4, 150–2.

Pearson, G., Teseder, J. and Yelloly, M. (Eds.) (1988) *Social Work and The Legacy of Freud: Psychoanalysis and Its Uses.* London: Macmillan.

Pels, D. (2000) Reflexivity One Step Up. *Theory, Culture and Society.* 17: 3, 1–25

Perelberg, R. J. and Miller, A. (Eds.) (1990) *Gender and Power in Families.* London: Routledge.

Pierson, J. (2002) *Tackling Social Exclusion*. London: Routledge.

Phillips, C., Palfrey, C. and Thomas, P. (1994) *Evaluating Health and Social Care*. London: Macmillan.

Pincus, A. and Minahan, A. (1973) *Social Work Practice: Model and Method*. London: Peacock.

Pinkerton, J., Higgins, K. and Devine, P. (2000) *Family Support: Linking Project Evaluation to Policy Analysis*. Aldershot: Ashgate.

Pithouse, A. (1998) *Social Work: The Social Organisation of an Invisible Trade*. Aldershot: Ashgate.

PIU (Performance and Innovation Unit) (2000) *Prime Minister's Review of Adoption*. London: Cabinet Office.

Platt, D. and Edwards, A. (1996) Planning A Comprehensive Family Assessment. *Practice*. 9: 2.

Pollock, S. W. and Boland, M. G. (1990) Children and HIV Infection. *New Jersey Psychologist*. 40: 3, 17–21.

Polwczyk, D. et al. (1993) Comparison of Patient and Staff Surveys of Consumer Satisfaction. *Hospital and Community Psychiatry*. 44: 6, 589–91.

Priestly, M. (1999) *Disability Politics and Community Care*. London: Jessica Kingsley.

Priestly, M. (2001) *Disability and The Life Course: Global Perspectives*. Cambridge Univerity Press: Cambridge.

Pritchard, J. (1995) *The Abuse of Old People*. 2nd edn. London: Jessica Kingsley.

Ramon, S. (1999) Social Work. In Bhui, K. and Olajide, D. (Eds.) *Mental Health Service Provision for a Multi-Cultural Society*. London: Saunders.

Reimers, S. and Treacher, A. (1995) *Introducing User-Friendly Family Therapy*. London: Routledge.

Richardson, J. and Joughlin, C. (2000) *The Mental Health Needs of Looked After Children*. London: Gaskill.

Rodgers, A., Pilgrim, D. and Lacey, R. (1993) *Experiencing Psychiatry: Users Views of Services*. London: Macmillan/Mind.

Rogers, C. (1957) The Necessary and Sufficient Conditions of Therapeutic Personality Change. *Journal of Consulting Psychology*. 21: 95–103.

Rogers, C. (1967) *On becoming a Person: A Therapists View of Psychotherapy*. London: Constable.

Rossi, P. H. (1992) Assessing Family Preservation Programmes. *Children and Youth Services Review*. 14: 77–97.

Royal College of Psychiatrists (2002) Parent-Training Programmes for the Management of Young Children with Conduct Disorders, Findings from Research. London: RCP.

Rutter, M. (1999) Resilience Concepts and Findings: Implications for Family Therapy. *Journal of Family Therapy*. 21: 119–44.

Sanderson, H. (1997) *Peoples Plans and Possibilities: Exploring Person Centred Planning*. Edinburgh: Scottish Health Services.

Save the Children (2001) Denied a Future? The right to education of roma/gypsy/traveller children in Europe. London: Save the Children.

Shah, R. (1992) The Silent Minority: Children with Disabilities in Asian Families. London: National Children's Bureau.

Shardlow, S. and Payne, M. (1998) *Contemporary Issues in Social Work: Western Europe*. Aldershot: Arena.

Sharkey, P. (2000) *The Essentials of Community Care. A Guide for Practitioners*. London: Macmillan.

Sheldon, B. and Chilvers, R. (2002) *Evidence-based Social Care: A Study of Prospects and Problems*. Lyme Regis: Russell House Publishing.

Sinclair, R., Garnett, L. and Berridge, D. (1995) *Social Work and Assessment with Adolescents*. London: National Children's Bureau.

Smale, G., Tunson, G., Biehal, N. and Marsh, P. (1993) *Empowerment Assessment, Care Management and The Skilled Worker*. London: HMSO.

Smale, G., Tuson, G. and Statham, D. (2000) *Social Work and Social Problems*. Basingstoke: Macmillan.

Social Exclusion Unit (2002) *Reducing Re-offending by Ex-Prisoners*. London: SEU.

SSI (2000) *Excellence Not Excuses: Inspection of Services for Ethnic Minority Children and Families*. London: HMSO.

Stephens, J. (2002) The Mental Health Needs of Homless Young People. London: MHF.

Stepney, R. and Ford, S. (2000) *Social Work Models, Methods, and Theories*. Lyme Regis: Russell House Publishing.

Stevenson, O. (1996) *Elder Protection in the Community: What Can We Learn From Child Protection?* London: Institute of Gerontology, Kings College London.

Stevenson, O. (1999) *Elder Protection in Residential Care. What Can We Learn From Child Protection?* London: HMSO.

Strachan, R. and Tallant, C. (1997) Improving Judgement and Appreciating Biases Within the Risk Assessment Process. In Kemshall, H. and Pritchard, J. (Eds.) *Good Practice in Risk Assessment and Risk Management 2: Protection Rights and Responsibilities*. London: Jessica Kingsley.

Summit, R. (1983) The Child Sexual Abuse Accommodation Syndrome. *Child Abuse and Neglect*. 7: 177–93.

Sutton, C. (1999) *Helping Families with Troubled Children*. London: Wiley.

Sveaass, N. and Reichelt, S. (2001) Refugee Families in Therapy: From Referrals to Therapeutic Conversations. *Journal of Family Therapy*. 23: 119–35.

Target, M. (1998) Approaches to Evaluation. *The European Journal of Psychotherapy, Counselling and Health*. 1: 1, 79–92.

Taylor, B. and Devine, D. (1993) *Assessing Needs and Planning Care in Social Work*. London: Arena.

Taylor, C. and White, S. (2000) *Practising Reflexivity in Health and Welfare*. Buckingham: Open University Press.

Taylor, P. J. and Gunn, J. (1999) Homicides by People with Mental Illness: Myth and Reality. *British Journal of Psychiatry*. 174: 9–14.

Thompson, N. (1995) *Theory and Practice in Health and Social Welfare*. Buckingham: Open University Press.

Thompson, N. (2000) *Theory and Practice in Human Services*. Buckingham: Open University Press.

Thompson, N. and Thompson, S. (2002) *Understanding Social Care*. Lyme Regis: Russell House Publishing.

Treacher, A. and Reimers, S. (1995) *Introducing User-Friendly Family Therapy*. London: Routledge.

Trevithick, P. (2000) *Social Work Skills*. Buckingham: Open University Press.

Tucker, S., Strange, C., Cordeaux, C., Moules, T. and Torrance, N. (1999) Developing an inter-disciplinary framework for the education and training of those working with children and young people. *Journal of Interprofessional Care*. 13, 3: 261–70.

United Nations (1993) *Rules on the Equalization of Opportunities for Disabled People*. Geneva: IDF.

United Nations (1994) Towards a Society For All Annex to: Implementation of the World Programme of Action Concerning Disabled Persons, Report of the Secretary General. Geneva.

United Nations (1998) *Human Rights Act*. Geneva: UN.

Van Dan Berg, I. and Grealish, E. (1996) Individualised Services and Supports through to wraparound Process: Philosophy and Process. *Journal of Child and Family Studies*. 5: 1, 7–21.

Vincent, J. and Jouriles, E. (Eds.) (2000) *Domestic Violence: Guidelines for Research Informed Practice*. London: Jessica Kingsley.

Walker, S. (2001) Tracing the Contours of Postmodern Social Work. *British Journal of Social Work*. 31: 29–39.

Walker, S. (2001) Family Support and Social Work Practice: Opportunities for Child Mental Health Work. *Social Work and Social Sciences Review*. 9: 2, 25–40.

Walker, S. (2002) Family Support and Social Work Practice: Renaissance or Retrenchment? *European Journal of Social Work*. 5: 1, 43–54.

Walker, S. (2003) *Social Work and Child and Adolescent Mental Health*. Lyme Regis: Russell House Publishing.

Watkins, D. and Gerong, A. (1997) Culture and Spontaneous Self-Concepts Among Filipino College Students. *Journal of Social Psychology*. 137: 480–8.

Weersing, V. and Weisz, J. (2002) Mechanisms of Action in Youth Psychotherapy. *Journal of Child Psychology and Psychiatry*. 43: 1, 3–29.

Weisz, J., Weiss, B. and Donenberg, G. (1992) The Lab Versus the Clinic: Effects of Child and Adolescent Psychotherapy. *American Psychologist.* 47: 1578–85.

Wolbring, G. (2001) Surviving Eugenics. In Priestly, M. (Ed.) *Disability and The Life Course.* Cambridge: Cambridge University Press.

Zavirsek, D. (1995) Social Innovations: A New Paradigm in Central European Social Work. *International Perspectives in Social Work.* 1.